BRITISH FIRST WORLD WAR PROPAGANDA

BRITISH FIRST WORLD WAR PROPAGANDA: FROM A TO Z

David Monger

BLOOMSBURY ACADEMIC
LONDON • NEW YORK • OXFORD • NEW DELHI • SYDNEY

BLOOMSBURY ACADEMIC

Bloomsbury Publishing Plc, 50 Bedford Square, London, WC1B 3DP, UK
Bloomsbury Publishing Inc, 1385 Broadway, New York, NY 10018, USA
Bloomsbury Publishing Ireland, 29 Earlsfort Terrace, Dublin 2, D02 AY28, Ireland

BLOOMSBURY, BLOOMSBURY ACADEMIC and the Diana logo are trademarks of
Bloomsbury Publishing Plc

First published in Great Britain 2025

Copyright © David Monger, 2025

David Monger has asserted his right under the Copyright, Designs and Patents Act, 1988,
to be identified as Author of this work.

For legal purposes the Acknowledgements on pp. ix–x constitute an extension
of this copyright page.

Cover design by Grace Ridge
Cover image: Vintage World War I poster of a British army hat © Vernon Lewis
Gallery/Stocktrek Images via Getty Images

All rights reserved. No part of this publication may be: i) reproduced or transmitted in
any form, electronic or mechanical, including photocopying, recording or by means of any
information storage or retrieval system without prior permission in writing from the publishers;
or ii) used or reproduced in any way for the training, development or operation of artificial
intelligence (AI) technologies, including generative AI technologies. The rights holders expressly
reserve this publication from the text and data mining exception as per Article 4(3) of the Digital
Single Market Directive (EU) 2019/790.

Bloomsbury Publishing Plc does not have any control over, or responsibility for,
any third-party websites referred to or in this book. All internet addresses given in this book
were correct at the time of going to press. The author and publisher regret any
inconvenience caused if addresses have changed or sites have ceased to exist, but
can accept no responsibility for any such changes.

A catalogue record for this book is available from the British Library.

A catalog record for this book is available from the Library of Congress.

ISBN: HB: 978-1-3503-8684-6
PB: 978-1-3503-8683-9
ePDF: 978-1-3504-1355-9
eBook: 978-1-3504-1354-2

Typeset by Newgen KnowledgeWorks Pvt. Ltd., Chennai, India
Printed and bound in Great Britain

For product safety related questions contact
productsafety@bloomsbury.com.

To find out more about our authors and books visit www.bloomsbury.com
and sign up for our newsletters.

CONTENTS

List of Illustrations — vii
Acknowledgements — ix
List of Abbreviations and Glossary of Propaganda Organizations — xi

Introduction — 1

1. Atrocities — 5
2. Britain — 13
3. Children — 21
4. Duty — 29
5. Empire — 37
6. Film — 45
7. Germany — 53
8. Humblebragging — 61
9. Information — 69
10. Jokes — 77
11. *Kultur* — 85
12. Locality — 93
13. Mother or munition worker — 101
14. Neutrals — 109
15. Organizations — 117

Contents

16.	Propagandists	125
17.	Quotidian propaganda	133
18.	Religion	141
19.	Soldiers	151
20.	Truth	159
21.	Unofficial propaganda	167
22.	Voluntarism	175
23.	War work	183
24.	X – Censorship	191
25.	Yanks	199
26.	Zero-sum bias	207

Bibliography 215
Index 227

ILLUSTRATIONS

Figures

1	Louis Raemaekers, *Thrown to the Swine*. The 'Land & Water' Edition of Raemaekers' Cartoons, I	6
2	Parliamentary Recruiting Committee, poster no. 104, 'Step Into Your Place', 1915	16
3	Detail from *Belgian Refugees Fund: A Children's Painting Book*	22
4	National Service poster W61, 'One Clear Call for Me'	32
5	Still from Lancelot Speed, *Britain's Effort*	41
6	1918 advertisement (in bright pink) for a National Service film event in South Molton, Devon	46
7	W. F. Blood, 'Holey War'	57
8	Cover of *Overseas*, August 1918	66
9	'10,000 Women Wanted for Farm Work'	74
10	'When You *Don't* Buy War Bonds'	80
11	National War Savings Committee leaflet A.C. 87	97
12	Septimus Scott, *These Women Are Doing Their Bit*	102
13	A selection of National War Savings Committee publicity material, including its use of the swastika as its organizational logo	120
14	*To Dress Extravagantly in War Time Is Worse than Bad Form, It Is Unpatriotic*	128
15	Draft National Service poster artwork	134
16	Reproduction of Bernard Partridge cartoon, 'The Last Crusade'	145
17	Reproduction of Bruce Bairnsfather cartoon, 'A Parcel Worth Holding on For'	156
18	Parliamentary Recruiting Committee poster no. 7, *The Scrap of Paper*, 1914	163
19	Poster advertising a CCNPO meeting, 1915	171
20	Press Bureau D notice D611, 12 December 1917	193
21	Cover of *Satire*, vol. 1, no. 10 (October 1917) in Press Bureau correspondence re. seditious propaganda	196
22	Roland Hill, 'Some Pitcher', *Welcome*, 3 July 1918, 163	204
23	Cover of the *Globe*, 18 January 1918	208

Illustrations

24 Cartoon in the *Railway Review* (National Union of Railwaymen),
    3 October 1919, 9   213

Table

1   Appearances of Percy James Brebner, 'The Home Offensive'   188

ACKNOWLEDGEMENTS

This book builds on nearly two decades of work on British First World War propaganda, and I have accumulated many debts over that time, some of which I apologize in advance for rudely overlooking here. Many of my ideas have been worked through in previous publications and enhanced by the editors and reviewers of Liverpool University Press (for my first book on the subject) and (in order of publication) *Sport in History, Cultural and Social History, Women's History Review, Twentieth Century British History, 1914-1918 Online: International Encyclopedia of the First World War, Journal of Transatlantic Studies, War & Society, History, The Historical Journal, First World War Studies* and *Historical Research*. Other pieces benefited from the editorial guidance of Troy Paddock and Sir Hew Strachan, while organizers and audiences of various talks at King's College London, the Institute of Historical Research, University of Oxford, Oxford Brookes University, Durham University, University of Adelaide, University of Canterbury, Te Papa Tongarewa, University of Exeter, University of St Andrews, Deakin University and the Canterbury100 Conference in Christchurch all aided my evolving thinking. Thanks also to Emily Drewe, Megan Harris and their anonymous reviewers at Bloomsbury Academic for aiding this project.

Different elements of my research were helped along the way by assistance from Ian Barrett (who found and photographed further official files for me at the UK National Archives after my move to New Zealand), Seth Thévoz (who gathered some of Lord Bryce's materials in Oxford for me) and Helen Leggatt (who substantially extended my identification of online materials relating to MI7b propaganda), to whose efforts I remain grateful. Grants of sabbatical research time and other research funding from the University of Canterbury, as well as Visiting Fellowships at the University of Oxford funded by the University of Canterbury's Erskine Office, are also gratefully acknowledged and enabled me to continue extending my knowledge of this area despite my substantial distance from the archives. The freely provided materials of online repositories including Internet Archive, Papers Past and Trove make distant research easier than it once was and are great and important assets to modern research that I hope will remain accessible to all of us in the future.

Discussing propaganda with some of my postgraduate students, particularly Greg Hynes, Tom Gilmour, Kate Pickworth and Daniel Steel has helped tighten my own thinking as well as revealing new insights, while colleagues in the History Department at the University of Canterbury have probably heard enough about seemingly similar aspects of the history of wartime propaganda from me over the last fourteen years. Timely 'resting' of a course I'd normally coordinate for the Department gave me valuable time to write this book, which would otherwise have waited rather longer. As well as this,

Acknowledgements

my knowledge and development of ideas about the war and propaganda (in particular) have benefitted from extended conversations with mentors, colleagues and friends including Maartje Abbenhuis, Steve Badsey, Santanu Das, Sue Grayzel, Adrian Gregory, John Horne, Kate Hunter, Jenny Macleod, Sarah Murray, Catriona Pennell, Jane Potter, Bill Philpott, Paul Readman, Noah Riseman, David Thackeray and Bart Ziino.

I moved to Aotearoa New Zealand in 2010 thanks to an academic job offer at Canterbury. My plan was to return to the UK after a few years, but I'm still here, now established as a citizen, fifteen years on. Final thanks, and love, belong to my wife, Heather Wolffram, fellow historian and enthusiast for travel, good food and inane television, who makes my life better simply by her presence near me.

ABBREVIATIONS AND GLOSSARY OF PROPAGANDA ORGANIZATIONS

ATL   Alexander Turnbull Library, Wellington

BLO   Bodleian Library, Oxford

BWNL   British Workers National League – an unofficial, 'patriotic labour' organization, developed in 1915 under the leadership of Victor Fisher. Connected with the Conservative Lord Milner. Strongly supported the war via propaganda and notorious for breaking up dissenting propaganda events. Leading figures elected as National Democratic Party candidates in 1918 election.

CCNPO   Central Committee for National Patriotic Organizations – an unofficial propaganda organization founded in 1914 by the historian G. W. Prothero, politician Harry Cust and colonial administrator W. Grey Wilson to promote the war effort in Britain. Absorbed by the NWAC in 1917.

DI   Department of Information – official Department founded in 1917 to coordinate all British propaganda under the direction of the novelist John Buchan. Absorbed Wellington House but was later absorbed itself into the Ministry of Information.

DNS   Directorate of National Service (also referred to as Department, then Ministry) – established in 1916 to recruit workers for work of national importance.

DORA   Defence of the Realm Act – a wide-ranging set of emergency regulations granting unusual powers to the government over things including working conditions, civil liberties and censorship.

FRM   Fight for Right Movement – unofficial propaganda organization founded in 1915 by the soldier and explorer Francis Younghusband to encourage patriotic support for the war. Lord Bryce was its first president.

ILP   Independent Labour Party – connected to the Parliamentary Labour Party but opposed the war based on its opposition to militarism.

IWM   Imperial War Museum, London

MI   Ministry of Information – established in 1918 to supersede the DI, with Lord Beaverbrook appointed minister. Intended to coordinate all British propaganda, but did not have authority over domestic propaganda (NWAC), while other propaganda groups (e.g. the NWSC) also operated separately.

Abbreviations and Glossary

MI7b	A branch of military intelligence established in 1916 with responsibility, among other things, for analysing enemy propaganda and for producing propaganda for use in imperial newspapers. Prominent members included A. A. Milne and Bruce Bairnsfather.
NCRB	National Committee for the Relief of Belgium – a charitable organization dedicated to Belgian relief.
n.p.d.	No publication details
NWAC	National War Aims Committee – parliamentary, 'officially unofficial' propaganda organization formed in July 1917 to provide propaganda for British civilians.
NWSC	National War Savings Committee – established in 1916 to promote the sale of war savings, loans and bonds.
PA	Parliamentary Archives, London
PB	Press Bureau – established in 1914 to oversee censorship of the press. Acted as conduit between government and press, claiming not to censor 'opinion'.
PRC	Parliamentary Recruiting Committee – parliamentary propaganda organization established in 1914 to recruit men for armed service.
RCI	Royal Colonial Institute – long-standing pro-empire society. Assisted distribution of MI7b propaganda during the war.
TNA	The National Archives: Public Record Office, Kew
TUC	Trades Union Congress
UDC	Union of Democratic Control – dissenting organization founded in 1914 by the MPs Ramsay MacDonald (Labour), Arthur Ponsonby and C. P. Trevelyan (Liberal), the activist E. D. Morel and economist Norman Angell. Strongest voice of dissenting propaganda.
WAAC	Women's Army Auxiliary Corps (later Queen Mary's Army Auxiliary Corps) – founded in 1917 to recruit women for non-combatant military roles.
WOCC	War Office Cinematograph Committee – founded in 1916. Produced full-length film propaganda as well as shorter 'topical budget' newsreels.
WSPU	Women's Social and Political Union – militant suffrage organization founded by Emmeline Pankhurst, who turned her attention to supporting the war as a propagandist.

INTRODUCTION

As the title shows, this book discusses British propaganda during the First World War. If you are interested enough in the topic to be browsing the introduction, you may well have existing knowledge of it from previous reading, documentaries or exhibitions. Or you may be interested in propaganda generally. It continues to be a controversial topic. I doubt anybody, today, refers to propaganda with a positive meaning. To identify something as propaganda is to dismiss it, or at least cast significant doubt and suspicion on it, and these suspicions build on a legacy that reaches back to the First World War.

That said, propaganda in the First World War was different and more varied than common stereotypes suggest. Broadly speaking, propaganda may be helpfully defined as organized communication intended to persuade people to act in desired ways or to accept or support a particular situation. As Chapter 20 argues in greater detail, however, British First World War propaganda might be more tightly defined as organized communication intended to persuade people through interpretations of truthful material. In this way, it differed from much of what propaganda came to represent in later thinking. British wartime propagandists were often prone to embellishment and exaggeration but very rarely undertook deliberate deception.

A generation of scholarship, particularly since the late 1990s, has tested, questioned and complicated its history.[1] Arguably, however, non-specialist understanding of the topic remains limited. Propaganda tends to be reduced to sensationalism and shame, recruiting and revenge. Common examples involve the most overblown claims of German atrocities towards civilians and recruiting posters intending to shame men into enlistment. These were, really, parts of a much wider enterprise. Likewise, its exponents – really numbered in thousands, many of them little more than names in committee minutes or a local press report – are easily reduced to its most famous names. Listing the gathering of writers recruited for propaganda work towards neutral and imperial Dominion audiences at Wellington House in September 1914 is common, as is reference to the 'Bryce Report' on German atrocities in the invasion of Belgium.[2] While this book certainly discusses eminent figures – James Bryce and the novelist John Galsworthy feature regularly, for instance – it also considers the far larger body of people involved with propaganda. That scale, in turn, reflects the very wide variety of purposes that wartime propaganda served. Besides recruiting for armed service, propagandists also recruited for civilian work, promoted investments in war loans, bonds and savings, attempted to attract sympathy and support overseas, discouraged excessive food consumption and advised how to make the most of wartime ingredients or simply tried to keep up public morale. Unofficial groups, including charities, special interest groups and critical organizations, meanwhile, also undertook propaganda promoting their causes and said so. In the 1910s, propaganda was a recognized form of persuasive communication used and acknowledged by groups of all kinds. While there were concerns about official involvement with propaganda activity, which contributed to the slow and poorly coordinated development of official propaganda – far short of any 'propaganda machine' – propaganda itself was not yet damned. Readers wishing to familiarize themselves with the structures of Britain's wartime propaganda before considering its content may wish to leap ahead in this book to Chapter 15, titled 'Organizations', which addresses these issues in more detail.[3]

Writers (and probably readers too) may lean towards the most exciting, striking and famous examples to capture the wider phenomenon, but propaganda was surprisingly diverse in both form and content. The most easily accessible visual form, posters, was accompanied by articles, pamphlets and books, new innovations like feature films and short newsreels and continued reliance on the publicly spoken word. Public meetings were the lynchpin of many propaganda campaigns, to the extent that, as discussed in Chapter 6, some organizations believed films needed speakers present to ensure they were properly understood. For all the emphasis on dramatic examples, much wartime propaganda could be surprisingly dull and skewed towards the plain provision of information. It was nonetheless important. This is not the writer's equivalent of telling readers they must also eat their vegetables. It relates to the function of propaganda as a form of persuasive communication. Understanding the duller stuff makes the dramatic more meaningful. Propagandists formed arguments intended to support whatever cause they were presenting, but following up the persuasive element often required some nuts and bolts. If a woman was inspired to enlist for national service work by a speech, pamphlet or film, for instance, she needed to know where to go and what to do, as well as why she should enlist.

British First World War propaganda was, thus, a vast, complicated, sometimes competitive and often contradictory enterprise. Rather than a 'complete history', this book provides a critical introduction to the subject via twenty-six short chapters. They include chapters addressing particular themes and ideas, methods and media such as jokes and films, and the groups and individuals involved in, or targeted by, propaganda. Each chapter stands alone as a short discussion focused on its topic (inevitably, there is some overlap across chapters), while, read as a whole, the book offers an overarching view of the key features of wartime propaganda, challenging some persistent assumptions through its examples and introducing up-to-date specialist interpretations. A combined abbreviation list and glossary help to keep the various organizations straight, while cross-references between chapters suggest connections. The A to Z offers a different structure for thinking about propaganda (one, indeed, that propagandists – lovers of lists – sometimes employed themselves). Read it cover to cover or dip into the topics that most interest you.

My serious interest in First World War propaganda began when I started a PhD on the domestic propaganda organization, the National War Aims Committee (NWAC), in 2005. At the time (in the thesis and book that followed, *Patriotism and Propaganda in First World War Britain: The National War Aims Committee and Civilian Morale*) my interest was, primarily, in the ways in which that organization discussed patriotism. The study suggested that, when read as a whole, NWAC propaganda content could be seen as a flexible patriotic narrative containing several elements used in varying combinations by different speakers, authors and artists. Since then, while an interest in patriotism remains, propaganda has edged itself to the forefront of my attention in research. From my initial, detailed work on a single organization operating only from July 1917 onwards, I expanded to other aspects of British wartime propaganda, including work conducted by many of the organizations discussed in this book. Bringing together those collected insights, alongside those of many others exploring the subject, consolidates nearly two decades of research. An introduction such as this book will not be the last word on the subject (indeed, I fear it won't even be *my* last word on the subject!), but I hope it helps readers see British First World War propaganda in a new light. From the humourist, soldier-propagandist and future beloved children's author, A. A. Milne, to a seconded zoologist's questionable guide to counteracting German propaganda, there is much to discover.

Notes

1   Important contributors focused substantially on Britain include, but are not limited to, Jim Aulich and John Hewitt, Stephen Badsey, Adrian Gregory, Nicoletta Gullace, Nicholas Hiley, John Horne and Alan Kramer, Brendan Maartens, Catriona Pennell, whose work features in later chapters.
2   For the Wellington House meeting in both specialist and general accounts, see, for example, D. G. Wright, 'The Great War, Propaganda, and English Men of Letters, 1914–1916', *Literature and History*, 7 (1978), 72; Peter Buitenhuis, *The Great War of Words: Literature as Propaganda, 1914–18 and After* (London, B.T: Batsford, 1989), 14; Samuel Hynes, *A War Imagined: The First World War and English Culture* (New York: Colliers, 1992), 26; Gary S. Messinger, *British Propaganda and the State in the First World War* (Manchester: Manchester University Press, 1992), 34–6; Philip Waller, *Writers, Readers, and Reputations: Literary Life in Britain, 1870–1918* (Oxford: Oxford University Press, 2006), 927; Adam Hochschild, *To End All Wars: A Story of Loyalty and Rebellion, 1914–1918* (Boston: Mariner, 2012), 148.
3   For another brief, online and open-access overview of this development and the groups and aims of propaganda, see David Monger, 'Propaganda at Home (Great Britain and Ireland)' in Ute Daniel, Peter Gatrell, Oliver Janz, Heather Jones, Jennifer Keene, Alan Kramer and Bill Nasson (eds), *1914–1918 Online: International Encyclopedia of the First World War* (Berlin: Freie Universität Berlin, 2016): https://encyclopedia.1914-1918-online.net/article/propaganda_at_home_great_britain_and_ireland.

CHAPTER 1
ATROCITIES

Nine eager pigs crowd around a bound female body in white, blood running from her corpse. The pigs wear spiked helmets, one a monocle (signifying an elite pig-soldier) and another has the German bravery medal, the iron cross, hanging from its tail. 'Thrown to the Swine. The Martyred Nurse', by Louis Raemaekers, first released in the Dutch press in October 1915, was reissued in colour in 1916, after Raemaekers moved to Britain and accepted his work's distribution as propaganda (Figure 1). It later appeared on the cover of Peter Buitenhuis's *The Great War of Words*, a critical account of deceptive literary propaganda that he said had worn out 'the integrity of language' in a 'climate created by the hate and atrocity propaganda against Germany'.[1] Such attitudes reflect the dominant perspective of British First World War propaganda, developed since the 1920s and still powerful today. Atrocities are thus the natural starting point for discussion.

Raemaekers's cartoon evokes the trial and execution of the British nurse, Edith Cavell, for espionage. Nicoletta Gullace notes she was 'undoubtedly guilty' (she hid British soldiers in German-occupied Belgium in 1914 and helped them escape). It thus, apparently, reflects Buitenhuis's argument – propaganda was twisting facts to promote disgust at Britain's enemy. Indeed, early studies of propaganda emphasized Cavell's guilt to discredit the outcry. Yet this was freely acknowledged in 1916. The dean of St Paul's, William Inge, described the execution, in a paragraph accompanying the cartoon, as 'not the worst of [Germany's] misdeeds', but 'probably the stupidest'. The 'pedantic condemnation ... by the letter of the law' had stirred English and American sentiment 'against an enemy whose moral unlikeness to ourselves becomes more apparent with every new phase in the struggle'.[2] Though legal, Cavell's execution was an 'atrocity': the violence was unnecessary and fit a larger pattern of deliberate German brutality since its invasion of Belgium in 1914.

By the war's later years, her death was routinely listed among other atrocious acts, which propagandists stressed were matters of policy:

> Everything that we thought secure among civilised men was defiled and destroyed – fidelity to the pledged word, reverence for age, the sanctity of womanhood, childhood and weakness; standards of honour, of justice and of clean fighting. And they were destroyed, not in an act of passion, but on a deliberate and calculated policy of 'frightfulness'.
>
> In military operations themselves, these bestialities formed a fitting preparation for the introduction of the torture of poison gas and of the flame-throwers. The slaughter of women and children and other non-combatants at Scarborough by

Figure 1 Louis Raemaekers, *Thrown to the Swine*. The 'Land & Water' Edition of Raemaekers' Cartoons, I.
Source: London: 'Land & Water', 1916, 25 (author's photograph). © Louis Raemaekers Foundation.

the raiding warships of Germany; the murder of Nurse Cavell; the indiscriminate destruction of civilian life by the Zeppelin and Gotha raids; the deliberate torpedoing of the *Ancona* and other hospital ships; the German submarine crew jeering at the struggles of the drowning passengers of the torpedoed *Falaba*; the sinking of the *Belgian Prince* when the very life-belts were taken from the drowning crew; the shooting of hostages, the burning of open towns; the looting and burning of Louvain; the poisoning of wells; these and similar acts received their immortal crown of cruelty when the *Lusitania* was sunk with over a thousand civilians, American and British.[3]

This litany was inaccurate – the *Ancona* was not a hospital ship, and the jeering at the *Falaba* was uncertain – and it overlooked Britain's own willingness to deploy poison gas and aerially bombard civilians. However, Germany's policy of 'frightfulness' was real enough. The army instructed soldiers to respond to resistance during its invasion of Belgium with exemplary punishment and posted public notices to that effect. In Les Rivages, a suburb of Dinant, seventy-seven civilians were executed on 23 August 1914 in reprisal for shots fired (by French soldiers) at the Germans, including '38 women and girls, and 15 children under 14, of whom seven were babies; seven of the men were over 70 years old'. German protests that criticism ignored threats against their soldiers cut little ice with wider opinion. Their explanation for shelling Rheims Cathedral – that the French had used it for military purposes – did not deter accusations of cultural desecration of a building described by an American author in a British propaganda pamphlet as 'more precious to the world's culture' than any building since the Parthenon. Claims that the RMS *Lusitania*, sunk in the Irish Sea at the cost of over a thousand passengers' lives, including over 100 US citizens, was carrying contraband material (it was, indeed, carrying some munitions) through a declared zone of submarine warfare did not deflect condemnation. Likewise, rejecting rumours that German soldiers cut ears off corpses, by reporting that an investigation found only one example, proved unsuccessful![4]

Germany's tone-deaf responses to atrocity propaganda often involved haughty dismissal of misconduct that aided further propaganda by admitting criticized actions. This merged with later claims of successful enemy (and failed German) propaganda, first by the defeated military leader, Erich Ludendorff, then Adolf Hitler. Ludendorff's Germany was 'helpless', 'hypnotized' by 'mischievous and lying' enemy propaganda, which Hitler claimed involved 'amazing skill and really brilliant calculation'. Thus, Ludendorff's mythologizing concluded, though 'victorious on the field of battle, Germany failed in the fight against the *moral* of the enemy peoples'. Propaganda and the Allied blockade ended the war, not military defeat, and Germany's post-war treatment was unjust.[5] As transatlantic conviction about the war's merits faded in the 1920s, propaganda helped explain why so many people willingly supported such a devastating conflict. Emphasizing deception, particularly through 'fabricated' atrocities, offered people who had changed their minds about the war an explanation for earlier views. For investigating authors they often provided cautionary tales against involvement in future wars.

US authors, including Harold Lasswell, H. C. Peterson and James Morgan Read, said both sides committed atrocities and produced propaganda attacking those of their enemies. Lasswell and Read explicitly rejected claims of German helplessness and inactivity. Nonetheless, Peterson affirmed 'it was the British who succeeded', and US intervention was 'the product of British propaganda ... [that portrayed] a simple conflict between good and evil ... In the minds of American leaders there was developed a blind hatred of everything German ... [that] distorted American neutrality.'[6] The United States was duped. Likewise, Britain's most prominent critic, Arthur Ponsonby, exploring 'an assortment of lies circulated' in the war, focused mainly on British examples since 'we are more concerned with our own Government and Press methods and our own national honour than the duplicity of other Governments'. 'Atrocity lies' had the most impact, according to Ponsonby's regularly reprinted polemic.[7]

Their importance to early studies and their undeniably frequent presence in propaganda mean atrocities remain central to most specialist accounts of the war's propaganda. One important work noted the 'continued association ... with lies and atrocity stories' to explain propaganda's poor reputation but also said propagandists 'exploited this theme ceaselessly and tirelessly' in their own summary of content. While discussing varied propaganda themes, Eberhard Demm recently concluded that 'only atrocity propaganda succeeded temporarily' in gaining British military recruits. Demm, acknowledging modern scholarly exploration of German atrocities in 1914 that verified over 6,000 civilian deaths at German hands, says atrocity propaganda worked for Britain mainly because Germany committed atrocities throughout the war.[8] Other, often more general, works likewise acknowledge real atrocities but rapidly point to further imagined or unverified crimes. Despite scholarly certainty that dismissing atrocities as 'the feverish imagination of Allied propagandists ... is no longer a tenable position', wartime propaganda continues to be dismissed as deceptive, with lurid atrocity stories as the key example of deception.[9]

Verifiable atrocious conduct like the Les Rivages example was shocking enough. Details of victimization of Belgian and French civilians were extended at the time, however, by the 'low resistance ... to myth and hysteria' of the committee headed by the former ambassador to the United States, Lord Bryce, to investigate the invasion of Belgium. Including many refugees' unverified claims extended the 1915 condemnation's impact, but the Bryce Report's flaws are repeatedly stressed in later discussions of propaganda. Only John Horne and Alan Kramer's scrupulous transnational study in 2001 settled the reality of atrocities during the invasion (though even this has been attacked).[10] Doubts about Bryce's efforts and atrocity propaganda also aided denial of the war's largest atrocity, the Armenian Genocide. Another report, compiled by the historian Arnold Toynbee (described in a leading work as 'something of a specialist in atrocity propaganda') in collaboration with Bryce and an international network of informants, has been dismissed as propaganda, partly through falsely connecting the reports and propaganda's poor reputation. Toynbee was, indeed, working for the British propaganda organization, Wellington House, during his work on the Armenian report, but its reports were thoroughly cross-checked and verified. Atrocity propaganda, more broadly, largely targeted Germany, even regarding the genocide driven by Germany's ally, the Ottoman

Empire.[11] This had serious consequences for later discussion of war crimes. Dishonest interpreters stressed inaccurate examples to discredit everything. Others assisted such doubts by acknowledging flawed evidence alongside actual crimes or suggesting genuine source material was 'tainted' by propaganda associations.

Tunnel vision on German responsibility encouraged later doubts about atrocities and genocide, but this focus makes more sense when wartime atrocity propaganda's purposes are understood. Propaganda aimed to persuade audiences to accept needs and arguments. Since Germany was Britain's primary adversary, and its defeat was key to ending the war, propagandists focused here. Multiple modern studies show the contexts and purposes behind atrocity propaganda were more complex than straightforward appeals to 'hate'. One persuasive account shows that violent crime against civilians provided a more relatable justification for Britain's war against Germany. Gullace shows that attacking Germany for breaking international law, through examples like the German Chancellor's protest that Britain was declaring war based on a 'scrap of paper' (the 1839 Treaty of London, guaranteeing Belgian neutrality), morphed into graphic accounts of atrocities against civilians. Soldiers assaulting civilians and the German state infringing neutrality were on the same spectrum. Germany and its people did not accept limits on conduct; thus, Britain must protect both international agreements and ordinary people:

> For those inclined to agree that a 'scrap of paper' was hardly a reason to fight, the Bryce Report and hundreds of other documents painted a harrowing picture of treaty violation that represented it as an issue of national, personal, and sexual concern.

Reporting crimes against vulnerable individuals was thus not about cheap thrills. It explained why first Britain, then neutrals – not themselves attacked – should uphold law through war. A more recent argument adds that British propaganda reflected 'genuine belief that war had become more civilised' – German willingness to brutalize civilians broke such 'optimism', and this worsened when British towns were shelled.[12]

From a different angle, another account shows that British condemnation of German actions moved relatively slowly to violence towards civilians. Much of the visual record of the war's early days instead focused on destroyed buildings – cultural destruction was then worsened by reports of civilian violence and attacks on British targets, steadily fixing a perspective of Germany as wilfully acting outside 'civilized' bounds. The public became more willing to believe (and assert) the worst – 'the iniquity of the enemy could largely be taken for granted'. Likewise, exhaustive investigation of the infamous 'corpse conversion factory' story – the suggestion that Germany rendered human corpses for fats, based on a misreading of the word *kadaver*, used only for animal remains – shows that the story was not created by propagandists at all, as critics like Ponsonby assumed. It circulated widely through several factors. These included the genuine industrial processes used to remove bodies from battle zones, examples of melted human remains found after bombardments, persistent jokes and rumours and German denials, which prompted republication. Most importantly, however, atrocity stories resonated in 1917 because atrocities continued to happen. While withdrawing from the Somme region in late 1916, deliberate 'devastation and looting' was conducted, and tens of thousands of civilians were displaced. In early 1917, Germany reintroduced unrestricted submarine warfare (previously halted because of outcry at civilian deaths at sea). Clear evidence of crimes made unclear rumours more plausible.[13]

Atrocity propaganda was not an end in itself. Rather, it enlivened drier calls for service and sacrifice needed in a total war effort. In later years, some officials believed public interest in atrocities and their meaning was weakened by 'constant repetition'. Nonetheless, they remained central to the domestic propaganda of the National War Aims Committee (NWAC, established in mid-1917), because they provided a negative context for public action. NWAC propagandists stressed duty, praised existing service and demanded more, celebrated 'British' civilizational values and promised post-war rewards. Alongside all this, atrocities efficiently reminded audiences of an even less tolerable alternative to wartime discomfort, as the barrister J. Bromhead Matthews suggested when sliding from atrocities to food economy in Malmesbury, Wiltshire:

> Think of the soldiers and sailors – the heroes who had gone, the heroes still fighting, and their sacrifices, what they had given up and were day by day giving up! … But go to Belgium, to Serbia, to Poland, to Montenegro, to Roumania. There they found, if possible, deeper sacrifices; … they found in addition bloody murders and atrocities, and every foul practice of the devil. They found the ruthless foe paid no regard to womanhood or childhood: cities lay in ruins, plains were devastated, everything prized in the country gone, and the whole countryside blasted and blotted out … Before the war it seemed as if we had got into a terrible state, but in a moment it was swept aside, and every Englishman sprang to arms, either in the Army or to do national work…
>
> When the thing happened, we got in, and they knew the rest. They knew what their own Wiltshire Regiment had done and won undying fame. (Applause.) … The struggle had been bitter, but we had got to suffer more if we meant to see it through. We were going to grumble about the tea and sugar – (laughter) – we were convinced that the men operating these things did not know their job. But we had got to learn … We might have to strap our belts closer, for there was going to be greater difficulty, and we must have
>
> MORE ECONOMY.
>
> He put it to himself that every little bit of food saved meant probably the life of a soldier or sailor saved. This thought helped them when they wanted 'another bit of toast', but it was true. The less ships they had coming with food, the less submarining, the less lives lost, the less time of the Navy, and the shortening of the war.[14]

For Matthews, recalling atrocities, praising servicemen, avoiding waste and winning the war went hand-in-hand. Atrocities were the shock reminder people needed of the cost of failing to meet wartime duties.

Seeing atrocity propaganda as persuasive communication, rooted in the fact of enemy violence, judged by most to be unwarranted, is less dramatic than earlier ironic scorn for bloodthirsty and sensational 'propaganda of hate'.[15] However, it underlines British First World War propaganda's basic purpose. Propagandists had to reason with the public to persuade it to commit to an increasingly unwelcome war effort and to gain other nations' support. Rather than encouraging random hate, atrocity stories put an undesired and exhausting war on a human scale for those (despite naval and aerial attacks) less directly confronted by its impacts.

Notes

1. *The "Land & Water" Edition of Raemaekers' Cartoon*, I (London: Land & Water, 1916), 25; Buitenhuis, *Great War of Words*, 144–5, 141.
2. Nicoletta F. Gullace, *'The Blood of Our Sons': Men, Women and the Renegotiation of British Citizenship during World War One* (New York: Palgrave, 2002), 99; H. C. Peterson, *Propaganda for War: The Campaign Against American Neutrality, 1914–1917* (Norman: University of Oklahoma Press, 1939), 61–3; James Morgan Read, *Atrocity Propaganda, 1914–1918* (New Haven: Yale University Press, 1941), 210–16; *"Land & Water" Edition*, 24.
3. Basil Mathews, *The Vista of Victory* (London: Hodder & Stoughton, 1917), 6. Mathews's book was written for the National War Aims Committee (NWAC), which oversaw domestic propaganda from July 1917.
4. John Horne and Alan Kramer, *German Atrocities, 1914: A History of Denial* (New Haven: Yale University Press, 2001), 50–1, 292–9; Alan Kramer, *Dynamic of Destruction: Culture and Mass Killing in the First World War* (Oxford: Oxford University Press, 2007), 18; Nicola Lambourne, 'First World War Propaganda and the Use and Abuse of Historic Monuments on the Western Front', *Imperial War Museum Review*, no. 12 (1999); Newell Dwight Hillis, *Murder Most Foul!* (London: Field and Queen, [1917]), 14; Nicoletta Gullace, 'Sexual Violence and Family Honor: British Propaganda and International Law during the First World War', *American Historical Review*, 102, no. 3 (1997), 740. Hillis's pamphlet was also supplied by the NWAC.
5. General Ludendorff, *My War Memories, 1914–1918* (London: Hutchinson & Row, 1919), vol. 1, 203, 361, 383; Adolf Hitler, *Mein Kampf*, trans. Ralph Mannheim (Boston: Houghton Mifflin [1925–6] 1972), 176.
6. Harold D. Lasswell, *Propaganda Technique in the World War* (London: Kegan Paul, 1927), 3; Read, *Atrocity Propaganda*, 104; Peterson, *Propaganda for War*, viii, 326.
7. Arthur Ponsonby, *Falsehood in War-Time: Containing an Assortment of Lies Circulated Throughout the Nations during the Great War* (London: Allen & Unwin, 1928), 28, 22. For discussion of Ponsonby's motives and impact on propaganda's reputation, see Adrian Gregory, *The Last Great War: British Society and the First World War* (Cambridge: Cambridge University Press, 2008), 41–4; Stephen Badsey, *The German Corpse Factory: A Study in First World War Propaganda* (Warwick: Helion, 2019), 28–31.
8. M. L. Sanders and Philip M. Taylor, *British Propaganda during the First World War, 1914–18* (London: MacMillan, 1982), 264, 137; Eberhard Demm, *Censorship and Propaganda in World War I: A Comprehensive History* (London: Bloomsbury, 2019), 184, 37–40. For other works emphasizing atrocities' impact, see Buitenhuis, *Great War of Words*; Cate Haste, *Keep the Home Fires Burning: Propaganda in the First World War* (London: Allen Lane, 1977); Stuart Wallace, *War and the Image of Germany: British Academics, 1914–1918* (Edinburgh: John

Donald, 1988). For an earlier work acknowledging the reality of German civilian killing (if not military policy), see Read, *Atrocity Propaganda*, 286.
9 For examples of a swift pivot from reality to fabrication, see Gerard J. DeGroot, *Blighty: British Society in the First World War* (Harlow: Longman, 1996), 187–91; Hochschild, *To End All Wars*, 148–51. For 'untenability', see Jay Winter and Antoine Prost, *The Great War in History*, 2nd edn (Cambridge: Cambridge University Press, 2020), 171.
10 Horne and Karmer, *German Atrocities*, 236; for their response to a work by Ulrich Keller dismissing their findings, see 'Wer schießt hier aus dem Hinterhalt', *Frankfurter Allgemeine Zeitung*, 1 March 2018, 14.
11 For discussion of the report and its connection to propaganda, which corrects these misleading associations, see David Monger, 'Networking Against Genocide during the First World War: The International Network Behind the British Parliamentary Report on the Armenian Genocide', *Journal of Transatlantic Studies*, 16, no. 3 (2018). For Toynbee's reputation, see Sanders and Taylor, *British Propaganda*, 145. Regarding inaccurate emphasis on German responsibility for the genocide, see Horne and Kramer, *German Atrocities*, 296–7; Stéphane Audoin-Rouzeau and Annette Becker, *1914–1918: Understanding the Great War*, trans. Catherine Temerson (London: Profile Books, 2002), 64–9; Demm, *Censorship and Propaganda*, 38; Daniel Steel, 'Genocide and the "Clean Fighting Turk" in First World War Britain and Ireland', *Historical Research*, 94, no. 264 (2021).
12 Gullace, 'Sexual Violence', quotation at 743; Emily Robertson, 'Propaganda and "Manufactured Hatred": A Reappraisal of the Ethics of First World War British and Australian Atrocity Propaganda', *Public Relations Inquiry*, 3, no. 2 (2014), quotation at 259.
13 Gregory, *Last Great War*, 40–69; Badsey, *German Corpse Factory*, ch. 4, esp. 215–34.
14 'National War Aims Campaign. Meeting at Malmesbury', *Wilts and Gloucestershire Standard, and Cirencester and Swindon Express*, 3 November 1917, 6. For discussion of atrocities as a negative context for wider issues, see David Monger, *Patriotism and Propaganda in First World War Britain: The National War Aims Committee and Civilian Morale* (Liverpool: Liverpool University Press, 2012), esp. chs. 4–5; quotation repetition at 27.
15 Read, *Atrocity Propaganda*, 5.

CHAPTER 2
BRITAIN

British propagandists addressed audiences on street corners in local towns, recruiting for armed service or war work, advocating war loan investments or restraint in food consumption, simply aiming to boost morale or, among some critical organizations like the Independent Labour Party (ILP) or Union of Democratic Control (UDC), condemning the war's effects on civil rights or international relations. Prominent and obscure figures wrote, drew and filmed propaganda for distribution in Britain and abroad. Organizations, from the War Propaganda Bureau set up in 1914 in Wellington House to MI7b, a branch of military intelligence that distributed thousands of articles to imperial newspapers in 1918, addressed a global audience of imperial or neutral minds. Wherever appeals were made, the central character was not Germany, regardless of heavy discussion of its atrocities, which, Chapter 1 suggested, provided a negative motivation for public action. Rather, British propagandists offered a fundamentally *positive* story with Britain as protagonist. Other nations were lauded – Belgium for its brave and noble resistance, the United States for its 'impartial' decision to take Britain's side – but this praise generally reflected further credit on Britain, the nation that supposedly entered the war to protect the rule of law, preserving the 'scrap of paper' protecting Belgium's borders.

Speaking in New York during a propaganda tour in 1918, the Archbishop of York, Cosmo Lang, flattered his audience that:

> We in England felt a new force had entered on April 6, 1917, more valuable than material power …
>
> You Americans have always been assured of the supremacy of your great ideals. You are learning now that they are not secure …
>
> Our joy was great when we beckoned for help and on that great and fateful day you answered, and came over and helped us. America brings to this enterprise not only her great material resources but chiefly a clear and disinterested vindication of the ideals of freedom, justice and peace …
>
> Now because these principles are at stake, we English speaking nations are partners in a great and inspiring enterprise.

Lang was subtle enough not to boast that those ideals were proclaimed as Britain's driving principles since the war's outbreak; nonetheless, the United States 'came over and helped', and now 'we English speaking nations are partners in a great and inspiring enterprise', after 'clear and disinterested vindication' of British ideas and actions. Like so many advocates of Britain's cause in the United States, Lang used civilizational ideals, which many British commentators happily claimed were forged by Britain, as a transatlantic bond. In another speech in London, reprinted as a propaganda pamphlet, Lang quoted the former US Secretary of State, Elihu Root, who had assured him the United States would 'continue to fight, with all the dogged persistency, the bull-dog courage, the incapacity to realise defeat ... and therefore the capacity for victory which we rightly inherit from the men who have made the liberty of the Anglo-Saxon race'.[1] The United States was thus simultaneously an independent actor, vindicating Britain by abandoning neutrality, and a descendant of the British bulldog that inherited British values. As another US commentator, gleefully reproduced by the NWAC, put it in 1918,

> What she has done in this war ... has surprised no one who knew British character, British stamina, and British history ...
> the stubborn, stick-to-it, bulldog British had decided to live or die with the French ...
> *Thousands of American lads will come home to us alive and whole* because thousands of our blood-brothers from the British Isles have been killed and mutilated.[2]

Late-war statements of certainty about British civilizational ideals, and US reinforcement of them, put a triumphalist edge on positive assertions of British virtues that propagandists had made since 1914. Glorying in the United States and wider 'vindication' of Britain's stance, however, showed an unease about Britain's position in world affairs that preceded the war. From late-nineteenth-century confidence as the world's only genuinely global power, Britain saw its industrial and economic dominance reduced by US and German competition, with those larger nations likely to overhaul Britain eventually. A sense of imperial overstretch, alongside declining European stability, encouraged deals and accommodations with the United States, Japan, France and Russia that relaxed Britain's security concerns but stiffened European diplomatic tensions before the war. Meanwhile, though the US anti-war commentator Randolph Bourne rejected claims of 'Anglo-Saxon' cultural ties and continued US enthusiasm for 'English snobberies, English religion, English literary styles, English literary reverences and canons, English ethics, English superiorities', British writers habitually toured the United States before 1914, eager for *American* acclaim and sales, while organizations like the elite Pilgrims Society actively cultivated Anglo-Saxonism (a belief in the cultural and racial superiority of the descendants of Anglo-Saxons).[3] Even before the war, Britain needed the United States as an economic, diplomatic and cultural friend. An early, unofficial, propaganda work, *King Albert's Book*, published at Christmas 1914 in support of Belgian relief funds, was ostensibly an international tribute to Belgian courage. However, its (primarily British) contributors made the collection an appeal to world opinion. Belgians were as courageous as the Spartans of Thermopylae; Britain kept its honour by defending Belgian neutrality. Contributors either expected or pleaded with neutrals to endorse Britain's actions and join its side. If not, the former prime minister,

Lord Rosebery, suggested, Britain might be overwhelmed and the United States would be next. The book's messages suggested neither British judgement nor British action, alone, was enough. The world must act. Its editor, the novelist Hall Caine – an enthusiastic veteran of US tours – later lamented the slowness of meaningful US action in response.[4] Nonetheless, earlier twentieth-century efforts to improve British–US relations aided Britain's later propaganda work there, and *King Albert's Book* provided an unofficial way to connect 'British' civilizational values with those of other nations.

Wartime propaganda was awash with discussion of values such as justice, honour, freedom and democracy. While these were often described as universal to 'civilized' people, commentators were rarely shy to emphasize Britain's special heritage of, and responsibility for, them. The Fight for Right Movement (FRM), founded in 1915 by the soldier and explorer Sir Francis Younghusband, saw its role as to 'confirm and deepen the conviction most men now have that we are fighting for something more than our own defence, and are battling for all humanity in order to preserve common human rights for the generations to come'. It aimed to inspire civilians already committed to the war and its ideals, those who were 'sound, but need support and encouragement' to bear the war's demands, as well as those not currently meeting their responsibilities. Since the government was too busy to produce this propaganda, Younghusband argued (official domestic propaganda for morale did not commence seriously until 1917), it was his movement's responsibility 'continually to remind the nation of the ideals and principles for which we were fighting; to demonstrate the value and importance of those ideals for our national life and for mankind as a whole'. The movement's president, Viscount Bryce, affirmed Britain was 'led to undertake the defence of those principles of humanity which we had believed to be recognized by all the civilized countries of the world'.[5]

Such sentiments are easily dismissed as overblown elite self-congratulation, but they continued a 'civilizational perspective' with which Peter Mandler suggests Britons of varied social and political backgrounds viewed their own, supposedly less selfish, culture from the late eighteenth century onwards. Most of the labour movement supported Britain's war, while retaining the right to criticize, Paul Ward argues, because its radical patriotism approved national defence of 'the natural home of democracy, liberty and free institutions'. Catriona Pennell's assessment of ordinary people's private writing in 1914, meanwhile, suggests they were not 'brainwashed' into accepting such ideals but invoked them themselves. In this interpretation, FRM's elite assertions echoed widely established views or, as Aldous Huxley suggested in the 1930s, 'The propagandist is a man who canalizes an already existing stream. In a land where there is no water, he digs in vain.'[6] Rightly or wrongly, enough Britons apparently believed their country represented 'special' values that harping on them was worthwhile.

If British values were shared by 'civilized' allies and others, propagandists took particular pride in voluntarism as a sign of unique qualities. Looking back at the military recruitment of two million volunteers, an MI7b article, intended for reuse by the press, stressed the remarkable achievements of the Parliamentary Recruiting Committee (PRC), in which

Tories and Radicals, Labour Members and Irishmen, hardly on speaking terms before the war, toured the country together in caravans, or made lightning journeys from the Land's End to Sutherlandshire to meet on the same platforms or at the same street corners to address their fellow-citizens.

Politicians, in this interpretation, voluntarily put aside differences to set an example and attract Britons of all backgrounds. This sentiment was exemplified in the PRC's poster, 'Step into your Place', in which miner and barrister, farmer and banker march together at the rear of a column that merges into military uniforms ahead (Figure 2). The 1916 turn to conscription was not a failure, MI7b said, but a 'revolution', smoothly accomplished, that went against 'British history for the last three centuries' as citizens accepted 'abandoning cherished habits and prejudices'. Such interpretations only partly chimed with critical voices. The ILP argued government ministers had continually celebrated voluntary recruitment and that 'freedom from conscription is one of the few great heritages of freedom that belongs to the British nation', while Labour's parliamentary leader, Arthur Henderson, rejected conscription because 'an army, entirely without precedent in the history of any country, has been secured on the voluntary principle'.[7] Nonetheless, all agreed that voluntarism best showed the UK's character.

Such character was also ascribed to Ireland. Irish voluntary enlistment further proved British liberty and justice and was an appropriate response to the concession of Home

Figure 2 Parliamentary Recruiting Committee, poster no. 104, 'Step Into Your Place', 1915.
Source: Public Domain (Wikimedia Commons).

Rule. In the wake of 1916's Easter Rising, launched by Irish republicans unwilling to accept the wartime delay to self-government and demanding more radical changes, Wellington House rapidly issued a pamphlet containing a New York speech by the Irish parliamentary leader, John Redmond (one of five it published under his name). Redmond suggested Ireland's participation in the war was

> true to all the principles which she had held through all her history ... the rights of small nations; the sacred principle of nationality; liberty and democracy ...
>
> this was the opinion of the overwhelming majority of the Irish people; it was the opinion which thousands of Irish soldiers have sealed with their blood by dying in the cause of the liberty of Ireland and of the world.[8]

'True' Irishmen like Redmond, propagandists suggested, shared Britain's civilized values and willingly fought for them because Britain had treated Ireland justly in granting Home Rule.

Even after conscription, propagandists still depicted Britain as a nation of volunteers. Propaganda for national service (civilian war work) stressed that efficient organization of manpower was essential to bring the war to an earlier close and preserve Britain's way of life. Thus 'every man who enrols will be able, with a clear conscience, to reflect that in the hour of our Nation's peril, he offered "to do his bit" by placing himself at the service of his country'. Likewise, a Ministry of Food poster depicted a merchant sailor at the wheel of his ship in heavy weather, with the message, 'I risked my life to bring you Food. Use it carefully – live on Voluntary Rations and Win the War', while a window card supplied to civilians declared those adopting these limits 'In Honour Bound'. Accepting smaller supplies thus matched British ideals, and civilians could display their patriotic restraint through the cards. Milder and less abrasive than more famous (and doubtfully effective) 'shaming' propaganda like the 'Daddy, what did *YOU* do in the Great War' poster, the national service appeals affirmed that, while military service was not always possible, voluntarism remained an option for all Britons. The subtext behind many such appeals was that compulsion was the unwelcome possible alternative.[9] Despite conscription, propagandists persistently announced their faith that Britons would choose the correct path themselves, thus flattering them as good citizens rather than berating them as bad ones.

If the beauties of civilizational principles might not appeal to all Britons, some propagandists calculated that the beauties of Britain itself would. A PRC recruitment poster showed a Scottish soldier pointing to cottages in rolling green countryside, asking, 'Isn't this worth fighting for?' NWAC propagandists, late in the war, meanwhile, regularly evoked the countryside's beauties in cartoons aimed at soldiers on leave, reminding them of the peaceful environment they fought to both preserve and return to. For the humorous author turned soldier-propagandist, A. A. Milne, writing for MI7b, 'Blighty' was, for soldiers, 'the life we knew before the war'. Whether in 'mean streets in a slum city [or] tumble-down cottages in a sleeping village', soldiers visualized a 'land where we can be happy'. Such 'images and homelands' for soldiers, Alex Mayhew has recently argued, were both 'collectively constructed' and very intimate ... drawn from personal experience and memory of particular scenes'. Lurking in these pleasant reflections, however, was possible destruction. Speaking at a 'War Anniversary' event in Battersea, South London, in August 1918, Rev. H. F. Pegg said he had recently returned from Devon:

> It was a part of this green and pleasant isle that had been made famous by Blackmoore, in Lorna Doone. ... Sitting there ... [h]e then thanked God for the peacefulness of the scene spread out before him, for the ships wending their way peacefully up and down the Bristol Channel. Why was it, he thought, that we had that peace ... Paris might have been in the hands of Germans. The Channel ports might have been in their hands. Famine might have been stalking through our land. We owed that peaceful scene to our fighting men.

Servicemen protected Britain so they could return to its beauties and comforts. Civilians should ensure the country held strong until servicemen returned.[10]

Pegg was one of many voluntary local speakers who contributed to public propaganda events. His literary allusion seemingly blurred William Shakespeare's 'sceptred isle ... other Eden, demi-paradise ... this England' of *Richard II*, with William Blake's 'green and pleasant land'. In 1916, part of Blake's 'And did those feet in ancient time' was set to music by Hubert Parry at the request of the poet laureate, Robert Bridges, for use at FRM events. Bridges explained that the final lines encapsulated the movement's 'crusade' to 'build Jerusalem in England's green and pleasant land'.[11] As later chapters elaborate further, propagandists promised civilians that the war would be worthwhile because a better society would emerge thanks to wartime sacrifices. Improved standards of living and international harmony would both ensure a better world for Britain's children.[12] Parry later had second thoughts about FRM, presenting his song, instead, to the women's suffrage movement.[13] Nonetheless, 'Jerusalem', one of modern Britain's most treasured and familiar songs, owed its formulation to British propaganda and its attempt to tell a positive story with Britain as its hero.

Notes

1 'Ideals Will Win, Says Archbishop', *New York Sun*, 4 March 1918, 14; *Hands Across the Atlantic: Personal Impressions of the United States at War by the Archbishop of York* (London: W.H. Smith, 1918), 22–3. For the frequent civilizational association of Britain and the United States in wartime propaganda, see, Jessica Bennett and Mark Hampton, 'World War I and the Anglo-American Imagined Community: Civilization vs. Barbarism in British Propaganda and American Newspapers', in Joel H. Wiener and Mark Hampton (eds), *Anglo-American Media Interactions, 1850–2000* (Basingstoke: Palgrave MacMillan, 2007).

2 *The Unboasting British: An American Tribute* (London: W.H. Smith, NWAC Searchlight leaflet no. 29, 1918); original emphasis.

3 Randolph S. Bourne, 'Trans-National America', *Atlantic Monthly* (July 1916), 88; Philip Waller, *Writers, Readers, and Reputations: Literary Life in Britain, 1870–1918* (Oxford: Oxford

University Press, 2006), ch. 16; Stephen Bowman, *The Pilgrims Society and Public Diplomacy, 1895-1945* (Edinburgh: Edinburgh University Press, 2018); Stuart Anderson, *Race and Rapprochement: Anglo-Saxonism and Anglo-American Relations, 1895-1904* (London: Associated University Presses, 1981), 11-12.

4   For full discussion, see David Monger, 'Speaking to or for the World? Britain, Presumed Authority and World Opinion at the Start of the First World War', *Historical Research*, 96, no. 1 (2023).

5   'The Fight for Right Movement', letter to the *Spectator*, 18 December 1915, 14; Sir Francis Younghusband, 'Preface' and Viscount Bryce, 'For the Right. The Defence of Right' [transcript of speech delivered in London, 21 March 1916], in *For the Right: Essays and Addresses by Members of the "Fight for Right Movement"* (New York: G.P. Putnam's, 1918), iii-iv, 2-3.

6   Peter Mandler, *The English National Character: The History of an Idea from Edmund Burke to Tony Blair* (New Haven: Yale University Press, 2006); Paul Ward, *Red Flag and Union Jack: Englishness, Patriotism and the British Left, 1881-1924* (Woodbridge: Boydell Press, 1998), 122; Catriona Pennell, *A Kingdom United: Popular Responses to the Outbreak of the First World War* (Oxford: Oxford University Press, 2012), 64; Aldous Huxley, 'Notes on Propaganda', *Harper's Magazine*, 174 (1936), 39.

7   Parliamentary Archives, London, Lord Beaverbrook Papers, BBK E/3/5, 'How Britain Has Raised Her Armies'; Parliamentary Recruiting Committee, *Step Into Your Place* (PRC poster no. 104, 1915); Independent Labour Party, 'The Perils of Conscription: An Appeal to the Organised Workers of Great Britain' (5 June 1915); 'Against Conscription. Success of Voluntary System', *Manchester Guardian*, 13 January 1915, 3.

8   *The Voice of Ireland: Being an Interview with John Redmond, M.P., and Some Message from Representative Irishmen Regarding the Sinn Fein Rebellion* (London: Thomas Nelson, 1916), 2-3.

9   'Twelve Good Reasons Why Every Able-Bodied Man Should Enrol for National Service' (Department of National Service, n.d.); League of National Safety/Ministry of Food, 'I Risked My Life to Bring You Food'; 'In Honour Bound We Adopt the National Scale of Voluntary Rations' (Ministry of Food card no. 9). On the wartime 'ethic of doing one's bit', see Gregory, *Last Great War*, 95. For the unrepresentativeness of the 'Daddy' poster, see Nicholas Hiley, '"Kitchener Wants YOU" and "Daddy, What Did YOU Do in the Great War?" The Myth of British Recruiting Posters', *Imperial War Museum Review*, 11 (1999). For fuller discussion of propaganda emphases on voluntarism, see David Monger, 'The Press and Propaganda', in Hew Strachan (ed.), *The British Home Front and the First World War* (Cambridge: Cambridge University Press, 2023).

10 *Your Country's Call* (PRC poster no. 87, 1915); for NWAC evocations of home, see David Monger, 'Soldiers, Propaganda and Ideas of Home and Community in First World War Britain', *Cultural and Social History*, 8, no. 3 (2011); A. A. Milne, '"Blighty"', *Wanganui Chronicle*, 18 October 1918, 7 (the article previously featured in a special war anniversary supplement of *Overseas* (journal of the Overseas Club and Patriotic League) in August and appeared in several other New Zealand papers subsequently); Alex Mayhew, 'English Patriotism and the Implicit Nation: Homelands and Soldiers' National Identity during the Great War', *English Historical Review*, 138, no. 594-5 (2024), 1295; 'Mayor and Councillors of Battersea Attend at St. Mary's', *Battersea Boro' News*, 9 August 1918, 2.

11 'Literature', *Otago Witness*, 28 June 1916, 66; see also 'The Poet Laureate as Chairman', *Manchester Guardian*, 24 March 1916, 6.

12 For extended discussion, see Monger, *Patriotism and Propaganda*, ch. 8.

13 Jason Whittaker, *Jerusalem: Blake, Parry, and the Fight for Englishness* (Oxford: Oxford University Press, 2022), 73-91; for brief earlier discussion, see John Ramsden, *Don't Mention the War: The British and the Germans since 1890* (London: Little, Brown, 2006), 100-2.

CHAPTER 3
CHILDREN

Britons, Chapter 2 concluded, were assured that wartime sacrifices would be compensated by a better Britain to come. If increasingly war-weary civilians would not act out of innate duty to their nation (despite propagandists' assertions), perhaps invoking the next generation would strengthen adults' resolve. Children were thus regularly present in propaganda as victims of enemy aggression (whether actual foreign or British children or potential victims), admirers of parental service or inheritors of the present generation's war effort. The Liberal MP Charles McCurdy, having rehashed common criticisms of militarized German *kultur*, indifferent to brutality (discussed in greater detail in Chapter 11), cautioned his readers:

> If from any weariness of soul, or infirmity of spirit, or in any hour of doubt, we were to abandon our task, we might for ourselves gain an easy peace; but we should be leaving to our children a heritage of wars more cruel, or burdens yet more difficult to bear.

Britons may be sick of war, but the current generation could not seek temporary relief at the cost of their children's futures. Speaking in Wigan in 1917, the Labour MP Stephen Walsh said:

> We are fighting now to bring about conditions which will enable every father and mother … to say that this shall be the last of diabolical wars of this kind, and that when we passed away from this earth we shall pass away with the conviction that we have not bequeathed an accursed legacy to our children or our children's children.[1]

As Rosie Kennedy notes, however, total war's demands also meant children, no less than parents, were expected to 'do their bit' via both 'physical participation and mental commitment'.[2] Wartime children were objects, subjects, targets and, sometimes, producers or distributors of propaganda. Nor was this solely a late-war push to use all resources. The *Belgian Refugees Fund: A Children's Picture Book*, from which Figure 3 is drawn, was released in December 1914 at the same time as *King Albert's Book* (discussed in Chapter 2). It was a commercially sponsored children's fundraiser with illustrations by the commercial artist John Hassall. In Figure 3, a boy reacts to the latest 'War Special' news by taking courage, despite the German threat, from his 'Indispensable Pesco Underwear'. In this A–Z picture book, charity fundraiser and crass commercial

Figure 3 Detail from *Belgian Refugees Fund: A Children's Painting Book.*
Source: London: Odhams, 1914. John Johnson Collection, Bodleian Library, University of Oxford (author's photograph).

advertisement, it was hardly children who were the targets reflecting on their wonderful underwear, but their parents.[3] Watching their child colour the image might induce a purchase. Similar, non-commercial, motivations apparently lay behind much more serious propaganda involving children.

Within propaganda, children were, unsurprisingly, frequently portrayed as victims of enemy brutality. A PRC leaflet reproduced a cartoon from the US cartoonist Rollin Kirby, first published in the *New York World*, showing apparitions of naked babies and small children haunting the German kaiser on a beach with the question, 'But why did you kill *us*?' The leaflet's reverse stated baldly that '129 Children perished, including 39 Infants' in the May 1915 sinking of the passenger liner, *Lusitania*, before quoting the Bryce Report on German atrocities involving children during the 1914 invasion. A PRC recruitment poster, meanwhile, depicted a small girl holding a baby in front of a ruined house, with a caption explaining that it was bombarded by the German navy in December 1914, killing four people, including two children. Over 300 women and children had been casualties, overall. The poster asked, 'Men of Britain! Will You Stand This?' Not only, the poster reminded people, were there bayonetted Belgian babies to avenge. *British* children were at direct risk. By contrast, an extensive report on German propaganda, produced to help British propagandists in their work, highlighted a German children's picture book, *Hurra!*, which depicted a small German child and his pet dog killing enemy troops and, in one image, dropping bombs from a Zeppelin, seemingly on London. British childhood innocence thus contrasted with a brutal German culture in which children's books glorified killing.[4]

However, children's links with propaganda went beyond simple representations of victims. They were also hailed as contributors to the war, encouraged to play roles and used to help propaganda messages reach their adult relatives. Andrew Donson suggests conventional representations of children in wartime propaganda embraced both innocent and heroic images. On the one hand, children were vulnerable to attack through no fault of their own. Whether portrayed as victims or participants of the war or inheritors of its outcomes, preserving childhood innocence offered a compelling motivation for adults. The reality, on the other hand, was that this total war did not permit children to be shielded. Thus, children's heroism could also be celebrated.[5] Far from a victim, Jack Cornwell, a sixteen-year-old gunner on HMS *Cheshire*, who died after the 1916 Battle of Jutland and received a posthumous Victoria Cross (VC), was hailed as an example to all. In a book seemingly aimed at children, the publisher and author, J. E. Hodder-Williams, supplied a biography of Cornwell. He 'had few of what people call advantages – he left school when he was fourteen – [but] he had a patriot for a father. And that's a very big advantage indeed.' Jack, apparently, always wanted to go to sea and responded to recruitment calls. His time in training was recounted in terms that stressed fun and adventure, and his exemplary record was noted:

> Now there's great danger that you and I look upon heroes like Jack Cornwell as so gifted, so naturally clever and brave, so out of the ordinary, that we say to ourselves it is no good our trying to follow in their footsteps ... but I do say, and say again, that this was a very ordinary boy as far as any one could judge at school, at the training ground and on his ship.

Jack's abilities, Hodder-Williams wrote, were fostered by his training and officers. When his ship came under fire and the men around him were killed, he kept to his gun, although wounded himself, until the *Chester* withdrew, later dying in a Grimsby hospital. 'Just an ordinary boy, but because he obeyed that call of Duty and Honour – think of it! his name goes down to the ages.' Nonetheless, the lesson for readers was not to simply admire Jack Cornwell's heroism:

> Were there boys and men on such ships whose heroism was as great as Jack Cornwell's? Very likely. Are there men and boys, women and girls, all over the world, in a thousand different ways, every day, showing the same pluck and courage and devotion? Yes, I think so. No one hears of them. They are unknown heroes – but heroes just the same.[6]

Cornwell, then, was an inspiration for all, not necessarily because everyone should join the navy and earn a VC but because he was an ordinary boy who accepted his duty, someone children and adults alike could admire and emulate through their own wartime service. Jack's childhood made him both remarkable, in dying a martial death, and one of millions of unremarkable similar children, equally capable of greatness.

Playing whatever role was possible within the war effort was a common propaganda call towards audiences of all kinds, including children. The National Service Department's Women's Section published a leaflet for children, asking them to collect stray wool from 'the hedges and thorns in your neighbourhood', which could be converted into blankets for soldiers.[7] Such inclusive propaganda messages meant everyone from field marshal to field labourer played a part in the war effort. In a positive sense, this meant every occupation that contributed to the war effort in any way was equally valuable, but in a more coercive sense it also meant everyone, including children, should relate every action and decision to wartime needs. For example, the National War Savings Committee promoted a play, *Patriotic Pence*, for performance by children in schools, in which a mother and children are taught to save their pennies by a fairy named Thrift, who sings:

> Follow me, one and all! and we will go
> To win fresh helpers and with them to show
> How one and all can join in Home Defence
> By mustering their Patriotic Pence!

The children's mother, meanwhile, tells a neighbour, 'The kids and I are trying to do their bit at home, as their Dad's doing his in the Navy.' Like the picture book discussed above, the play had multiple targets. It provided a performative lesson in saving for children and also targeted parents, watching their children perform. Similarly, the Ministry of Food promoted songs and essay competitions in schools on the need for food economy. Meanwhile, a talk aimed at schoolchildren, produced for the unofficial imperial propaganda group, the Victoria League, by a member of the London Teachers' Association, presented 'Gallant Belgium' as the Biblical David facing Goliath. All boys and girls could relate to this as 'a great spirit in a little body'. Having heard of Britain's honour in standing up for Belgium, the children were encouraged: 'Take this home to your parents, and read to them the story of how Britain has always stood by the small nations.' Parents should be informed that a longer book on the subject was available for them. Thus, messages about British protection could be imparted to children directly and related back or read to parents by their children, while these adults could then read in greater depth on the subject. As Kennedy notes, schoolchildren were also mobilized to grow and prepare food for the nation by the Board of Education, again with expectations that such lessons would filter home.[8] Using children as vehicles for propaganda in these ways broadened the means by which organizations could reach the public, alongside campaigns directly addressing adult civilians.

These were not the only ways that children participated in propaganda work, however. Organizations like the Boy Scouts and Girl Guides were mobilized for war work throughout the conflict. A 1915 recruitment poster depicted a Scout handing ammunition to a soldier, alongside further images of a sailor, nurse, munitions worker and ironworker, with the question 'Are YOU in this' directed towards a final, idle man to the side. Scouts also played active parts in propaganda – for instance, distributing pamphlets in Cornwall and Devon for the NWAC in 1918 – while they also formed part of parades organized for the fourth anniversary of Britain's entry into the war on 4 August 1918.[9] By this time, capitalizing on the youth voluntarism of the Scouts and Guides was already routine. Advising on the organization of the National Service campaign in early 1917, the Director of Enrolment, Major C. G. C. Hamilton, MP, suggested using 'boy scouts or girl guides or any other volunteers' to put up posters if possible, before paying local billposters, while in Brighton Scouts earned 'war service' badges for their part as messengers in a local war savings campaign which raised over £4,000. By 1918, a female NWAC propagandist suggested that, with the demands of war work increasing, women had found new status. Not only that,

> We shall find that old ladies who live in country houses and have pony carts, and Girl Guides, and any small boys and girls with bicycles, will help to deliver goods or to fetch them from the market town if anyone suggests to them that their work will be useful.

Once again, the call of duty was assumed to resonate in every ear, including, if not especially, those not usually expected to fulfil public duties.[10] As Kennedy notes, Girl Guides – 50,000 strong by 1916 – were encouraged to set an example to the public by undertaking useful work for the war effort. Random patriotic displays would have little effect, but meaningful effort, particularly that channelled into tasks 'appropriate' for girls, would inspire others.[11]

If it was hoped children could inspire civilian effort, either to protect children from such a war in future or to match their wartime service, another group for whom children were presented as inspiration were servicemen. While attention often focuses on recruitment of servicemen by propaganda, by the war's later years propagandists also recognized the need to try to motivate (or remobilize) those in armed service. C. E. Montague – himself a wartime propagandist – suggested that '"can't believe a word you read" had long been becoming a catch-phrase in the army' due to unrealistic press depictions of their exploits.[12] Late-war propagandists, producing material for a free newspaper for soldiers on leave, thus avoided talk of glory, focusing instead on things presumed to still motivate servicemen. In particular, comforting images of home were regularly portrayed. *Welcome*'s masthead showed soldiers exiting a lorry on one side of a village road, with a woman, child and dog waiting at an open gate on the other side. Home was still presumed to be where soldiers' hearts lay. Several front-page illustrations by the artists Wilmot Lunt and W. F. Blood showed happy soldiers at home with children. 'Daddy's Little 'Un' showed a soldier holding up his son with a gifted German helmet dropping over his eyes. 'Daddy's First Kiss' saw another soldier presented with his baby for the first time amid home's comforts. 'Waiting for Daddy' showed a mother, boy scout and girl guide waiting at 'Sweethome' station, while 'Reveille in Blighty' saw a father surprisingly pleased to be awakened by a small boy with a trumpet! The prominence and repetitiveness of these depictions suggest a propagandist perspective that even those disenchanted with the war could still find motivation in their children's happiness.[13] While Lunt and Blood's pictures provided soft and soothing reassurance, another cartoon, by Roland Hill, took a more humorous approach, encouraging a sense of mutual mischief between father and son. Challenged on what his father would say about a young Scottish boy fishing on the Sabbath, the reply came, 'Weel, uncle, the last time he said – "Where the H-ll's the fish"?' Here, the emphasis was on (moderate and controlled) disobedience – a link between servicemen, barely restrained by military discipline, and their sons, supposedly answerable to adults.[14] Such propaganda aimed to reassure soldiers that their cherished normal lives awaited their return.

Whether as victims or heroes, examples, conduits for propaganda or the comforting reward for soldierly toil, children were routine symbols of wartime service, sacrifice and duty. If children could learn to save or grow their own food, their parents had no excuse. If those parents wanted to retain their children's happiness and innocence, meanwhile, they must keep contributing to the war effort. Brutality towards children in other war zones reminded British audiences that worse privations than wartime shortages and armed service were possible. Children assisted the delivery of a core propaganda message of duty despite adversity. If audiences were increasingly sceptical of claims about public duty to the state or empire, promoting the duty to protect and nurture the next generation gave a message that reduced duty to someone's nearest and dearest before, as Chapter 4 discusses, scaling this up from the family to the local, national and supranational community.

Notes

1. Charles McCurdy, *To Restore the Ten Commandments: The Basis of a Permanent Peace for Europe* (London: Hodder & Stoughton, n.d. [1917]), 15; 'To Combat Pacifism. A Week's Campaign at Wigan and Ince', *Wigan Examiner*, 28 September 1917, 7.
2. Rosie Kennedy, 'Children' in Strachan, *British Home Front*, 564. For broader comments on propaganda and children, see Demm, *Censorship and Propaganda*, 96–104.

3 *Belgian Relief Fund: A Children's Painting Book* (London: Odhams, 1914), 'I'.
4 'But Why Did You Kill *Us*?' (PRC leaflet no. 44); 'Men of Britain! Will You Stand This?' (PRC poster no. 51); P. C. M. [Peter Chalmers Mitchell], Report on the Propaganda Library (MI7b, August 1917), 3. A copy is held at The National Archives: Public Record Office, Kew (henceforth TNA), CAB17/196. A digitized copy is accessible via the British Library catalogue; Herbert Rikli, *Hurra!: ein Kriegs-Bilderbuch* (Stuttgart: Loewes Verlag, 1915), 21.
5 Andrew Donson, 'Children and Youth', in Ute Daniel, Peter Gatrell, Oliver Janz, Heather Jones, Jennifer Keene, Alan Kramer and Bill Nasson (eds), *1914–1918 Online: International Encyclopedia of the First World War* (Berlin: Freie Universität Berlin, 2014).
6 Anonymous [J. E. Hodder-Williams], *Jack Cornwell: The Story of John Travers Cornwell, V.C., 'Boy – 1st Class'* (Toronto: Hodder & Stoughton, 1918), 14, 19, 32–3, 78.
7 Imperial War Museum [henceforth IWM], MS Women, War and Society, 1914–1918: Women at War Collection, EMP49.1/24, 'National Wool Collection. Notice to Children' (National Service leaflet W53).
8 Mrs Horace [Mary] Porter *Patriotic Pence or The Home Fairy: A Musical War Savings Play for Young People* (London: Evans Brothers, n.d. [1917]), 17, 15. For fuller discussion, see David Monger, 'Tangible Patriotism during the First World War: Individuals and the Nation in British Propaganda', *War & Society*, 37, no. 4 (2018); W. J. Pincombe, *Britain and Gallant Belgium: A Talk to the School Children of Britain* (Victoria League leaflet no. 6, London: J. Wyman, n.d.), 3, 7; Rosie Kennedy, *The Children's War, 1914–1918* (Basingstoke: Palgrave Macmillan, 2014), 125–8. For schools, see also Barry Blades, *Roll of Honour: Schooling and the Great War, 1914–1919* (Barnsley: Pen & Sword, 2015), esp. chs. 3–4.
9 'Are YOU in this?' (PRC poster no. 112, 1915); Monger, *Patriotism and Propaganda*, 58. For examples of Scouts' presence at War Anniversary parades, see 'Remembrance Day in Croydon', *Croydon Times*, 7 August 1918, 1; 'Mayor and Councillors of Battersea Attend at St. Mary's', *Battersea Boro' News*, 9 August 1918, 2; 'Evesham. Remembrance Day at Evesham', *Evesham Journal and Four Shires Advertiser*, 10 August 1918, 6.
10 Bodleian Library, Oxford (henceforth BLO), John Johnson Collection, 'National Service. Addresses by Lord Rhondda and Mr. Neville Chamberlain to Representatives from National Service Committees. Problems of Organization Explained in Questions and Answers by Major C.G.C. Hamilton, M.P.' (National Service pamphlet P15, 6 March 1917), 20; 'Throughout the Country', *War Savings*, 1, no. 11 (July 1917), 116–17; Margaret Osborne [E. M. Goodman], 'Not Too Old at Forty – or Even Sixty', *Nuneaton Observer War Supplement*, week ending 4 May 1918, 2.
11 Kennedy, *Children's War*, 115–19. On Guides and the war, see also Michelle Smith, 'Be(ing) Prepared: Girl Guides, Colonial Life, and National Strength', *Limina*, 12 (2006).
12 C. E. Montague, *Disenchantment* (London: Chatto & Windus, [1922] 1924), 98.
13 Wilmot Lunt and W. F. Blood (all), 'Daddy's Little "Un"', *Welcome*, 8 May 1918, 61; 'Daddy's First Kiss', *Welcome*, no. 24, 11 September 1918, 277; 'Waiting for Daddy', *Welcome*, 21 August 1918, 241; 'Reveille in Blighty', *Welcome*, 27 November 1918, 97. For fuller discussion of the use of comforting images of home in propaganda to soldiers, see David Monger, 'Soldiers, Propaganda and Ideas of Home', esp. 342–6.
14 Roland Hill, untitled ('Fishing'), *Welcome*, 28 August 1918, 256. Details of the cartoon title are from TNA T102/19, NWAC Production Department ledgers.

CHAPTER 4
DUTY

A pamphlet reproducing a piece by the eminent soldier Lord Roberts, shortly before his death in November 1914, began with Roberts's assertion that all Britons' duty was to surrender everything to the state:

> There is but one duty for the British citizen at the present time – men and women, young and old, rich and poor, all alike must place everything at the service of the State. Nothing must be kept back – time, energy, money, talents, even life itself, must be freely offered in this supreme crisis.

Thirty-one further pages then drily summarized the breakdown of European relations into war, asserted German culpability (unusually, however, Roberts suggested caution about believing tales of German war crimes, perhaps recalling criticism of his army's actions during the Second Boer War) and stressed Britain and its empire's virtues, before calling for further volunteers.[1] Less industrious readers, who did not go beyond the first paragraph, however, had already received the pamphlet's core message. Duty was the cornerstone of nearly all wartime propaganda. Though other elements – particularly atrocity propaganda – provided more vivid content, they generally provided context for a call for Britons to meet their duties. As Chapter 3 noted, Britons were reminded of their duty to see the war through for the sake of their children and future generations. This was, perhaps, the most intimate of several layers of duty: civilians had duties to serve because servicemen bore greater burdens; communities were duty-bound to economize to the greatest possible extent because other communities may not be able to; Britain met its duty to protect small nations and, in the process, preserved wider civilization. John Galsworthy, one of several eminent writers recruited to write propaganda for neutrals on behalf of Wellington House, brought some of this together in a piece published in the *New York Times' Current History* magazine in 1914. Declaring himself a lover of peace and hostile to militarism, he nonetheless argued that

> there is a national honour charged with the future happiness of man, that loyalty is due from those living to those that will come after; that civilisation can only wax and flourish in a world where faith is kept; that for nations, as for individuals, there are laws of duty, whose violation harms the whole human race.[2]

With such high stakes asserted and, according to Pennell, widely accepted from the war's earliest days, all Britons, from schoolchildren to pensioners, should 'do their bit'.[3]

Propagandists made this demand inclusive by emphasizing that virtually all activities, from spring cleaning to preserve domestic health, to savings campaigns, to shell manufacture, were important contributions to the war effort.[4] Commercial organizations exploited such messages of duty too – Royal Vinolia face cream, for instance, depicted a munition worker in action with the motto 'Beauty on Duty has a Duty to Beauty', emphasizing that, while taking on new wartime roles, women still had beauty standards to maintain.[5] Everyone was thus not only included in the war effort but also, implicitly, accountable for the part they played.

Early recruitment propaganda stressed heavily men's duty to enlist – for example, a mother was depicted telling her son, 'Go! it's your Duty lad' – but as the war progressed, particularly after the introduction of conscription in 1916, propaganda increasingly focused on civilians' duties to servicemen.[6] Like Hodder Williams's depiction of the sailor Jack Cornwell as an ordinary boy doing extraordinary things, A. A. Milne, writing pieces for colonial newspapers for MI7b in 1918, evoked a simple man, bound by duty, joining the army and finding a place among his fellow soldiers:

> He didn't look like a soldier … In private life he had been some sort of a clerk, and I can see him taking his wife and children very regularly to church on Sundays. The war must have come as a shock to him in his quiet life, but he joined up from a strong sense of duty, no doubt. There was Belgium, you see …
>
> Now a sense of duty is a very fine thing, and to some people it may be sustaining under hardships, but with others it does not last. It saw him through his training in England, but when he got to France he began to feel himself very seriously in need of something else. And, again unconsciously, he found something; some sustaining thought, which enabled him, so far from home, to bear himself cheerfully. His discovery was this – he was 'one of the boys'. …
>
> Anybody less like 'one of the boys' could hardly be found in the British army. But the realization that he was out there with them 'doing his bit', … became his spiritual nourishment.

In Milne's hands, this awkward clerk (a signal officer, like Milne himself) accepted his national duty but found fulfilment in comradeship. At the end of the piece, the soldier is carried away, mortally wounded. Milne's emphasis on civilian soldiers' ordinary heroism seemingly sanitizes the brutality of military service. Despite common claims of public ignorance, however, audiences had little doubt of the war's realities. Rather, Milne's account elevated even the least martial soldier as an example to all of duty, forbearance and sacrifice.[7] The subtext was that, if the clerk could manage – 'Well, we must keep smiling, I'm doing my bit out here' – civilians' modest discomforts should be borne willingly.

Emphasis on civilians' duty to servicemen varied from indirect examples like Milne's to blunter confrontations like the poster, described in Chapter 2, reminding civilians that sailors' lives were risked to import food. This accompanied similar appeals, like that of the Food Controller Lord Devonport, that claimed by 'strict control of our daily bread we can best help the men who are gallantly fighting on sea and land to achieve victory'. The NWAC, meanwhile, issued a pamphlet, *An Infantryman on Strikes*, describing the hard conditions of soldiers, 'fighting, dying at a shilling a day', to invalidate industrial action,[8] while Milne, in another article, took a more confrontational tone. In 'The Infantryman's Friend', he depicted a British unit under aerial bombardment, unhindered by British opposition:

> I speak for the infantry. I am one of them. We do the dirty work. We are there to be shot at. You who read this have a brother or a son or a husband in the infantry – anyhow a friend? Of course you have; we all have. Do you realise what the aeroplane means to that son of yours, that friend? …
>
> He is in an old trench line, in support. His trench, not much of a one at the best, is being shelled to the devil. Why? Because a German aeroplane has spotted troops in that trench, and has turned on the German guns … Why was that German aeroplane ever allowed to come there? Why is it allowed to stay? Because we haven't enough aeroplanes to look after that part of the line. Why not? Oh, well, there's a bit of a strike on.[9]

Similarly, in a message to 'fellow War Savers' in 1917, the NWSC's chairman, Sir Robert Kindersley, wrote that

> public opinion must be so strong that the blatant spender becomes a social outcast.
>
> We must make people realise that whoever amongst us is prosperous to-day, that prosperity is only possible because of the sacrifice of life and limb on the part of those who we at home have sent out to fight for us, and that therefore every shilling we earn beyond what is necessary for our health and efficiency is in the nature of a sacred trust …
>
> Let us remember that while our fighting forces are making such great sacrifices, it is our duty and our privilege to do our utmost to keep the nation financially sound … In other words, if we weaken the economic fabric of the nation by our self-indulgence we are betraying those whom we have sent to fight.[10]

As long as soldiers did their duty it was a stated assumption that civilians do likewise. In all the examples above, propagandists called on Britons to accept privations and hardships not so much for the abstract health of the nation but for the real help of servicemen who 'we all' knew personally.

Appeals to duty also targeted a sense of community. A call for Women's Army Auxiliary Corps (WAAC) volunteers, placed in several newspapers in June 1917, by Grace Curnock, press representative of the National Service Department's Women's Section, suggested:

> The soldiers of Devon and Cornwall, of Somerset and Dorset have proved themselves to be among the most gallant in the country …
>
> It lies now with the girls and women of the South-west to show how great can be their patriotism and self-sacrifice in the country's cause … not only in nursing

… but now in actually releasing fit men for the fighting line by undertaking office and sedentary work which has kept the soldiers at the base …

The country looks to the girls of this district to 'join up'.

A version of the article appeared in the *Western Times* on 29 June, beneath the article 'Another Example of Patriotism at Exeter', describing several brothers on active service (one of whom had been killed) while their sister worked in munitions production and a notice of a missing Devonian soldier.[11] Here, Curnock's original notice was accentuated by editorial choices that made the stakes clearer to readers. Propaganda work, whether in the form of paid notices or of events in local communities, frequently benefited from local press accompaniment or commentary. Calls to 'release a fit man', meanwhile, were increasingly made to women as manpower concerns grew – a national service poster, for instance (Figure 4), printed for use in Leeds, affirmed that 'every girl' who joined the WAAC released 'a man' for the army. Young women's service was not only elevated by emphasizing that WAAC workers wore khaki but also downgraded by describing young women, required to be over twenty, as 'girls' whose lesser role allowed men to fight.

Nonetheless, historians have pointed to the impact of propaganda appeals to duty, and groups' acceptance of the demands, as influential in changing perspectives of citizenship in Britain. Gullace argues that wartime propaganda 'facilitated a fundamental shift in the parameters of citizenship'. Rather than assigning citizenship based on ideas of men's 'physical force', wartime promotion of soldiers and sailors as the best of Britain, but male 'shirkers' as the worst, led to an emphasis instead on national service. Women's active embrace of wartime service, including answering the calls to release fit men for fighting, made demands for full citizenship much harder to resist, even if many young

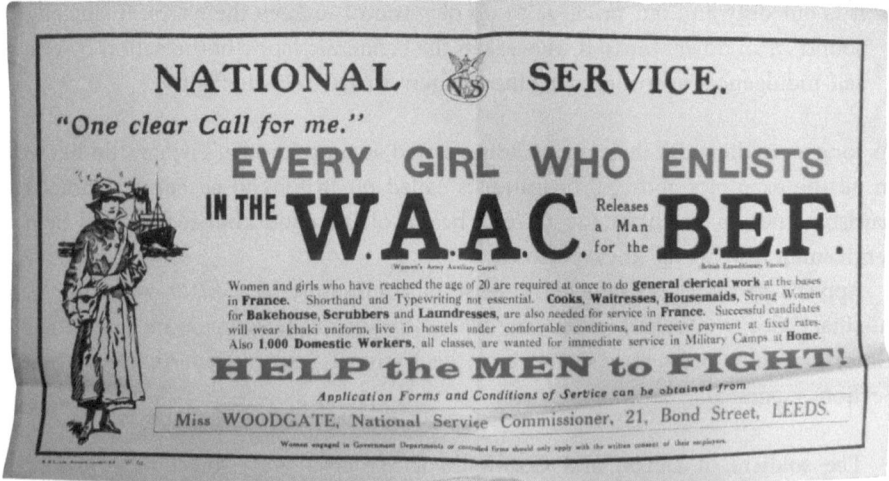

Figure 4 National Service poster W61, 'One Clear Call for Me'.
Source: National Archives, Kew (TNA), NATS1/109 (author's photograph).

women who answered the call were excluded by the over-thirty age restriction on women's enfranchisement in 1918.[12] Politicians, including the fierce pre-war opponent of women's suffrage, former prime minister Herbert Asquith and the independent Irish Nationalist D. D. Sheehan, argued in propaganda speeches or writing that women's war service advanced their claims to citizenship. Further, widespread propaganda assertions that nearly every act, including housework, could be a patriotic contribution to the war effort meant not only enlistment in formal national service, nursing or munitions work qualified women for citizenship. Housewives and mothers, keeping the home fires burning and nurturing the nation's future, also saw their service recognized as what the female journalist and propagandist E. M. Goodman labelled part of a 'citizen's duty', while women workers' health was prioritized in some wartime and post-war regulations.[13]

Duty and service remained fundamental elements of propaganda appeals to the war's end. Particularly by the war's later years, however, propagandists recognized that simply demanding more and more from civilians was unlikely to yield desired results. A common approach by groups like the NWAC, NWSC, national service and food control propagandists was thus to mix acknowledgements of the duties civilians had already met with calls for further effort. Speakers at NWAC events in Liverpool, Sheffield and Keighley in Yorkshire and Brecon in South Wales all highlighted local communities' particular achievements and virtues, before emphasizing the need for still more.[14] At Bretforton in Worcestershire, meanwhile, at another NWAC meeting

> Mr. J.B. Wright said the Central War Savings Committee desired him to thank them for the splendid work they had done in Bretforton. The children had done splendidly, and there were none better. He asked them to make a new effort, and so end the war quicker.[15]

Overlapping messages from propaganda bodies (in this case, the NWSC followed by the NWAC) kept up a steady message of ongoing need for civilian effort. Some weeks could see multiple organizations holding meetings. At Gloucester, J. T. Brownlee, chairman of the Amalgamated Society of Engineers, began his appeal at a 1917 national service meeting by tying his members' willingness to suspend peacetime workplace conditions to military achievements:

> If, as was the case, it was to the eternal credit of their Belgian comrades that they delayed the progress of the Huns in the opening days of the war, the skilled workmen of this country, by relinquishing at the call of the nation their hard-won and established workshop conditions, had gained no less an honour and placed no less a debt upon future generations.

Nonetheless, there was still more to do:

> If the people were desirous of maintaining the honourable traditions of the British race and of showing to the despots of mid-Europe that they stood by voluntaryism

and damned compulsion, let them all enrol in the National Service movement and make compulsion unnecessary.

Brownlee's fellow trade unionists, then, had already shown patriotic valour in accepting harder working conditions but had a 'bounden duty to support the nation' through national service.[16] Men, women and children and cities, towns, villages and organized labour alike were thus praised for their collective efforts as precursors to further requests for dutiful service. Voluntarism, as a later chapter discusses, exemplified the UK's unique character in civilians' free choice of duty (even after conscription). Even in Ireland in 1918, two years after the Easter Rising's bloody repression, which poisoned Irish public sentiment, a nationalist leader of a voluntary recruiting scheme, despite attracting limited numbers, believed the attempt had 'achieved "good educative results in the broad principles of citizenship"'.[17] Offering opportunities for voluntary enlistment, even in such a disturbed environment, maintained the link between service and citizenship that nationalist Home Rule advocates made from the beginning of the war. William Redmond, reflecting on Irish leaders' decision to support the war effort, prior to his own death in combat, noted that, with Home Rule granted, 'the King and representatives of the British people had conceded [Ireland's] claim. Was it conceivable then that Ireland should refrain from carrying out her pledged word?'[18] For nationalists like Redmond, like so many British propagandists, real citizenship meant accepting citizens' duties in order to preserve citizens' rights.

Notes

1. Field-Marshal Earl Roberts, *The Supreme Duty of the Citizen at the Present Crisis: The Last Message to His Fellow-Countrymen* (London: Williams & Norgate, n.d. [1915]), 1, 30–1. Roberts's comments originally appeared in the *Hibbert Journal* in 1914.
2. John Galsworthy, 'A "Credo" for Keeping Faith', *Current History*, 1, no. 1 (1914), 102–3. Galsworthy later published a revised version as 'Credo', in *A Sheaf* (London: William Heinemann, 1916), quotation at 170. For the recruitment of writers, see, for example, Buitenhuis, *Great War of Words*, 1, 14.
3. Pennell, *Kingdom United*, 57–67; Gregory, *Last Great War*, 95; Kennedy, 'Children', 564.
4. For spring cleaning, see David Monger, 'Nothing Special? Propaganda and Women's Roles in Late First World War Britain', *Women's History Review*, 23, no. 4 (2014), 528–9. On wartime promotion of domestic management, see also Paul Ward, 'Empire and the Everyday: Britishers and Imperialism in Women's Lives in the Great War', in Philip Buckner and R. Douglas Francis (eds), *Rediscovering the British World* (Calgary: University of Calgary Press, 2005). For the fostering of local competitive pride in war savings, see David Monger, 'Familiarity Breeds Consent? Patriotic Rituals in British First World War Propaganda', *Twentieth Century British History*, 26, no. 4 (2015), 519–24.
5. Luci Gosling, 'Saving Face – Beauty for Women Workers during the First World War', *Picturing the Great War: The First World War Blog from Mary Evans Picture Library*, 16 December 2013: https://blog.maryevans.com/2013/12/saving-face-beauty-for-women-workers-during-the-first-world-war.html (accessed 1 November 2023).
6. 'Go! It's Your Duty, Lad' (PRC poster no. 109, n.d. [1914]).

7   2nd-Lieutenant A. A. Milne, 'One of the Boys', *Mercury* (Hobart), 1 May 1918, 8. On public knowledge of soldiers' conditions, see, for example, Helen B. McCartney,*Citizen Soldiers: The Liverpool Territorials in the First World War* (Cambridge: Cambridge University Press, 2005), ch. 5, esp. 109–16.
8   BLO, John Johnson Collection, Box 19, 'Rationing': Ministry of Food circular no. 67, 29 May 1917; Sergeant H. V. Holmes, *An Infantryman on Strikes: An Appeal to the Workers of Great Britain* (n.p.d. [NWAC, 1918]), 19.
9   A. A. M., 'The Infantryman's Friend', *Otago Witness*, 13 February 1918, 55.
10 TNA NSC 6/105, 'The National War Savings Committee', pamphlet A.C.16 (1917).
11 TNA NATS 1/1320, 'Girls for France. Women's Army Auxiliary Corps', sent to 19 papers, 26 June 1917; 'Girls for France', *Western Times*, 29 June 1917, 7.
12 Gullace, *Blood of Our Sons*, quotation at 196. Cf. the distinctions drawn by Janet S. K. Watson, *Fighting Different War: Experience, Memory and the First World War in Britain* (Cambridge: Cambridge University Press, 2005) between those who considered their war work dutiful service and those who took a more material view.
13 Monger, *Patriotism and Propaganda*, 188, 209–10; Monger, 'Nothing Special?', Goodman quotation at 534; Susan R. Grayzel, *Women's Identities at War: Gender, Motherhood, and Politics in Britain and France during the First World War* (Chapel Hill: University of North Carolina Press, 1999), esp. ch. 3.
14 Monger, *Patriotism and Propaganda*, 189–94; 'Picton Hall. Mr. Asquith & Unruly Women', *Liverpool Daily Post & Mercury*, 12 October 1917, 6.
15 'District News. Evesham. National War Aims. Meetings in Evesham District', *Evesham Journal & Four Shires Advertiser*, 20 October 1917, 6.
16 'National Service', *Gloucester Journal*, 24 March 1917, 3.
17 A. M. Sullivan, cited in Brendan Maartens, 'For "Common Christianity": War, Peace and the Campaign of the Irish Recruiting Council, 1918', *English Historical Review*, 136, no. 579 (2021), 392. For further discussion of appeals to duty in Ireland, see Catriona Pennell, 'Presenting the War in Ireland, 1914–1918' in Troy R. E. Paddock (ed.), *World War I and Propaganda* (Leiden: Brill, 2014); Monger, 'The Press and Propaganda', 502–5.
18 William Redmond, 'From the Trenches: A Plea and a Claim', reprinted from the *Dublin Review*, April 1917, in *Major William Redmond* (London: Burns & Oates, 1918), 27.

CHAPTER 5
EMPIRE

The call of the great adventure for the defence of Empire, for the freedom of small nations, for those principles of loyalty to the given word, of even-handed justice and of personal liberty which are the secret of the British Raj, had no sooner sounded than every province of the Empire sprang to arms. English and Boers, Scots and Canadians, Irish and Indians, men of Australia, New Zealand, Newfoundland and Africa, even the little island peoples of Fiji and Niué and the Cook Islands, offered their lives.[1]

If Ireland, treated more like a colony than integral to the UK, was reminded of and commended for dutiful conduct, so was Britain's empire. The NWAC's 1918 handbook, quoted above, provides a typical perspective on imperial participation, here meant for domestic audiences. The willing involvement of imperial subjects, propagandists opined, showed that Britain's empire was virtuous and benevolent and that its war was just. Imperial contributions were regularly celebrated and imperial figures acted as propagandists, again validating British conduct. The South African statesman Jan Christiaan Smuts, an armed opponent of Britain during the Second Boer War at the turn of the century, emerged as a celebrated advocate later in the war, and others also took propaganda roles, from low-level speakers to leadership. By 1918, the Canadian press magnate, Lord Beaverbrook, as Minister of Information, was British propaganda's parliamentary face. Just as Britain's war was global and imperial, so was its propaganda.

Imperial fellow-feeling was not taken for granted, as demonstrated by extensive efforts to disseminate official propaganda to the empire via organizations like Wellington House and MI7b. Wellington House relied on various steamship and railway companies to distribute written propaganda to imperial territories alongside neutral nations – a 1916 report claimed three million pamphlets were thus distributed – as well as working with groups like the Overseas Club (whose membership certificate proclaimed the empire 'to stand for justice, freedom, order and good government' and committed members to its active promotion and protection). MI7b, similarly, worked with the Royal Colonial Institute (RCI) to distribute articles to newspapers in Britain's settler Dominions. It claimed to have produced 60–70 articles per week by 1918, offered over 40,000 articles to the press and recorded over 8,000 instances of publication.[2] Such efforts accompanied those by existing groups like the Victoria League (VL), who continued promoting the empire's cause.[3] From the war's start to finish, then, empire loomed as both reassurance and concern.

British authorities were reassured by imperial contributions to the Boer War between 1899 and 1902, and discussions at the 1907 Imperial Conference led to the granting of Dominion status, by 1910, to Britain's settlement colonies – Australia, Canada, Newfoundland, New Zealand and South Africa. This conference also discussed possible 'Imperial Partnership for defence … operated on an agreed basis of equality of sacrifice', but a contemporary Canadian commentator suggested any results would not be known till the future.[4] At the war's outbreak, the Dominions and India declared war on Germany alongside Britain, but threats to imperial unity appeared. A rebellion in South Africa in 1914, against plans to invade German South-West Africa at British request – labelled by André Wessels as 'a farce in the veld' – was overcome by South African government forces. Second, the Ottoman Empire's declaration of *jihad* against Britain and its allies, encouraged by Germany, called on over 100 million Muslims in Britain's empire to join the Ottoman Empire's fight. While this call did not produce mass Islamic uprisings, it provoked small-scale mutinies, substantial 'counterpropaganda' in Britain's Asian and African imperial territories and sustained focus on the Middle East.[5] Britain's Press Bureau (PB), which generally censored information affecting British security, issued notices to newspaper editors to avoid referring to 'a war of Christian versus Moslem', citing the possible offence to many Muslims within the empire.[6] While both threats were contained, empire could not be treated casually by propagandists. Later controversies over the proposed introduction of conscription – accepted despite protests in Canada and New Zealand, rejected in Australia and hastily withdrawn in Ireland – further demonstrated that imperial support was neither absolute nor unquestioning but required cultivation.

For domestic consumption, nonetheless, empire was largely a positive presence in propaganda. PRC publications quickly highlighted imperial contributions. One quoted a lengthy speech by Prime Minister Asquith, who praised the supposedly spontaneous assertions by 'Canada, Australia, South Africa, New Zealand and Newfoundland, children of the Empire … not as an obligation but as a privilege' that they would provide money, supplies and soldiers. In India, every 'class and creed, British and native, princes and people, Hindus and Mahomedans, vie with one another' to show support because they were part of 'an Empire which knows no distinction of race or caste'. A second pamphlet, *The Rally of Our United Empire*, gloated that Germany had expected an Indian uprising against Britain: 'India, it is true, has risen as one man – in enthusiastic support of her Emperor King.' It then listed the contributions of Britain's Dominions, crown colonies and India before calling for British volunteers.[7] The Victoria League, meanwhile, published a pamphlet by the pro-British Indian administrator, Bhupendranath Basu, which suggested the war provided India's 'great opportunity', not to escape British rule but to '[claim] to hold an equal position with other parts of the Empire'. This would see a future of 'the East and the West, India and England, marching onwards in comradeship'. As Matthew Hendley suggests, regular assertions of Indian loyalty indicate uncertainty more than confidence that this was true. Santanu Das adds that widespread professions of loyalty were accompanied by ambitions for changes to Indians' status, similar to and beyond those stated by Basu, which war service might assist. In 1918, Mohandas Gandhi, already promoting campaigns of non-violent resistance, voluntarily assisted military recruitment, asserting that military service enhanced ambitions for *swaraj* (self-rule).[8]

Gandhi was not the only prominent imperial figure to assist British propaganda. From statesmen to sportsmen, imperial voices and administration were welcome contributions. Multiple exhibitions were held of military rugby teams, with crowds in their thousands attending games involving Dominion troops, although an announced tour of New Zealand players in early 1917 was hastily cancelled as unseemly. Nonetheless, the appeal of trans-imperial sporting rivalry seemingly remained later in the war, with one of A. A. Milne's MI7b articles for Dominion consumption using a charity match between armed forces England and Dominion XIs, featuring C. B. Fry and the Australian test players Charlie Kelleway and Charlie Macartney, to offer wistful reflections on the peacetime luxury of a day's cricket.[9] Ordinary servicemen from the Dominions were also sometimes seconded for platform speaking. In North Devon, for instance, Lt. P. H. Aspinall appeared at an NWAC event alongside local Conservative and Liberal politicians – who later contested the 1918 election – and the prominent Devonian, Earl Fortescue. Aspinall suggested Dominion contributions should not be celebrated as exceptional. Despite being able to fit the British Isles 'twenty-five times into Australia', and his nation's record of sending 350,000 troops from a population of only 5 million, Aspinall argued:

> To say they came here to fight for the British was wrong; they were part and parcel of the British Empire just as much as Ilfracombe was, and they fought as such. Every Australian, even those who had never been to England spoke of 'going home'.

Aspinall's speech thus drew his audience's attention to the size and potential of Britain's empire, while suggesting no meaningful difference between his continent and the small Devon towns he addressed. Nonetheless, in a cheered nod to local pride, the Liberal politician Lt. J. T. Tudor Rees chided Aspinall that, for all Australia's grandeur, it could not match the local scenery.[10] As a fellow soldier, Tudor Rees could tease his Dominion guest without insulting servicemen.

Elsewhere, imperial politicians wrote and spoke on behalf of the war effort. Like Aspinall, Smuts proved adept at uniting the very specific and very broad. Touring industrial areas of Britain, he connected the desires of workers in Sheffield or Tonypandy with the wartime aims of Britain and its empire. Social progress could best be achieved through a victory that ended the threat of war, allowing Britain to redirect resources to social reform. The fact that he, as a former enemy, was now a member of the war cabinet and advocated Britain's cause was evidence of the empire's justness, while discussion of a possible League of Nations neglected that Britain's 'Commonwealth of Nations' was 'not an Empire. Germany is an Empire, so was Rome, and so is India, but we are a system of nations, a community of states and of nations', which set an example for the world. Implicitly, the British empire, not the United States and President Wilson, led efforts to form a collaborative international community.[11] Smuts's exclusion of India from his Commonwealth went against some wider claims that the war had changed imperial relations more fundamentally, with the Canadian prime minister, Sir Robert Borden, on a platform shared with Smuts elsewhere, celebrating India 'for the first time taking her place at the national council of Empire' at the 1917 Imperial Conference in London.[12] However, it chimed with other examples of selectivity, as discussed later. Nonetheless, Smuts, perhaps more effectively than any other propagandist, combined the priorities of individual workers, Britain's national war effort, its claimed ideals and the wider proclaimed values of empire in seeking to invigorate British audiences.

As noted above, British propaganda was disseminated to the empire by organizations including Wellington House and MI7b, with assistance from commercial organizations and imperial groups like the RCI and VL. A 'Supplementary Imperial Service', supplied by Reuters News Agency at the request of the Department of Information, added to the flow of propaganda into the Dominions from 1917. However, propaganda was also developed separately within imperial territories, while figures like Beaverbrook, or the Canadian Campbell Stuart, who played a prominent role in Lord Northcliffe's Department of Enemy Propaganda in 1918, ensured British propaganda *received* imperial perspectives, as well as informing them.[13] Beaverbrook influenced several areas of propaganda, seeing to the promotion (in some people's view, overstatement) of Canada's efforts via the Canadian War Records Office, extending film propaganda through his chairmanship of the War Office Cinematographic Committee (WOCC) from 1916 and heading the Ministry of Information (ostensibly, though not actually, overseeing all British propaganda) from 1918.[14] British propaganda to empire was thus at least partly a dialogue rather than monologue. New Zealand's propaganda, Greg Hynes shows, relied considerably on British material but adapted it to local needs. For instance, it edited the PRC poster, 'The Empire Needs Men', depicting a lion with younger lions behind it: where the original named the young lions as 'the overseas states', New Zealand's version specifically named Australia, Canada, India and New Zealand (identifying India, rather than South Africa, as one of the most stable parts of empire), and was widely disseminated. Like Britain, which recruited many leading writers and artists to work for Wellington House and other organizations, the official Australian response to ineffective earlier recruiting propaganda was to enlist the talents of the artist Norman Lindsay to enliven the appeals. Also like Britain, unofficial organizations in Australia took arguments to greater extremes.[15] Meanwhile, India ran War Loan campaigns targeting large and small investors alike in 1917–18. While the British press suggested the campaign lacked the vigour of British equivalents, the first and second (1918) Indian War Loans raised funds well beyond what had been hoped and used many similar techniques to British campaigns, organizing meetings addressed by local notables, attracting attention through examples of military technology, which the loans would support, publishing lists of subscribers and appealing to material self-interest. At the same time, however, similarly to Gandhi's expectation that military service might enhance calls for self-rule, the war loans were promoted by official voices as a means to enhance India's status within the empire.[16]

Such recognition was only partially given. As the NWAC handbook indicated, India, as well as small colonies, were celebrated, with India discussed first. In the Ministry of Information's 1918 animated film, *Britain's Effort*, India's depiction as coming to

Empire

Figure 5 Still from Lancelot Speed, *Britain's Effort*.
Source: Ministry of Information, 1918. © Imperial War Museum (IWM 514).

Britain's aid atop an ornately dressed elephant through a jungle was no more exotic than the Canadian soldier riding a moose in a mountainous wilderness, the Australian hopping to duty astride a kangaroo, the South African hugging a wary springbok in front of Table Mountain or the New Zealander with his arm inexplicably draped over an extinct moa next to a marae (Figure 5).[17] Yet non-white contributions were often treated with what Das describes as 'racist condescension'. In Jamaica, Richard Smith's survey of propaganda notes many familiar themes from Britain – among them the brutality of Germany and the virtues of Britain's empire – that were tailored to avoid encouraging criticism of imperial rule or disruption to racial hierarchies. Colonial contributions were 'often overshadowed' by emphases on the Dominions and India. A propaganda piece, *The Eyes of Asia*, in which Rudyard Kipling imagined various Indian soldiers writing letters home (drawing on copies of real letters handed to him by military intelligence), depicted them as 'naive, semi-educated and wholly beholden to empire', smoothing over the more complex source material he borrowed from.[18] Such treatment embraced elements of personal propaganda, too. While New Zealand troops visiting London had free rein, Indians were only allowed supervised tours. Censors, meanwhile, urged British newspapers not to publish pictures of 'European nurses attending our wounded native soldiers'. While African, Asian and Caribbean imperial troops were welcome to fight for the British empire, the PB (at the request of the Director of Military Operations) claimed that images of mixed-race medical care 'have a bad effect on discipline'.[19] Such limitations suggest Britain's imperial unity, much trumpeted by propagandists, was far from absolute. Nonetheless propaganda of and to empire was a substantial feature of wartime discussion.

Notes

1. *Aims and Effort of the War: Britain's Case after Four Years* (London: NWAC, 1918), 55.
2. TNA INF4/5, 'Second Report on the Work Conducted for the Government at Wellington House', 1 February 1916, 17–19; INF 4/1B, 'Military Press Control: A History of the Work of MI7b' (1920), 19, 22; Alexander Turnbull Library, Wellington, New Zealand (henceforth ATL), Eph-C-ASSOCIATION-O-1911, Overseas Club membership certificate for Edmund Goodbehere, 13 September 1911.
3. Matthew Hendley, *Organized Patriotism and the Crucible of War: Popular Imperialism in Britain, 1914–1932* (Toronto: McGill-Queen's University Press, 2012), ch. 3.
4. Richard Jebb, *The Imperial Conference: A History and Study*, vol. 2 (London: Longmans, Green, 1911), 178.
5. Hew Strachan, *The First World War: To Arms* (Oxford: Oxford University Press, 2001), 550–5, 702–12; André Wessels, 'Afrikaner (Boer) Rebellion (Union of South Africa)', in Ute Daniel, Peter Gatrell, Oliver Janz, Heather Jones, Jennifer Keene, Alan Kramer and Bill Nasson (eds), *1914–1918 Online: International Encyclopedia of the First World War* (Berlin: Freie Universität Berlin, 2015); Eugene Rogan, 'Rival Jihads: Islam and the Great War in the Middle East, 1914–1918', *Journal of the British Academy*, 4, no. 1 (2016); John Slight, 'Reactions to the Ottoman Jihad *Fatwa* in the British Empire, 1914–18', in Robert Johnson and James Kitchen (eds), *The Great War in the Middle East: A Clash of Empires* (London: Routledge, 2019); Lumbini Sharma, 'Anti-Imperialist Pamphleteering: Understanding Global Jihad in Wartime India, 1914–1918', *British Journal for Military History*, 8, no. 1 (2022).
6. TNA HO139/43, D186, 16 March 1915; for a further request, see HO139/45, D607, n.d. (November 1917). On the PB's role, see Nicholas Wilkinson, *Secrecy and the Media: The Official History of Britain's D-Notice System* (London: Routledge, 2009) ; David Monger, 'The Press Bureau, "D" Notices, and Official Control of the British Press's Record of the First World War', *Historical Journal*, 65, no. 2 (2022).
7. *"To a Victorious Conclusion." The Prime Minister's Appeal to the Nation* (London: PRC pamphlet no. 5, 1914), 8–9; *The Rally of Our United Empire* (London: PRC leaflet no. 14, 1914), 1–2. For some of the realities behind this claimed unity, see the references to Rogan, Slight and Sharma in n. 5.
8. Bhupendranath Basu, *Why India Is Heart and Soul with Great Britain* (London: Macmillan, 1914), 8. On Basu and the Victoria League, see Hendley, *Organized Patriotism*, 156–7; Santanu Das, *India, Empire and First World War Culture: Writings, Images, and Songs* (Oxford: Oxford University Press, 2018), ch. 1 – on Gandhi, see 56–67.
9. Tony Collins, 'English Rugby Union and the First World War', *Historical Journal*, 45, no. 4 (2002), 806–7; A. A. Milne, 'A Day at Lords', *The Mercury* (Hobart), 19 October 1918, 8.
10. 'War Aims of the Allies', *Ilfracombe Gazette and Observer*, 2 November 1917, 3; 'War Aims Campaign. Meeting at Ilfracombe', *Ilfracombe Chronicle*, 3 November 1917, 3.
11. General Smuts, *The British Commonwealth of Nations: A Speech Made by General Smuts on May 15th, 1917* (London: Hodder & Stoughton, 1917), 5. For fuller discussion of Smuts' propaganda, see Monger, *Patriotism and Propaganda*, esp. 100–1, 149–52, 190–1; Monger, 'Press and Propaganda', 505–7.

12. *The Empire and the War: The Voice of the Dominions* (Empire Parliamentary Association, 1917), 11.
13. Peter Putnis and Kerry McCallum, 'Reuters, Propaganda-Inspired News, and the Australian Press during the First World War', *Media History*, 19, no. 3 (2013); Emily Robertson, 'Propaganda at Home (Australia)', in Ute Daniel, Peter Gatrell, Oliver Janz, Heather Jones, Jennifer Keene, Alan Kramer and Bill Nasson (eds), *1914-1918 Online: International Encyclopedia of the War* (Berlin: Freie Universität Berlin, 2015); Stephen Badsey, 'Propaganda and the Defence of Empire, 1856-1956' in Greg Kennedy (ed.), *Imperial Defence: The Old World Order 1856-1956* (London: Routledge, 2008), 226-7.
14. Tim Cook, 'Documenting War and Forging Reputations: Sir Max Aitken and the Canadian War Records Office in the First World War', *War in History*, 10, no. 3 (2003); Messinger, *British Propaganda*, ch. 9; Nicholas Reeves, *Official British Film Propaganda during the First World War* (London: Croom Helm, 1986), 61-4; Luke McKernan, *Topical Budget: The Great British News Film* (London: BFI, 1992), 36-8.
15. Gregory Hynes, '"We New Zealanders Pride Ourselves Most of All Upon Loyalty to Our Empire, Our Country, Our Flag": Internalised Britishness and National Character in New Zealand's First World War Propaganda', in Michael Walsh and Andrekos Varnava (eds), *The Great War and the British Empire: Culture and Society* (London: Routledge, 2017), esp. 82-9; Robertson, 'Propaganda at Home (Australia)'.
16. Radhika Singha, 'India's Silver Bullets: War Loans and War Propaganda, 1917-18', in Maartje Abbenhuis, Neill Atkinson, Kingsley Baird and Gail Romano (eds), *The Myriad Legacies of 1917: A Year of War and Revolution* (Cham: Palgrave Macmillan, 2018); for comparison with British war loan propaganda, see Stefan Goebel, 'Exhibitions', in Jay Winter and Antoine Prost (eds), *Capital Cities at War: Paris, London, Berlin, 1914-1919*, vol. 2, *A Cultural History* (Cambridge: Cambridge University Press, 2007), 157-61; Gregory, *Last Great War*, 220-33; Monger, 'Familiarity Breeds Consent', 519-24.
17. Speed, Lancelot, *Britain's Effort* (Ministry of Information, 1918), IWM 514: https://www.iwm.org.uk/collections/item/object/1060008269.
18. Das, *India, Empire, and First World War Culture*, 186-92, quotation at 189; Richard Smith, 'Propaganda, Imperial Subjecthood and National Identity in Jamaica during the First World War', in Paddock, *World War I and Propaganda*, 189, quotation at 89.
19. Felicity Barnes, *New Zealand's London: A Colony and Its Metropolis* (Auckland: Auckland University Press, 2013), 56-7; see also Tim Barringer, 'An Architecture of Imperial Ambivalence: The Patcham Chattri', in Walsh and Varnava, *Great War and British Empire*, 230-2; D225 (June 1915), cited in Monger, 'Press Bureau', 446.

CHAPTER 6
FILM

The animation, *Britain's Effort*, discussed in Chapter 5, was only one of many examples of an emerging form of wartime propaganda – film. Britain's propaganda substantially continued pre-war forms of communication (written, spoken and visual), but the adoption of film added a new element, which needed to fit into the wider approach. The most famous propaganda film, *Battle of the Somme*, shot during the 1916 campaign itself, was seen by millions in cinemas from late August. However, it was accompanied by a letter from the then war secretary David Lloyd George, explaining its significance, read live on opening night or added as intertitle text to the film thereafter. As late as 1918, a tour of national service films, projected onto walls or sheets by mobile cinema vans, required accompaniment by live speakers such as local notables, MPs or soldiers to ensure viewers obtained the proper lessons from the films (Figure 6), while all London cinemas, theatres and gathering places received another message from Lloyd George (now prime minister) on the war's fourth anniversary in August 1918. Film's value as an attraction to audiences was recognized, but it remained an emerging propaganda medium, with a preference for 'factual' material until late in the war. The mixed media approach both echoed earlier (and ongoing) methods of projected lantern lectures (talks illustrated with slides) and reflected cinemas' dubious reputation in 1914 as a rowdy, dark place where 'improper practices' occurred. Hence, as Roger Smither notes, unlike other fields of propaganda, when film was embraced in Britain, it was often specifically labelled 'official'.[1]

Thus, the most potentially dynamic area of propaganda was slowly and cautiously embraced in Britain despite the existence, as Nicholas Reeves notes, of a clear 'worldwide audience' for film. Indeed, *The British Army Film*, shot before the war as a recruiting tool, showed existing official awareness of film's potential. However, both the Admiralty and the War Office (led until 1916 by Lord Kitchener, whose criticism during the Second Boer War left him mistrustful of the press) attempted to keep media away from the fleet and front. Meanwhile, propaganda advocates like Charles Masterman (head of the War Propaganda Bureau at Wellington House) and representatives of the film trade agreed that film propaganda's potential value lay in real footage, not fictionalized material, meaning they could produce little film propaganda independent of the service departments. While official work began slowly, various film companies immediately dispatched cameramen to Europe at the outbreak of war, with British companies also purchasing film shot by neutrals, to produce short films, including Topical Films' *The German Occupation of Louvain* (a Belgian university city devastated by Germany's invasion), which Luke McKernan credits with depicting the 'shock of invasion' without

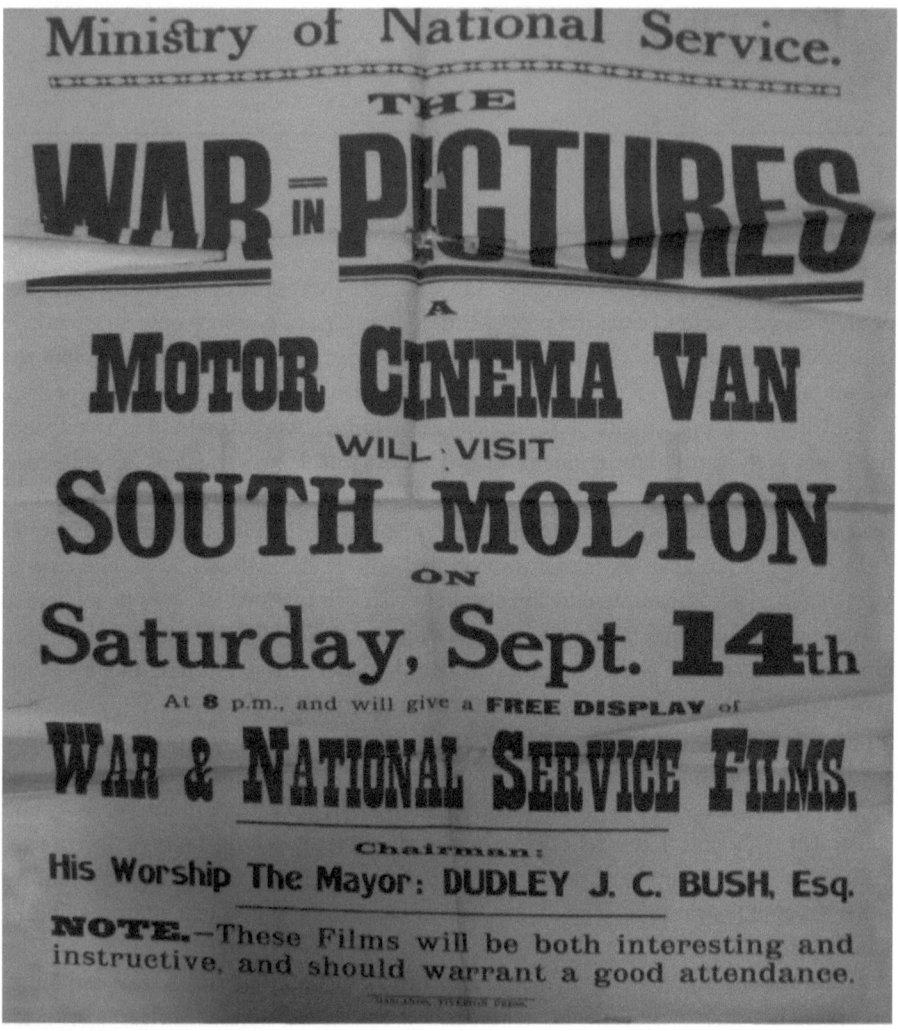

Figure 6 1918 advertisement (in bright pink) for a National Service film event in South Molton, Devon.
Source: TNA NATS1/110 (author's photograph).

resorting to melodramatic commentary. Topical, Pathé and Gaumont competed to provide newsreels for cinemas, though they struggled with restricted access to the front.[2]

By mid-1915, with press attached to Canadian forces and evidence of German and French film propaganda, negotiations began to allow film-makers access to British forces, eventually resulting in an agreement by October. With this in place, a first film, *Britain Prepared*, premiered in December and was distributed worldwide by March 1916, offering over three hours' footage, with limited textual intertitles to explain the scenes of military training, munitions production – including the role of women workers – and naval activity. Further films in early 1916, with restrictions on what film-makers were permitted to film, led to 'a propaganda startlingly low-keyed', although Reeves suggests they did show 'the harsh reality of life at the front' in depicting the difficult conditions of trench life.[3]

However, film propaganda reached new heights with *Battle of the Somme*, released in August 1916. Shot before and during the battle's early days in July, the film, over an hour long, became a 'phenomenon', seen perhaps twenty million times in Britain in the following weeks and, according to a 1917 report, by sixty-five million US viewers. Relatively close images of soldiers apparently dying in battle were staged later (due to the technical difficulties of live filming), but a shot of distant soldiers advancing showed some actual casualties, while Reeves notes that lingering shots of bodies in situ or being buried further confronted the audience with death. Michael Hammond suggests the film trod a fine line in trying to acknowledge suffering, provide an exciting sense of what battle was 'really' like and encourage patriotic duty. One of the cinematographers involved, Geoffrey Malins, suggested it 'takes you to the grave, but it cannot leave you there ... the film must finish with a touch of happiness'. Contemporary press commentary dwelt on the film's reality, although soldiers who saw it were less convinced.[4]

Following its success, film propaganda was brought more fully under government control with the establishment of the WOCC, chaired by Lord Beaverbrook. It took over from Topical Films both the production of feature films and its regular *Topical Budget* newsreels, which became the *War Office Official Topical Budget* in 1917. Assuming *Battle of the Somme* had shown the winning formula, similar films like *Battle of the Ancre* followed, but with decreasing success, before the WOCC branched out into other approaches. By this time, it faced competition in film production, with the Department of Information (DI, established in 1917, theoretically to centralize propaganda organization) aiming to run its own film section, while the NWAC, focused on domestic propaganda for public morale, invested heavily in an abortive feature film.[5] All this reflects wider patterns of competing and overlapping propaganda organizations, but it also shows that film was now considered a key part of propaganda operations.

Growing competition between organizations and propagandists' shifting priorities were both illustrated in 1917 by arrangements to support a new fictional film on the war by US director D. W. Griffith, creator of the hugely controversial – and successful – *Birth of a Nation*. The former journalist, T. L. Gilmour, in charge of the DI's film section, wrote to Beaverbrook, seeking help to arrange for 'the greatest living film producer', to visit and film sections of the front to aid later studio work. 'I am convinced', Gilmour wrote, 'that the new film will be the biggest thing in Propaganda that we can have in the States. Over forty millions ... saw his "Birth of a Nation", and as many more have seen "Intolerance"', his most recent film. 'It is good business for us to help him all we can.' While Beaverbrook seemed uninterested in April, by June he was ready to help. A squabble then developed between Gilmour and the DI (closely tied to the Foreign Office) and Beaverbrook and the WOCC (tied to the War Office), with both denying responsibility for organizing Griffith's logistics. 'That' Beaverbrook claimed, 'must rest with the Propaganda Department', adding 'it seems a great misfortune that a good plan should be lost simply because the Propaganda Department cannot agree to it's [*sic*] share of the work'.⁶

Ultimately, however, the WOCC supported Griffith's film, which told the story of a US-French couple separated by the man's war service and the woman's survival of German attacks before reuniting with her fiancé. *Hearts of the World*, Reeves notes, was the only completed and shown full-length fictional film tied to British propaganda, appearing shortly before the war ended. Another, planned by the NWAC, featured a script by the novelist Hall Caine, musical works by Edward Elgar and Alexander Mackenzie, direction from the prominent Irish director Herbert Brenon and several noted British actors including Ellen Terry. It would have sought to inspire public resolve by depicting a German invasion of Chester with accompanying war crimes. However, the film had to be reshot after the original was lost in a fire, and the war had ended by the time it was ready. The Treasury hoped to recover its costs by peacetime distribution, but a viewing confirmed that the film's emphasis on atrocities made it unsuitable and that linking invasion to strike action might even be 'dangerous' in 1919's industrial mood.⁷

If feature films were the most substantial and noted film propaganda of the war, however, they were far from the most common productions. Short films, whether shown as cinema newsreels or in independent 'cinemotor' tours run by the NWAC, Ministry of National Service and others, were more frequent. Topical Budget, taken over by the WOCC, produced two editions of the *War Office Topical Budget* (later the *Pictorial News (Official)*) per week, showing several short films of war-related material, often mixing armed forces and domestic topics. For instance, in a little less than six minutes, no. 322-1, produced in October 1917, began with images of 'Battleships at Anchor', moved to a section on 'Americans nearing the day of battle', with scenes of US artillery officers at an airfield, preparing to take off on a flight, then showed the Queen and Princess Mary inspecting Woolwich Dockyards, the King presenting medals at Buckingham Palace, before concluding with a section telling viewers to 'save your money and save the world!'. This showed prominent politicians attending the Albert Hall to hear Lloyd George discuss the economy. While the royal sections at least showed inspections and presentations, the naval, military and political sections contained very little action – ships at anchor; a group of men milling around a plane; and several politicians arriving at the venue. The intertitles did most of the work, touching on ideas of the navy as Britain's great defence, the imminent active intervention of US forces, industrial and particularly women's work, military gallantry, royal endorsements and the need for war economy. Newsreels could thus cover significant thematic ground in a short time, reaching substantial audiences, even if their message was largely conveyed by intertitles. Around twenty million cinema tickets were sold weekly to people mainly interested in fictional films. Like previously discussed propaganda towards children, which might filter through to parents, newsreels could thus reach audiences that might avoid street meetings or written propaganda. Over time, the official newsreels became increasingly widely shown at cinemas. Some of this success reflected the work of Captain W. Holt-White, brought in by Beaverbrook from the Canadian War Records Office to improve the newsreels' content, who sought connections with various government offices to ensure livelier material.⁸

Officials did not only work through Topical Budget or the WOCC, however. They also commissioned work from other film-makers, while propaganda events were also captured as news in themselves (again, similarly to public meetings filtering through to larger audiences through press reports). For example, the Hertfordshire and Essex War Agricultural Committees created a women's farming competition in 1917 to promote women's wartime work. Grace Curnock, press representative of the National Service Women's Section, notified the press, and the event was captured by Pathé.[9] Here, the overlap between official and private efforts was hazy, but the effects were similar. Propaganda around food production and consumption was likewise addressed on film. Stella Hockenhull identifies several newsreels dedicated to the subject by Pathé, showing ordinary adults and children growing food, as well as a commercial, fictional film, *Everybody's Business*, commissioned by the Ministry of Food. In this thirty-minute film, the unimaginatively named middle-class Briton family and their servants convey a lesson in food economy. Mrs Briton has to persuade both the cook and her husband that a restrained menu is suitable for the return of her soldier son on leave. During the meal, the son and daughter (a munitions worker) discuss their war work, thus painting the middle-class family as responsible and identifying food economy as a similar fulfilment of duty. Despite seemingly patronizing depiction of working-class characters, their portrayal by well-known actors apparently made the film a hit. In Scotland, meanwhile, George Green Ltd produced a film for the Ministry of Information (MI) and Ministry of Food, *Patriotic Porkers*, again dealing with food waste. Evidently Scottish in its depictions of local tenements and men in kilts, it nonetheless toured Britain as part of NWAC cinemotor tours in 1918. According to one post-war report, the NWAC controlled all film displays outside cinemas, for instance, showing nightly films at the foot of Nelson's Column in Trafalgar Square to promote the final War Loan.[10]

Cinemotors took films out of the paid confines of cinemas and directly into local communities. Projecting onto a wall, large sheet or screen, they brought informational films to the public, who traded free entertainment by new media for exposure to official messages. As noted, such events sometimes paired films with speeches and talks, reflecting the still transitional place of film in public campaigns. However, cinemotors again provided a bridge to more reluctant audiences, whether civilians tired of street meetings and pamphlets, or an increasingly hostile Irish public. Two NWAC cinemotors toured the areas outside Dublin from September to December 1918, seemingly managing to impart some messages even at this late stage through the novelty of film.[11]

Besides addressing domestic audiences, British films also served purposes abroad. A report collated before the Second World War suggested British propaganda films were sent to over fifty nations, excluding the empire. In neutral Spain, British film propaganda evaded Spanish censorship restrictions through private screenings at embassies and consulates or events organized by supportive groups like the Patriotic League of Britons Overseas and various overseas clubs. It reached 'all cities and provinces' by 1918, extending Britain's general messages in Spain of 'British courage, justice, and ability to wage war', Spain's 'economic dependence on Great Britain … and the benefits of a friendly neutrality'. In India, another report noted that from August 1916, Wellington

House arranged for films to be shown in many towns via a 'mobile generating plant and projector'. Meanwhile, as noted, *Battle of the Somme* had a large US audience. However, this was not obtained without effort. The film producer, Charles Urban, travelled to the United States in 1916 to arrange distribution of *Britain Prepared*, then returned to do the same for *Battle of the Somme*. However, controversy arose because of a deal supposedly struck with a film company tied to William Randolph Hearst, the anti-Entente (if not pro-German) US news mogul, which led to criticism and, more importantly, removed the pretence of independent commercial work that Urban was sent to undertake. Several deals and new film distribution companies were made and formed in following years, including after the United States entered the war. By war's end, Urban claimed that the *Official War Review* that he had overseen since 1 July 1918 – which merged *War Office Topical Budgets* with other films in Urban's possession – was seen by 3.5 million people daily, while twenty-six longer British films were distributed. However, McKernan suggests film propaganda's US impact was 'relatively minor' compared to other methods.[12]

Nonetheless, film added a new dimension to British propaganda, and a means to attract attention from those perhaps disinclined to receive more conventional propaganda. The material largely matched messages in other media – the virtues of Britain, the duties and service of ordinary people and the iniquities of Germany – and was sometimes incorporated within traditional communication structures, but moving pictures arguably brought those ideas to life. Though still an emerging medium in the war, Smither notes that many film methods and messages used in propaganda after 1939 – including, he suggests, something akin to the 'Blitz spirit' – were pioneered before 1918.[13]

Notes

1 Hynes, *A War Imagined*, 122–3; Monger, 'Familiarity Breeds Consent?', 515–18; '"Hold Fast." The Premier's Message to the Empire', *Norwood News and Dulwich Advertiser*, 10 August 1918, 2; Roger Smither, 'Film/Cinema', in Ute Daniel, Peter Gatrell, Oliver Janz, Heather Jones, Jennifer Keene, Alan Kramer and Bill Nasson (eds), *1914–1918 Online: International Encyclopedia of the First World War* (Berlin: Freie Universität Berlin, 2015). On cinema's reputation, see Nicholas Hiley, 'The British Cinema Auditorium', in Karel Dibbets and Bert Hogenkamp (eds), *Film and the First World War* (Amsterdam: Amsterdam University Press, 1995); Paul Moody, '"Improper Practices" in Great War British Cinemas', in Michael Hammond and Michael Williams (eds), *British Silent Cinema and the Great War* (Basingstoke: Palgrave Macmillan, 2011).

2 Nicholas P. Hiley, '"The British Army Film", "You!" and "For the Empire": Reconstructed Propaganda Films, 1914–1916', *Historical Journal of Film, Radio and Television*, 5, no. 2 (1985), 167–9; Reeves, *Film Propaganda*, 44–50; McKernan, *Topical Budget*, 20–35.

3 Reeves, *Film Propaganda*, 46, 50–7; 142–4, 157.

4 Badsey, *German Corpse Factory*, 153–7; Reeves, *Film Propaganda*, 157–69; Michael Hammond, '*The Battle of the Somme* (1916): An Industrial Process Film that "Wounds the Heart"', in Michael Hammond and Michael Williams (eds), *British Silent Cinema and the Great War* (Basingstoke: Palgrave Macmillan, 2011); quotation from Geoffrey Malins,

How I Filmed the War (1920), 181 in Reeves, *Film Propaganda*, 158. On the film's reception, compare Nicholas Reeves, 'Cinema, Spectatorship and Propaganda: "Battle of the Somme" and Its Contemporary Audience', *Historical Journal of Film, Radio and Television*, 17, no. 1 (1997) and Chris Grosvenor, '"He Sees Now What He Looked Like": Soldier Spectators, Topical Films, and the Problem of Onscreen Representation during World War I', *Film History*, 30, no. 4 (2018).

5   Reeves, *Film Propaganda*, 62–76.
6   Parliamentary Archives, London (henceforth PA), Beaverbrook Papers, BBK/E/2/4, Gilmour to Beaverbrook, 11 April 1917; BBK/E/2/7, correspondence between Gilmour and Beaverbrook, 1–6 June 1917 (quotation 6 June); Reeves, *Film Propaganda*, 119–22.
7   Reeves, *Film Propaganda*, 122–30, 212–16, 240–2; Michael Paris, 'Film/Cinema (Great Britain)', in Ute Daniel, Peter Gatrell, Oliver Janz, Heather Jones, Jennifer Keene, Alan Kramer and Bill Nasson (eds), *1914–1918: International Encyclopedia of the First World War* (Berlin: Freie Universität Berlin, 2014); Monger, *Patriotism and Propaganda*, 132–3.
8   McKernan, *Topical Budget*, 38–50; IWM NTB, *War Office Official Topical Budget*, 322–1, 25 October 1917: https://www.iwm.org.uk/collections/item/object/1060005434 (accessed 5 December 2023); for weekly cinema attendances, see Hiley, 'British Cinema Auditorium', 162.
9   Monger, *Tangible Patriotism*, 260.
10 Stella Hockenhull, 'Everybody's Business: Film, Food and Victory in the First World War', *Historical Journal of Film, Radio and Television*, 35, no. 4 (2015), 584–8; David Archibald and Maria Velez-Serna, 'Kilts, Tanks, and Aeroplanes: Scotland, Cinema, and the First World War', *NECSUS: European Journal of Media Studies*, 3, no. 2 (2014), 166–70; TNA INF4/2, 'Extract from "British Propaganda during the Great War, 1914–1918." Basic Document B.53', 2.
11 Pennell, 'Presenting the War in Ireland', 60–2.
12 TNA INF4/2, 'Extract from "British Propaganda during the Great War, 1914–1918." Basic Document B.53', 3–6; Marta García Cabrera, 'The British Film Campaign in Spain during the First World War (1914–1918)', *War & Society*, 41, no. 4 (2022), quotations at 322, 314; TNA INF4/2, G. Hughes Roberts, extracts from J. Brooke Wilkinson, '"Films and Censorship in England", Ch. XI, The War Years', 20 June 1939; Luke McKernan, 'Propaganda, Patriotism and Profit: Charles Urban and British Official War Films in America', *Film History*, 14, no. 3–4 (2002), quotation at 386.
13 Roger Smither, 'Anticipating the Blitz Spirit in First World War Propaganda Film: Evidence in the Imperial War Museum Archive', in Hammond and Williams, *British Silent Cinema*.

CHAPTER 7
GERMANY

That the NWAC's abortive 'National Film' involved a fictitious German invasion of Britain is unsurprising. This book argues firmly that there was much more to British propaganda than attacks on Germany. Nonetheless, Germany was clearly propaganda's villain to Britain's hero. As the early propaganda researcher Harold Lasswell noted, 'There must be no ambiguity about whom the public is to hate.'[1] Propagandists identified several adversaries – including Britain's other declared enemies, Austria–Hungary, the Ottoman Empire and Bulgaria, generic domestic 'shirkers', 'pacifists' and 'defeatists' and, after the October Revolution, Russian Bolsheviks – and addressed them significantly across the wide propaganda narrative provided to audiences. Yet, Germany always remained the foremost obstacle to victory, peace and a better post-war world. As noted in Chapter 1, this focus had serious and troublesome effects on later understanding of the war's events. Tying the Armenian Genocide, committed by the Ottoman Empire with limited German assistance (beyond lack of interest or intervention), to German *direction* in both propaganda and wider commentary had serious implications. Despite genocide deniers' whining about supposed propaganda fabrications, the major inaccuracy of wartime propaganda relating to the Genocide was not its discussion of well-established and documented mass crimes but its regular attachment of Germany to them.[2] Such attention, arguably, contributed to declining interest in Armenia after the war and enabled the century of denial that followed. Nonetheless, with the narrower horizons of wartime propagandists – whose role was, fundamentally, to assist Britain's victory over its main opponent – it made sense to attach Germany to the war's greatest crime. This extended the picture already established by its invasion of Belgium and Northern France as a brutal regime willing to go beyond wartime norms in its pursuit of power.

Regular atrocity propaganda should not obscure the more complex discussion of Germany, however. As in all areas of propaganda, Germany was not portrayed in black and white but in multiple shades of grey, including army *feldgrau*. Besides atrocities, discussion included German politics and philosophy. Propagandists exploited German voices and actions outside battle zones to discredit it and used humour and ridicule as much as horror and vitriol, not least because creating an image of an unstoppable monster was hardly good for morale. Additionally, some propaganda distinguished redeemable 'good Germans' (whether individuals or sections of society) from others poisoned by 'Prussian militarism'. The novelist H. G. Wells, for example, resigned from a senior role with Lord Northcliffe's enemy propaganda organization at Crewe House in 1918 when he felt his efforts to appeal to good Germans were undone by indiscriminate commentary elsewhere (particularly in Northcliffe's newspapers). Meanwhile, the zoologist Peter Chalmers Mitchell, seconded from London Zoo to a War Office role in military intelligence due to his fluent German and friendship with an undersecretary, produced a report on German propaganda, which identified fourteen (largely political) major themes and seven more for German home consumption. All of these, supposedly, needed counteraction by British propagandists.[3] Atrocities fulfilled some specific propaganda purposes, but a wider picture of Germany was needed.

One of the greatest assets for British propaganda about Germany was Germany itself. Besides the ill-considered efforts to justify atrocious conduct (discussed previously), Germany's general conduct of the war provoked neutral criticism. Despite US objections to many British actions – including its blockade and the brutal reaction to the 1916 Easter Rising of Irish nationalists – British officials, especially the Foreign Secretary Edward Grey (whose actions showed 'the absence of any complacency about the United States', according to Ernest May), took care to avoid pushing US patience too far either in its wartime activities or in the amount of overt propaganda it distributed there. By contrast German high-handed assertions of their right to conduct necessary actions (particularly its submarine campaigns) irritated US opinion. For President Woodrow Wilson, British infringement on property rights and US sovereignty through its blockade was less provocative than German submarines taking civilian lives. Meanwhile, German sabotage of munitions in US ports, while not notably hindering supplies to Britain, 'gave British propagandists horrible examples in America which served to illustrate dramatically that the Germans were America's enemies' and increase anti-German sentiments. Even when Grey's caution was replaced by stricter blockading in 1916, US objections were restrained by continued German misconduct.[4]

Propagandists thus paid close attention to what individual Germans said and did. This began (as noted in Chapter 1) with Chancellor Bethmann-Hollweg's objection to the British ambassador that Britain intended to declare war because of a 'scrap of paper' – the treaty signed by Britain and Germany, guaranteeing Belgian neutrality. Presented with an ultimatum, Belgium honourably defended its territory, and Britain honourably came to its aid. New York Senator (and former secretary of state) Elihu Root discouraged Lord Bryce from attempting to make a statement to influence US opinion, suggesting it was already with Britain as a result of published documents:

> I think the absence of argument helped the process. The conclusion reached has been much strengthened by the … 'scrap of paper' conversation. That phrase is in everybody's mouth and, taken in connection with the destruction of Louvain and the dreadful sufferings imposed upon innocent Belgium, has produced a profound impression.[5]

Reasonable arguments for British consumption would reach US audiences, Root suggested, but direct appeals would be counterproductive. Such restraint did not last, of course, although at least parts of the effort in the United States were indirect. However, emphasis on the 'scrap of paper' as shorthand for German contempt for law continued throughout the war. In 1916, Hodder & Stoughton published *Scraps of Paper*, featuring reproduced posters from occupied towns, threatening reprisals for civilian misconduct, with accompanying translations. By 1918, propagandists added examples of German treaty-making to their evidence. The harsh peace terms extracted from Russia and Romania proved that the 1917 resolution by Germany's elected lower house, the Reichstag, that Germany should seek peace without annexations or indemnities, was meaningless. Smuts suggested, 'like the treaties of her Government, the resolutions of her Parliament are mere scraps of paper.' 'We can always have peace on the terms on which "Russia" has it', the labour activist W. S. Sanders added. 'To say that Germany gave us an "opportunity of peace" in 1916 [through Bethmann-Hollweg's peace note] is merely to say that she gave us an opportunity of kissing her tyrannical sceptre.' Using material from the *Leipziger Neueste Nachrichten* on German debates about possible restoration of Belgium or acquisition of Baltic or French territory, meanwhile, A. A. Milne scoffed in an article for Dominion readers that

> It is easy for Germany to 'adopt a principle'; any principle you like – you've only to mention it; adopting a principle costs nothing. Putting your name to a form of words also costs nothing. For the principle can be made elastic, and the words can always be juggled with; and, as a last resort, the scraps of paper can be torn up.

Such examples used Germans' own words and deeds to suggest patterns of thought and behaviour. While the US propaganda organization, the Committee on Public Information, noted in its handbook that Bethmann Hollweg disputed his statement's meaning, the phrase stuck as shorthand for German willingness to ignore the law.[6]

In early 1918, propagandists received an 'unexpected boon' from an unlikely source. The former German ambassador to Britain Prince Lichnowsky circulated a private memorandum in 1916 to acquaintances, outlining his efforts to prevent war in 1914. This work, originally in eight copies, was reproduced and circulated more widely in Germany despite official efforts to suppress it that were supported by Lichnowsky himself. Nonetheless, it reached a Swedish newspaper in 1918, which serialized it, including Lichnowsky's assertions that Germany had encouraged Austria–Hungary to attack Serbia and blocked attempts at mediation, thus bringing on the world war. Gleeful propagandists rapidly exploited the memoir – the NWAC alone produced three separate publications in a short period that substantially discussed it, squabbling with the Ministry of Information about the merits of free versus commercial publication. These included the Liberal MP Charles McCurdy's *Guilty! Prince Lichnowsky's Disclosures* (also published in Welsh), a short leaflet summarizing the main claims, and the journalist A. G. Gardiner's *The Blast of Truth*, which stressed that the 'evidence of [the kaiser's] guilt does not depend on us. It comes from his own side', while everyone knew Lichnowsky was an honourable man. German efforts to reject Lichnowsky's claims and paint him as an incompetent diplomat backfired. The former foreign minister Gottlieb von Jagow's attempted rebuttal accepted parts of Lichnowsky's statements, encouraging attempts to add it to a Swiss edition by British propagandists as further evidence.[7] Once again, not only did the initial story damage Germany, but also German attempts to change opinion deepened doubts, at least outside Germany. Milne produced another mocking article, highlighting Lichnowsky's loss of rank after his 'imprudent' revelations: 'It most certainly does not pay to be an honest gentleman in Germany.' The Crewe House administrator, Campbell Stuart, meanwhile, felt that use of the text had been 'encouraging' (it was, apparently, distributed with some success to German prisoners of war) but that Germans still largely accepted their government's official explanations.[8]

Milne's reputation as a humourist was built before the war as assistant editor of *Punch*. His MI7b propaganda articles mixed humour with more serious pieces that both leaned on his soldierly status and went against his usual style. He and his fellow propagandists obtained regular material from the large library of German propaganda, analysed by Chalmers Mitchell, as well as monitoring of German cable and wireless communication. Several of Milne's articles targeted Germany using such materials, mixing humorous and sarcastic comments on inaccurate wireless claims or political debates. In 'At Ease in Zion', inspired by a pamphlet found in a German trench providing patriotic prayers, he reimagined the Lord's Prayer in the same vein, with lines including 'give us this day our daily bread, if possible with a little less potato peel in it' and 'lead us not into the temptation to make peace without annexations or indemnities'. On other occasions, he used imagined farces to suggest German delusion or duplicity. A series of reports from a German battlefront begins with grand claims about a major offensive and goes through several continually positive phases of lesser claims until finally confirming the eventual German retreat as a victory that allowed a shorter line of defence. In another imagined scene, a German officer, masquerading as an independent delegation from Lithuania, asks the kaiser for annexation.[9] Such pieces ridiculed prominent Germans like Ludendorff and the kaiser while still conveying more serious messages – German shortages, military failures or anti-democratic attitudes. Making the discussion a little more light-hearted may have attracted readers less interested in formal discussion, as well as diminishing the enemy by mockery.

Visual propaganda, too, used humorous depictions to undermine any image of Germany as a terrifyingly invincible ogre. For every Louis Raemaekers producing outraged cartoon denunciations, there were others who focused on making Germans absurd. In 'Holey War', for instance (Figure 7), the cartoonist W. F. Blood lampooned Germany's pompous leadership of its alliance and futile attempt to incite a jihad against Britain, depicting the kaiser in spotless uniform lecturing a bruised and bandaged 'Abdul' (representing the Ottoman Empire) about their 'holy war'. 'Yes, Wilhelm', replied Abdul, 'I get most of de holes'. Another Blood cartoon showed the kaiser, suffering from a head cold with a scarf wrapped absurdly round his *pickelhaube*. He stares at the mercury sliding down on his giant 'Victory' thermometer, labelled 'Made in Germany' – a nod to a pre-war phrase related to British and German commercial rivalry, which was repurposed in wartime as an ironic label for things either dishonest or failing.[10] Absurdity was also the preserve of humorous writers. Besides Milne's efforts, his MI7b colleague, the Anglo-Irish fantasy novelist Lord Dunsany, wrote a piece attributing the outbreak of war to the kaiser's barber, which was published for the entertainment of New Zealand readers:

> This preposterous inspiration of the absurd young barber madman was nothing less than a moustache that without any curve at all, or any suggestion of sanity, should go suddenly up at the ends very nearly as high as the eyes! …

Figure 7 W. F. Blood, 'Holey War'.
Source: *Welcome*, 15 April 1918, 33. Bodleian Library, University of Oxford (author's photograph).

> It was probably about the time that the Emperor dismissed Bismarck, certainly the drawings of that time show him still with a sane moustache ...
>
> I believe the absurdity of that barber to be among the great evils that brought death nearer to man ... For just as character is outwardly shown, so outward things react upon the character; and who, with that daring barber's ludicrous fancy visible always on his face, could quite go the sober way of beneficent monarchs?

In another absurdist explanation, the actor Sir Herbert Tree imagined the kaiser's chiropodist, alarmed at the idea of war, faltering on the point of giving him poison because of the award of an honour. Meanwhile, the kaiser decides upon war because the length of cheering outside his castle window has shortened, with one of his advisers informing him that he was 'twelve minutes and fifteen seconds less popular than you were at midnight, your Majesty'.[11] Tree's 1914 playscript and Dunsany's 1918 musings accompanied extensive and more serious discussion of Germany's responsibility for the war, conducted since 1914 and revitalized by Lichnowsky's memoir. Close analysis of documentary evidence and absurd speculations on the disastrous actions of imaginary servants coexisted – audiences could choose between dry as dust or daft as a brush. Flippant treatment reflected assumptions that everyone already understood Germany's responsibility for the war's outbreak.

Thus, British propaganda about Germany covered a wide spectrum, from deadly serious accounts of German war crimes and war guilt to seriously silly images of a rigid moustache, so absurd that the kaiser had to strike equally idiotic poses in eccentric garb, all of which affected his mind. The message underlying this varied commentary was that Germany was indeed a serious threat to Britain and the 'civilized' world, but one that tripped upon its own sword and could not get its story straight. Propaganda audiences should be horrified by evidence of German crime and thus determined to prevent its spread. Thus they should volunteer for armed or civic service and donate their money to the cause. 'Prussian militarism', as Chapter 11 discusses further, had to be destroyed. Once it was, 'good Germans', freed from bad government, could bring their nation back into the civilized fold. At the same time, however, audiences needed to be assured that British victory *would* come. An invincible Germany might undermine morale. As Chapter 8 shows, the same was also partially true in reverse. Audiences could be reassured Britain would succeed, but the need to inspire public action meant this could not be taken for granted. As such, propagandists sometimes depicted Britain, the largest and most powerful empire of the modern world, as a plucky underdog – the David to Germany's Goliath.

Notes

1. Lasswell, *Propaganda Technique*, 47.
2. Steel, 'Genocide'. For detailed discussion of Germany's (far from spotless) involvement with the Genocide, see Wolfgang Gust, *The Armenian Genocide: Evidence from the German Foreign Office Archives, 1915–1916* (New York: Berghahn, 2014); Stefan Ihrig, *Justifying*

Genocide: Germany and the Armenians from Bismarck to Hitler (Cambridge, MA: Harvard University Press, 2016).
3. On Wells, see Messinger, *British Propaganda*, 185-99; David Monger, '"A Not Uncongenial Task": British Propaganda Veterans and Propaganda's Post-First World War Reputation', *First World War Studies*, 13, no. 1 (2022), 9-10. For Chalmers Mitchell, see David Monger, 'Know Your Enemy: Peter Chalmers Mitchell, British Military Intelligence and the Understanding of German Propaganda in the First World War', *History*, 103, no. 358 (2018). For a discussion of the varying 'shades' of propaganda, see Garth S. Jowett and Victoria O'Donnell, *Propaganda and Persuasion*, 4th edn (London: Sage Publications, [1986] 2006), 16-22.
4. Ernest R. May, *The World War and American Isolation: 1914-1917* (Cambridge, MA: Harvard University Press, 1959), 29, 339-44; Sanders and Taylor, *British Propaganda*, 167-79; Peterson, *Propaganda for War*, 145-51.
5. BLO, Bryce Papers, MS Bryce 9, Root to Bryce, 23 September 1914.
6. *Scraps of Paper: German Proclamations in Belgium and France* (London: Hodder & Stoughton, 1916); *Smuts' Message: The World Awakened* (London: NWAC, 1918), 7; William Stephen Sanders, *Those German Peace Offers* (London: NWAC, German Aims series no. 3, 1918), 2, 6; A. A. M., 'The German Mind', *New Zealand Times*, 4 April 1918, 2; "Scrap of Paper", in Frederick L. Paxson, Edward S. Cordin and Samuel B. Harding (eds), *War Cyclopedia: A Handbook for Ready Reference on the Great War* (Washington: Committee on Public Information, Red White and Blue series no. 7, 1918), 247.
7. Harry F. Young, *Prince Lichnowsky and the Great War* (Athens, GA: University of Georgia Press, 1977), 145-60. Charles A. McCurdy, *Guilty! Prince Lichnowsky's Disclosures* (NWAC German Aims Series, 1918); *Germany Condemned By Her Own Ambassador* (NWAC Searchlight series, no. 18, 1918); A. G. G. (of the *Daily News*), *The Blast of Truth* (NWAC Searchlight series, no. 13, 1918). For brief discussion of the NWAC and Ministry of Information's dispute, see Monger, 'Know Your Enemy?', 796-7.
8. A. A. M., 'The Imprudent Prince', *Maitland Daily Mercury*, 16 July 1918, 6; Campbell Stuart, *Secrets of Crewe House* (London: Hodder & Stoughton, 1920), 162. For distribution to prisoners, see TNA CAB24/75 GT6839, 'Report on the Work of Propaganda in Enemy Countries' (n.d.), 39.
9. A. A. Milne, 'At Ease in Zion. Or How Germans Pray', *The Register* (Adelaide), 11 May 1918, 7; A. A. Milne, 'A German Offensive. By "Our Special Correspondent at German Headquarters"', *Dominion*, 4 October 1918, 6; A. A. Milne, 'Self-Determination. How Germany Wants It', *Star* (Christchurch), 24 October 1918, 7.
10. W. F. Blood, 'Holey War', *Welcome*, 15 April 1918, 33; Blood, 'The Teutonic Thermometer', *Welcome*, 14 August 1918, 235.
11. Captain Lord Dunsany, 'Kaiser's Barber. An Investigation. The Causes and Origins of the War', *New Zealand Times*, 17 October 1918, 6, also republished in Lord Dunsany, *Tales of War* (New York: G.P. Putnam's, 1918), 106-12; Herbert Tree, 'The Ultimatum; or Every Man Has His Price' in Caine, *King Albert's Book*, 93-6.

CHAPTER 8
HUMBLEBRAGGING

Earlier chapters noted that British propagandists placed much emphasis on Britain's virtues and the unity of its empire, while Chapter 7 concluded that propaganda included mocking material intended to avoid a view of Germany as an invincible foe. However, propagandists addressed multiple audiences. Some might be reassured by comments on the empire's unmatched global strength and wealth. But others may not respond well to open assertions of strength. Domestic critics condemned suggestions that Britain might gain materially from the war and needed to be mollified. Neutrals, especially the United States, might be less likely to support or fight alongside a nation too assertive and confident about its power. Sympathetic domestic audiences, too, had to be motivated to continue their physical and financial contributions to the war effort. Thus, while rejecting German strength on the one hand, propagandists sometimes reduced Britain's position on the other, identifying the modern world's most powerful empire as a plucky underdog.

One method for achieving this was humblebragging. This term, coined in the social media era, describes posts that seem modest and self-deprecating but actually show something the author is proud of. Such posts seek positive reactions, reversing the false modesty, from audiences but can be transparently insincere. Despite complaining about or disavowing something, the author ultimately expects praise. While the term was not used in the early twentieth century, versions of the humblebrag already existed. When Colonial Secretary Joseph Chamberlain called, in 1902, for imperial territories to bear a greater share of the burdens of imperial administration by declaring that 'the weary Titan staggers under the too vast orb of its fate',[1] for example, he both expressed British vulnerability and demanded admiration for the efforts already expended. Wartime expressions of British vulnerability likewise carried expectations of sympathy and admiration.

Humblebragging is clear in pieces like the novelist and journalist A. J. Dawson's 'John Bull at War':

> Britain has been harshly criticised for her extreme unpreparedness for war ... Her people probably deserve the blame that has been laid at their door. Certainly they were utterly unprepared. Certainly, also, they had been warned many times of their danger by authorities ... But, whether or not we may regret it, Britain's unpreparedness for this war – the persistent scepticism of her people as to the possibility of its coming – was entirely in keeping with the general attitude and temperament of this people, and with the national character.

> The British people may be insular, careless, and not over gracious ... The average Englishman, for example, might smile or sniff in a most irritating and, if you will, foolish manner over what he regarded as a peculiarity in any foreigner. But he has always been the slowest man in the world to suspect foreign individuals or nations of baseness, of criminal intentions ...
>
> That, in the last analysis, is why Britain was totally unprepared for this war. It took the average Briton many weeks to realise that Germany really had committed this unforgivable crime. Months had to pass before his radically good-natured, easy-going mind fully grasped the stark fact that Germany had coldly prepared for this crime for many years ... Then quietly, slowly, with extraordinary but quite characteristic deliberateness, the average Briton in the street made up his mind about it all ...
>
> John Bull may deserve blame for having been totally unprepared for Germany's murderous aggression. The attack did find him unready; but it drew no whimpering from him because of that ... The mere unreadiness of his hands proves, at all events, that they were clean.[2]

Dawson was already an experienced propagandist before 1914, having worked for the National Service League, advocating Britain's military preparedness. He became the first organizing secretary of the unofficial propaganda group, the Central Committee for National Patriotic Organizations (CCNPO), before later playing leading roles at MI7b and organizing propaganda for the Royal Air Force.[3] In the extract above, he writes at length about supposed flaws in British character – Britons are too trusting, prone to silly dismissal of foreigners and slow to act. Hence, Britain was totally unprepared for war. All this, however, ultimately proved the justice of British actions and the greatness of its war effort, fought with 'one hand ... to hold the garrotter at bay' while building up capacity and only taking a full military part from the Battle of the Somme onwards. In its way, Dawson implied, Britain's willingness to fight unprepared was as difficult and admirable as Belgium's resistance to Germany's invasion. Propagandists like Dawson played on familiar self-deprecating parodies of Britons to both identify peril and boast of British achievement.

Throughout the war, propagandists used gentle caricatures of Britishness and latched onto suggestions of British weakness and vulnerability. To domestic audiences, this often reflected an in-joke – Britons could afford to laugh at themselves because they largely assumed their superiority to others. For other nations, by contrast, playing down British strength and emphasizing flaws was a way to soften potentially negative views of Britain as an aggressive world power. Propagandists embraced (and may well have invented) the German kaiser's description of the small British Expeditionary Force initially sent to France as a 'contemptible little army'. The PRC published a poster and leaflet referring to the 'Kaiser's Insult' and urging men to enlist, and the soldiers were soon referred to as 'Old Contemptibles'. The abusive term instead became a shorthand for resilience and bravery, arguably serving a similar symbolic function to the post-Crimean War idea of the British Army's 'thin red line', protecting nation and empire. However, this apparent gratitude was tinged with doubt. The patriotic poet Rudyard Kipling noted common suspicions of soldiers, except when a 'Thin red line of 'eroes' was needed 'when the drums begin to roll'.[4] Contemptibility in 1914 sat well with these older ideas.

Probably the most famous later depiction of these troops came from the caricatures of the crotchety 'Old Bill' and his comrades, drawn by Bruce Bairnsfather, initially published for the *Bystander*. In an introduction to a wartime collection, *Fragments from France*, the magazine's editor Vivian Carter noted it was

> a fixed condition of the national life that wherever Britons are working together in any common object, whether in school, college, profession, or even warfare, they must never *appear* to be regarding their occupation too seriously …
>
> It ranks as a colossal German defeat that successive bloodthirsty assaults upon us by land, sea and air should produce a Bairnsfather, depicting the 'contemptible little Army', swollen out of all recognition, settling humorously down to war.

Britons, Carter suggested, were incapable of taking even the most urgent issues wholly seriously, but Bairnsfather's habitual depictions of 'fed up' soldiers only captured another British trait. Behind the jokes and grousing lay determination, he suggested. Bairnsfather's popularity was such that he was summoned to official propaganda work with Dawson's MI7b, later being sent to visit allied forces and try to draw similar caricatures of US troops, before touring the United States giving talks.[5]

Meanwhile, the propaganda newspaper, *Reality*, aimed mainly at industrial workers, published an article, 'More "Contemptibles"', in August 1917, noting that the German press now spoke of the US military in similarly dismissive terms. It cited the centrist German politician Matthias Erzberger's 1914 query about Britain's decision to seek only five hundred thousand volunteers: 'Has England then fallen so low that she can jest in this serious hour?' From the start, the article (like the comment on Bairnsfather) implied, Germans misunderstood British resolve and now misread US efforts too. The none-too-subtle humblebrag in this piece was not so much that Britain played an effective military part, despite German scepticism, but that the United States' present slow deployment mirrored Britain's earlier challenges. Here, the United States was less Britain's saviour, as it was frequently depicted elsewhere, but its inheritor. This was a relatively frequent secondary theme in the NWAC's discussion of the United States. The NWAC's papers and pamphlets not only fulsomely praised President Wilson's pledge to 'make the world safe for democracy' and establish a League of Nations but also seized on and reprinted his comparison of George Washington with the authors of Magna Carta, suggesting the United States' democratic instincts were fundamentally British. As an editorial for its newspaper for soldiers on leave, *Welcome*, noted in an edition focused on US Independence Day,

> When the American Colonists broke away from the mother-land in 1776, they carried with them the root principles of liberty and self-government, which had already developed here. In the altered circumstances of their case they were able

to carry forward those principles further and faster than could have been done in Britain of those times.⁶

The US, then, had surpassed Britain's democratic development, but only, the humblebragging editor suggested, because it had the advantage of building from British principles.

Nonetheless, propagandists worked hard to present a gentle picture of Britain for foreign audiences. The novelist John Galsworthy, a long-time producer of propaganda for neutral and imperial audiences via Wellington House, wrote an article for the *Yale Review* shortly before the war's end seeking to explain British differences from the United States, admitting,

> I have never held a whole-hearted brief for the British character. There is a lot of good in it, but much which is repellent. It has a kind of deliberate unattractiveness ...
>
> But this British self-consciousness is no mere fluffy gaucherie, it is our special form of what Germans would call *Kultur*. Behind every manifestation of thought or emotion, the Briton retains control of self ... This stoicism is good in its refusal to be foundered; bad in that it fosters a narrow outlook; starves emotion, spontaneity, and frank sympathy; destroys grace and what one may describe roughly as the lovable side of personality ...
>
> Americans, whose attitude towards their own country is that of a lover to his lady or a child to its mother, cannot ... understand how Englishmen can be critical of their own country, and yet love her. Well, the Englishman's attitude to his country is that of a man to himself, and the way he runs her down is part of that special English bone-deep self-consciousness.

Here, Galsworthy dealt with common perceptions of Britons as aloof and unemotional, emphasizing the negative consequences of (in reality) elite upbringings, including his own. Doing so sought to disarm critics (in what he, perhaps tactlessly, labelled a 'huge, still half-developed country'), who he noted were sometimes put off by British attitudes.⁷ Galsworthy then finished his discussion by emphasizing the need for ongoing US and British cooperation since, in spite of their differences, they shared common commitments to democracy and freedom. Galsworthy had provided a previous analysis of his countrymen, originally for Dutch readers (subsequently republished in the United States) in 1915. 'The Englishman must have a thing brought under his nose before he will act ... Want of imagination makes him, philosophically speaking, rather ludicrous; in practical affairs it handicaps him at the start; but once he has "got going" – as we say – it is of incalculable assistance to his stamina.' The English, this account seemingly suggested, were the ethnic equivalent of a stodgy bowl of porridge, slowly releasing energy over time, compared to the faster, but less enduring, energy release of a sugary breakfast. Once again, a rather unflattering portrait played up to assumptions about English character, before Galsworthy, like Dawson above, concluded that such a withdrawn and 'half-surly, half-good humoured manner' was ideal for the long war now required.⁸

While the regular willingness to acknowledge negative views of Britain and its people may suggest weakness and deference to others, it is noteworthy that all of Dawson and Galsworthy's comments ultimately came around to an idea of British self-assurance. Fundamentally, their writing suggested, Britons knew other people found them unattractive but did not care. Acknowledging foibles made the case for British achievements stronger. Similar tones are evident in propaganda by John Hay Beith, who wrote under the pseudonym Ian Hay. Beith's 1915 book, *The First Hundred Thousand*, mixed light-hearted pictures of soldiers' lives (again highlighting the refusal to take anything completely seriously) with emphasis on the importance of the fighting. It sold hundreds of thousands of copies and resulted in Beith undertaking propaganda in the United States. *The Last Million*, published after the war, discussed the intervention of US troops, but its introduction contains a 'welcome' Beith wrote for distribution on US troop transports in 1918. In it, he acknowledged several familiar US criticisms of Britain, including the inability to find cold drinks, driving on the left side of the road, poor weather, confusing currency and the unwillingness to talk, before explaining all of this at length. For the final issue, Beith suggested, 'An Englishman's ambition in life was to get a [railway] compartment to himself. That principle, for good or ill, prevails through all our habits.' Thus, US troops should not be surprised to find Britons withdrawn – it was not a snub to foreigners: 'No Englishman ever speaks to another Englishman if he can help it', and Britain was likely to be even less welcoming than usual given the strain of war it had borne. After twenty-five pages of explanation, however, Beith's conclusion (like Galsworthy's) was that Britain and the United States needed to work together and understand each other.[9] Once again, behind the apparent self-criticism was a strong defence of Britishness – Britons were different from Americans for a good reason and even more restrained than normal due to the war.

Not all humblebragging was directed at foreign audiences, however. Propagandists also consistently used it to inspire and flatter British civilians. In particular, by suggesting civilians were 'only' attempting to match the example of armed service, they simultaneously minimized and enlarged civilian service – while it could never really reach that of servicemen it was still recognized as part of a spectrum of effort. A regular column for local newspapers, written by the Liberal Publications Department official E. W. Record for the NWAC, regularly used this method. Like Dawson, Galsworthy and Beith, in one piece he noted, 'We are all John Bullish. We are slow to begin a new move, but when we do begin it we have plenty of capacity to carry it through with competence and efficiency.' In another, he quoted a book (which, in turn, quoted a recruiting message by David Lloyd George) that suggested

> some can render one service, some another; some here, some there. Some can render great assistance, others but little; but there is not one who cannot help in some measure, even if it is only by *enduring cheerfully* his share of the discomfort.[10]

Civilians, Record argued, could all make some contribution, no matter how small – only being more cheerful would be something, setting themselves to a task they may

Figure 8 Cover of *Overseas*, August 1918.
Source: Public Domain.

not previously have realized was needed would be even better. Such arguments about the importance of even the smallest contributions were commonplace in domestic propaganda: nobody was excluded from the war effort because everything related to the war. Civilians' efforts could never be enough because servicemen were suffering greater hardships, but trying their utmost to play their part could bring them closer to servicemen's example, like the mother and children in the war savings play, *Patriotic Pence* (discussed in Chapter 3), 'trying to do their bit at home, as their Dad's doing his bit in the Navy'. Similarly, a 1918 discussion of British women's wartime work drafted by the New Zealand journalist Kate Isitt and signed by Viscountess Rhondda, published in the Overseas Club and Patriotic League's journal, *Overseas*, spent considerable space outlining the work. However, the piece concluded it 'would be an impertinence to praise the women of Great Britain because, like her men, they have done their duty'. Since all war work contributed to the war effort, and women were unable to take up arms, Isitt and the suffragette Rhondda suggested women had only done what was expected. In downplaying such efforts, through this final humblebrag, they reinforced the equivalence of women's and men's war service.[11] As later chapters discuss, special emphasis on both armed servicemen and women's service were common propaganda themes.

The cover of *Overseas*, in which Rhondda's article appeared (Figure 8), featured a brightly coloured cover depicting a wooden ship, emblazoned with English flags, and a Tennyson verse: 'We sailed wherever ships could sail / We founded many a mighty state / Pray God our greatness may not fail / Through craven fears of being great'. Balancing the reality of British imperial strength with a preferred image of restraint in wartime evidently continued earlier attitudes. Humblebragging allowed propagandists to present an image of Britain and Britons, to its own people and others, as modest and restrained. It combined continued assumptions by many that Britain did, in fact, occupy a special place in the world with an understanding that British strength was not a subject relished by all. Downgrading service as something to be expected or acknowledging flaws in British character as part of larger discussions aimed to win over potentially sceptical audiences to the wider points made. Taking a matter-of-fact tone was supposedly in keeping with British national character – another point of distinction from the supposedly more ambitious and boastful Germans. As Chapter 9 discusses, matters of fact were also a substantial component of wartime propaganda, which existed to provide necessary information, as well as to inspire.

Notes

1 'Mr Chamberlain's Opening Speech', *The Times*, 4 November 1902, 5.
2 Captain A. J. Dawson, 'John Bull at War', in *Back to Blighty* (London: Hodder & Stoughton, 1917), 1–7.
3 'Major A.J. Dawson', *The Times*, 7 February 1951, 8; TNA INF4/1B, 'Military Press Control: A History of the Work of MI7' (1920), 20.
4 'The Kaiser's Insult' (PRC poster no. 6, 1914): https://www.iwm.org.uk/collections/item/object/27775 (accessed 4 January 2024); 'The Kaiser's Insult' (PRC leaflet no. 13, 1914); Rudyard Kipling, 'Tommy' [1890] in Jon Stallworthy (ed.), *The Oxford Book of War Poetry* (Oxford: Oxford University Press, [1984] 2008), 143.
5 'Foreword' in Bruce Bairnsfather, *Fragments from France* (New York: G.P. Putnam's, 1917), n.p.; For brief summaries of Bairnsfather's wartime propaganda, see Robert Whiter, 'Bairnsfather's "Fragments from France"', *Military Heritage*, 9, no. 1 (2007): https://warfarehistorynetwork.com/article/bairnsfathers-fragments-from-france/ (accessed 4 January 2024); Monger, 'A Not Uncongenial Task', 13.
6 'More "Contemptibles"', *Reality*, no. 89, 14 August 1917, 2–3; Monger, *Patriotism and Propaganda*, 145; 'Editorial Notes', *Welcome*, 1, no. 14 (3 July 1918), 159.
7 John Galsworthy, 'American and Briton', *Yale Review*, 8, no. 1 (October 1918), 18–19, 22. On Galsworthy's wartime propaganda, see Wright, 'The Great War, Government Propaganda,

and English Men of Letters', 84–7; Buitenhuis, *Great War of Words*, 42–3; Messinger, *British Propaganda*, 41–2; Monger, 'A Not Uncongenial Task', 6, 16.

8   John Galsworthy, 'Diagnosis of the Englishman' (originally published in the *Amsterdamer Revue*, 1915), *A Sheaf* (New York: G.P. Putnam's, 1916), 257–8.

9   Ian Hay, *The Last Million* (London: Hodder & Stoughton, 1919), ix–xxxv, quotations at xxix, xxxi; Buitenhuis, *Great War of Words*, 113–16.

10 'A Letter from London. By "Thought-Reader"', *North Devon Herald*, 18 April 1918, 3 and 9 May 1918, 3; Lloyd George's words appeared in *"Partners in One Great Enterprise." An Appeal for Sacrifice and Service* (PRC leaflet no. 36, 1915).

11 Viscountess Rhondda, 'The Women of Great Britain', *Overseas*, 3, no. 31 (August 1918), War Anniversary Supplement, xix–xx; details of Isitt's authorship, alongside a galley proof of the piece, are in TNA NATS 1/1290, Hesta Chesshire (assistant editor, *Overseas*) to Mrs [Helen] Archdale, Ministry of National Service, 8 July 1918. For wider comments on renegotiation of women's place as citizens through wartime service, see Gullace, *Blood of Our Sons*; Monger, 'Nothing Special?'.

CHAPTER 9
INFORMATION

When David Lloyd George became Britain's prime minister in December 1916, one of his first acts was to ask the newspaper editor Robert Donald to review the present state of Britain's propaganda. Donald's rapid investigation suggested disorganization, competition and wastefulness between the various official and unofficial groups that had produced propaganda since 1914. Following his report, a Department of Information was established, led by the novelist John Buchan, which was meant to coordinate all Britain's propaganda efforts. However, this failed to resolve competition between groups connected to the Foreign Office and War Office and paid little attention to domestic propaganda (which, instead, became the NWAC's focus from July 1917). A second attempt was made to bring all propaganda under the single direction of a Ministry of Information, led by Lord Beaverbrook, in 1918, but again was incomplete – the Foreign Office continued some activities independently, as did the NWAC and Lord Northcliffe's enemy propaganda organization at Crewe House. Nonetheless, the Ministry provoked political suspicion. During a parliamentary debate in August 1918, the Liberal MP Leif Jones protested the secrecy with which it had been established and now operated:

> It exists, and was announced to us through the Press, though up to now we have been kept in the dark as to its constitution, its purposes, its methods and its relation to other Departments of State ... Before the War there was not Government propaganda from public funds in this country, and there was no Press Bureau for the selection and manufacture of news and views.

Jones then identified several people with professional and business backgrounds involved with the Ministry's operations:

> These gentlemen represent the most formidable combination at the Ministry of Information. The interests represented are banks, electric power companies, gas, railways, newspapers, rubber, insurance, iron, steel, Pullman cars, ships, and tobacco – a wholly formidable combination.
>
> I find it impossible to believe that this great combination of business interests is building up in the closing years of the War propaganda work proper, for that work, in regard to the attitude of this country, and so forth, is practically at an end. The matter is decided, and the world knows that for which we are fighting. I find it impossible to believe that this immense organisation is being put up solely for war purposes...

> I regard the whole thing with suspicion. I admit I am prejudiced, but I think the whole thing is detestably vulgar. But that is not the worst thing. It is a real danger to the freedom of this country.

Jones's criticism reflected wider concerns about government interference with press freedom and discomfort with propaganda current at the time.[1] Later associations of propaganda almost entirely with deception and manipulation, meanwhile, make the Ministry of Information seem an Orwellian institution, with 'information' a euphemism for dishonest communication.

'Information' was certainly a euphemism for 'propaganda', but in this period it was arguably less sinister and more accurate than it seems. Before and during the war, propaganda was quite openly used as a term to describe public communication. A 1912 *Times* article, for instance, announced the Liberal government's 'Active Propaganda' in support of national insurance, highlighting the organization of meetings and leaflets to explain the scheme. Meanwhile, even relatively late in the war, organizations continued to openly refer to propaganda work. At a meeting at the Albert Hall, the Chancellor of the Exchequer Andrew Bonar Law announced he had 'entrusted' to the NWSC 'the whole duty of propaganda' for war savings and bonds, while newspapers reported conferences called by the NWAC in Liverpool and Norwich to arrange local propaganda.[2] There was not yet consensus that propaganda was a negative phenomenon. Further, substantial wartime propaganda genuinely focused on information. Discussion of propaganda often focuses on sensational content or on arguments and ideas intended to persuade people to act, but, as Chapter 8 on humblebragging noted, propaganda took varied forms. Even with sensational or persuasive material, substantial effort was often made to inform. The mass audience for the *Battle of the Somme* film (discussed in Chapter 6) showed the public's appetite for such material, even if particular interpretations or omissions were made by the creators. However, much propaganda material was also mainly informative. Alongside material for military or civilian recruitment that explained why service was needed, for instance, was substantial supporting material addressing technical details (such as where to go to enlist or an explanation of the process of buying and redeeming War Savings Certificates).[3] Though far less interesting, retrospectively, than elaborate arguments for service, or visual depictions of atrocities, providing necessary information was essential to wartime propaganda. Once a civilian was inspired to take up war work in a particular industry, they needed to know how to actually do it. Such material is overlooked partly because its plainness goes against modern assumptions. Propaganda is a means of communication intended to persuade an audience to act or to accept something, but part of this persuasion involves giving people information that they need.

One element tied to propaganda and information (as Chapter 24 discusses in more detail) is censorship, as noted in Jones's inclusion of the Press Bureau (PB) as part of his parliamentary challenge. After criticism during the Anglo-Boer War (1899–1902), government departments involved with the armed forces took greater interest in press coverage. By 1912, an Admiralty, War Office and Press Committee (AWOPC) existed to liaise with newspapers about potentially sensitive news, but after the outbreak of war, an official PB was established, which oversaw censorship of press content, as well as issuing notices to editors either containing information or prohibiting publication of information at a government department's request. The result was over 750 'D' and 'Ireland D' notices, limiting what could be discussed. While these included some dubious restrictions (like the racist ban on showing white nurses with non-white troops noted in Chapter 5), particularly regarding Irish nationalism, most D notices focused on information that might cause security damage. Most frequently, these concerned the movement or location of military units, ships, prominent people or sites of industry, which might assist enemy planning or create targets for naval or aerial attack. Security was defined widely: newspaper weather forecasts were forbidden in case of assistance to enemy, which one of the PB's directors, the journalist Edward Cook, later justified with evidence of a failed air raid caused by an inaccurate report. Cook also noted that the PB was sometimes excessively cautious because of the risk to lives and stressed that it censored dangerous information, not opinion (as demonstrated, for instance, by press criticism in the 1915 'shells scandal' that forced a change of government).[4]

More broadly, Britain's wartime control of information needed editors' cooperation. The AWOPC continued its liaison role and was supplemented by regular communication with the Newspaper Proprietors' Association, led by Sir George Riddell, owner of the *News of the World* and a confidante of Lloyd George. Newspapers chose whether to submit articles for PB scrutiny. The D notices, as well as the Defence of the Realm Act, provided legal means to prosecute if bounds were overstepped. As Badsey notes, this collaborative system 'only worked through considerable agreement between the censors and the London press', while Sanders and Taylor suggest press obedience to government restrictions reflected 'willing acquiescence' more than 'coercion'.[5] Editors, who often moved in the same social circles as government ministers, traded such obedience for increasing access to information. Over the first two years, opposition to journalists' presence in military zones, particularly from the War Secretary, Lord Kitchener, was slowly overcome by press insistence (including from Beaverbrook) on the need for decent information. At the same time, editors grew frustrated with departments issuing what they considered 'editorial paragraphs' or 'trade notices' containing information they expected published, which Riddell protested often involved 'dull matter which interests only a few people'. Seemingly responding to the stated desire for information that journalists could make readable, meanwhile, MI7b began issuing technical information 'as a basis for articles' newspapers could write themselves.[6] Anticipating this chapter's contention that more dramatic content overshadows plainer information, one of these briefings suggested,

> It is a trite reflection that modern science has revolutionised methods of warfare. But the more obvious instances which such reflection calls to mind – gas, tanks, liquid fire, and so forth – have, by reason of their sensational character, obscured many more significant developments, which have taken place unnoticed and passed almost without comment.

To put this right, the briefing provided four pages of detail on developments in frozen and preserved meat for army use! Other than briefly noting the 'patriotic contribution of our own dominions', the piece stuck to facts and statistics.[7]

Given widespread admiration for servicemen, and the many civilians linked to them, the information most desired was up-to-date news of the battlefronts and servicemen themselves. This was also most limited by security concerns, but information did reach Britain. Older assumptions that the public was ignorant of military conditions have been rejected in modern scholarship. Helen McCartney, for instance, notes that despite censorship rules, Liverpool newspapers published letters from soldiers in local battalions, early in the war, that left little doubt of the war's costs. Likewise, while *Battle of the Somme* did not show graphic violence, lingering scenes of bodies and grave-digging again meant that millions of viewers were confronted by death.[8] Propaganda largely presented servicemen's experiences indirectly in the war's early years, via imagined characters on posters, tales of heroic individuals like Jack Cornwell (discussed in Chapter 3) or the words of senior military figures. As the war continued, however, servicemen increasingly appeared as propagandists themselves, providing audiences with 'authentic' and authoritative voices. Increasingly (as discussed in a later chapter), soldiers appeared at propaganda events as speakers, validating the event by their presence, as well as in print. Some soldier-propagandists, like Milne writing for MI7b, tried to balance information and inspiration. Through much of 1918 he wrote a weekly column on 'The British Front', which was published in various Australian papers. The column was seemingly insulated from security risk by appearing weeks after the events described. Milne had a double propaganda value. As a famous writer known for his humour through his assistant-editorship of *Punch*, he might attract readers, while as a soldier writing about military matters he also carried weight. His British Front pieces mixed accounts of recent fighting, often focused on the heroism of individual soldiers or units, swipes at Germany and elements in which he seemed to confront readers with some realities of military service. A column published in mid-July (discussing events of mid-April) 1918 dwelt on heroic fighting around Flanders, including descriptions of troops fighting to the last man, mentioned German misuse of prisoners of war as labourers and the capture of German prisoners and concluded with discussion of aerial fighting. The final anecdote added a chilling detail

> to the surprise of those who were watching the British machine turned southwards and disappeared from the battle. Where it went nobody knows, but more than two hours later it came to the ground nearly 20 miles behind our lines. The petrol tank was empty, and the two occupants had been dead for some time, killed by the same bullet. For over two hours it had flown by itself, carrying its ghostly burden.[9]

Milne's propaganda often trod a fine line, sticking mainly to conventional patriotic lines and anti-Germanism, using his own humorous style but also confronting readers with sombre details – here, technology disrupted a conventional death for the airmen.

As noted, propaganda usually contained at least a persuasive edge. Calls for civilian service often stressed duty. At a meeting in Haywards Heath in Sussex, announcing a national service campaign, the main speaker, Mr Ellis, chairman of the Urban District Council, declared that the 'nation has got to be saved. We have got to make up our minds that our time for sacrifice has come.' He asked 'citizens to show their patriotism' and noted that Germany had introduced compulsory service, but Britons should act voluntarily, and local men should match the example of Haywards Heath's soldiers. All this was typical propaganda language. Yet Ellis spent much of his address outlining the process involved in volunteering for national service, the pay rates and allowances provided and the kinds of areas where work was particularly needed. He stressed that, even if men believed they were already doing work of national importance, they should volunteer and would be left in those roles if so. In the same month, a mass meeting at the Albert Hall called for women's national service. It was attended by the Queen and the wives of the commander-in-chief, several Dominion politicians and the Archbishop of Canterbury and several women already prominent in war work. The Director of National Service Neville Chamberlain read a message from the Admiralty commending work already done by women on its behalf. May Tennant, director of the Women's Section of National Service, noted that women had not been put off munitions work despite a lethal explosion, as well as requesting help in wool-gathering. The president of the Board of Agriculture, R. E. Prothero, then outlined needs for agricultural labour, noting the organization of selection committees, provision of free uniforms, travelling expenses and free training. He assured women that they 'would not be left on the land alone in isolated farms' and would have welfare inspectors to support them. The bulk of his discussion addressed practicalities, and only in concluding did he note that, while the work was hard and dirty, this made it 'comparable' to 'the men folk in the trenches'. Finally, the War Secretary, Lord Derby, and Tennant's assistant, Violet Markham, stressed the importance and efficiency of women who volunteered sticking to a single role.[10] While some elements of this event aimed to inspire, like Chamberlain and Derby's descriptions of service already rendered by women or Prothero's comparison between agricultural and military service, most aimed to state clearly the work and its conditions. Similarly, Figure 9, calling for 10,000 female farm workers, relied solely on the role's terms and conditions for persuasion.

Comparable balances of attempted inspiration and information existed elsewhere. Brendan Maartens notes that PRC military recruitment efforts extended beyond its well-known posters and meetings. It also operated a Householder Return and Information Sub-Department, responsible for canvassing all households about men's willingness to enlist and following up with respondents, either to organize their enlistment or to answer questions they asked.[11] Food control and war savings propaganda, in particular, balanced attempts to motivate civilians with practical guidance. There was no point in simply telling people to eat less. While wealthy people might substitute one expensive ingredient for another, it was harder for poorer people to simply 'eat less bread' as it was a necessary, affordable staple, as the food propagandists Dorothy Peel and Maud Pember Reeves noted. Hence, they arranged practical demonstrations of cookery with different

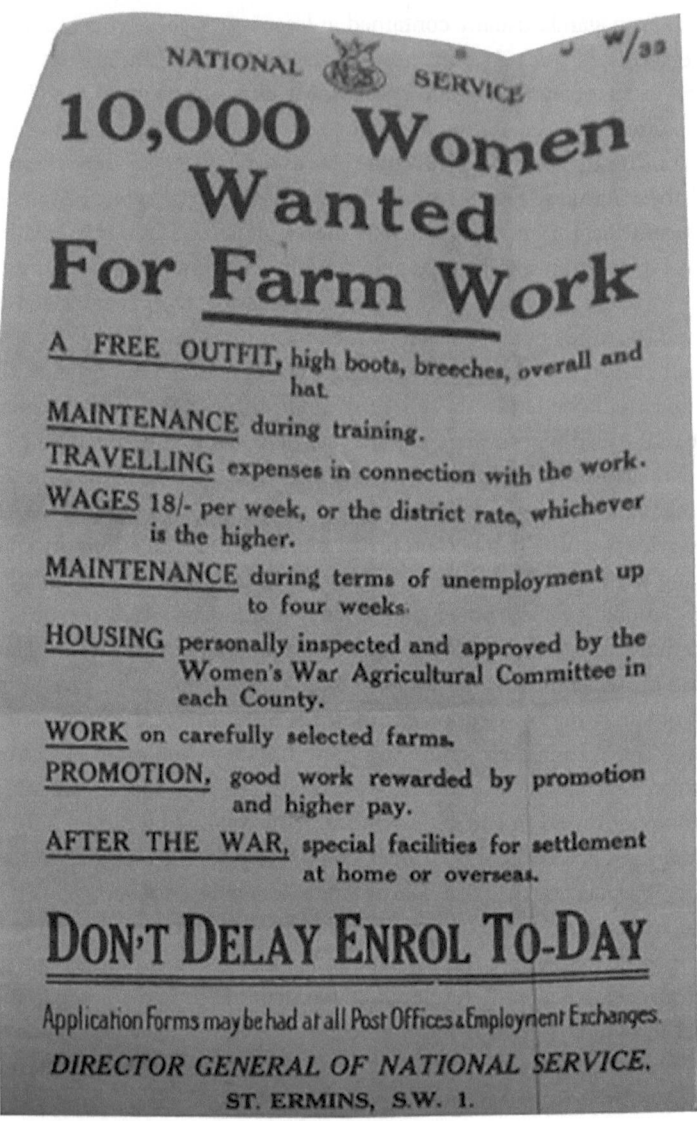

Figure 9 '10,000 Women Wanted for Farm Work'.
Source: National Service poster W/33, TNA NATS 1/1318 (author's photograph).

ingredients to accompany their speaking tours.[12] Similarly, war savings propaganda included multiple campaigns to motivate civilians to invest money in war bonds and savings, such as 'Tank Week', 'Businessmen's Week' and 'War Weapons Week', which tried to stimulate interest by adding a competitive element – people needed to invest a certain amount within a specified week to have an artillery piece, tank or plane named after their town or village. At the same time, however, the NWSC issued publications simply explaining the technicalities behind the investments. *How to Invest Small Sums in the War Loan* provided a question-and-answer leaflet explaining the investment. While it mentioned that this would help 'our country win the War', it largely focused on benefits and risks, when the government might repurchase the stock and how investors could sell their stock if they wished. *Why Your Money Is Safe If You Invest in the War Loan* offered an even simpler explanation – the loan was overseen by the government and Post Office, did not require an investor's management, would receive regular interest and could be sold at market value.[13] In all areas of civilian service and investment, propaganda not only had to inspire action through stirring concepts but provide necessary details too.

Though dry, such informational components of propaganda were essential to the whole. Audiences could not be motivated solely by abstract discussions of duty or shocking accounts of atrocities. Such things might frame requests for action, but people often needed practical guidance on how to meet the demands. Recipes and investment guides accompanied more dramatic content throughout the war. Such essential but stodgy fare made the regular use of jokes, discussed in Chapter 10, all the more valuable.

Notes

1. Speech of Leif Jones, in Hansard, *Parliamentary Debates Commons* (5), vol. 109, 5 August 1918, cols. 947–8, 958, 961. On the formation of the Department and Ministry, see Sanders and Taylor, *British Propaganda*, 55–88; for further discussion of suspicions about corruption (focused on the NWAC), see Monger, *Patriotism and Propaganda*, 217–28.
2. 'The Liberal Insurance Campaign. Active Propaganda', *The Times*, 11 March 1912, 7; 'Things Said at the Albert Hall', *War Savings*, 2, no. 3 (November 1917), 32; 'Allies' War Aims. Conference in Liverpool', *Liverpool Courier*, 12 October 1917, 4; 'Lest We Forget. What We Are Fighting For. National War Aims', *East Anglian Daily Times*, 27 November 1917, 5.
3. For example, *Recruiting: List of Commands, Military Districts and Regimental Areas* (PRC pamphlet no. 4); *£1 for 15s. 6d. War Savings Certificates on Sale at Post Offices and Banks* (NWSC pamphlet no. 90).
4. For extended discussion, see, most recently, Monger, 'Press Bureau', as well as Deian Hopkin, 'Domestic Censorship in the First World War', *Journal of Contemporary History*, 5, no. 4 (1970), 151–69; Wilkinson, *Secrecy and the Media*, sections 1–3.
5. Badsey, *German Corpse Factory*, 99; Sanders and Taylor, *British Propaganda*, 31.
6. For Riddell's protests of 1916 and 1918, see Monger, 'Press Bureau', 458–60.
7. MI7b, 'A New Way of Supplying an Army with Meat', in PA, BBK3/5.
8. McCartney, *Citizen Soldiers*, 104–16; Reeves, *Film Propaganda*, 158–9.
9. A. A. Milne, 'The British Front From Week to Week', *Darling Downs Gazette*, 18 July 1918, 2.
10. 'National Service', *Mid-Sussex Times*, 13 March 1917, 2; 'Women in National Service', *The Times*, 19 March 1917, 4.
11. Brendan Maartens, 'The Great War, Military Recruitment and the Public Relations Work of the Parliamentary Recruiting Committee, 1914–1915', *Public Relations Inquiry*, 5, no. 2 (2016), esp. 178–9.
12. Dorothy Peel, *A Year in Public Life* (London: Constable, 1919), 23–6. For brief discussion of Peel and Reeves, see Monger, 'Tangible Patriotism', 248–57; this discussion also draws on the current work of my PhD student, Kate Pickworth.

13 *How to Invest Small Sums in the War Loan* (Parliamentary War Savings Committee, leaflet no. 7); *Why Your Money Is Safe if You Invest in the War Loan* (Parliamentary War Savings Committee, leaflet no. 5). On the special campaigns, see Gregory, *Last Great War*, 220–33; Monger, 'Familiarity Breeds Consent', 519–24.

CHAPTER 10
JOKES

Previous chapters on information in propaganda and on 'humblebragging' showed two ways that propagandists departed from more obvious approaches such as sensational accounts of enemy wrongdoing, appeals to heroism or claims of virtuous British aims. Another element, also seen in passing in earlier chapters, was the persistent use of jokes and humour. Like providing dry but necessary information, or attempting to disarm audiences through humblebragging, jokes helped take the edge off the very serious wartime situation. Propagandists were often ready to assert the war's absolute gravity or criticize audiences for lacking full commitment. Both propagandists and audiences also understood the very substantial human costs of the war. Nonetheless, there was no shortage of humorous content. It is well known that soldiers used humour to help cope with their service. Bairnsfather's ironic cartoons of Old Bill and his friends (discussed previously) were reportedly favoured by soldiers compared to others depicting more conventional heroism. Soldiers' trench journals – most famously, the *Wipers Times* – featured a 'prevailing tone' of humour, mocking the absurdity of their situation at the front.[1] Propaganda aimed at soldiers picked up on this and included humorous content while avoiding pompous commentary on soldiers' heroism. However, propaganda to civilians also included humour to attack and undermine various enemies or, more gently, to lighten the mood of speeches or articles. Notable humourists, including Bairnsfather, Milne, the cartoonist H. M. Bateman and the singer and comedian Harry Lauder, were brought into propaganda work and assisted the British habit, identified by Bairnsfather's editor, Vivian Carter, of refusing to take anything wholly seriously.

Previous chapters have noted jokes and humour in propaganda content, including the imperial contributors associating with representative animals in Lancelot Speed's film *Britain's Effort*, harsh and absurd mockery of Germany and self-mocking portraits. Even information propaganda was not above joking. At the Albert Hall meeting calling for women's national service, discussed in the last chapter, Neville Chamberlain attempted humour when reminding women 'that men were less adaptable than they. Although women had learned to make shells, keep accounts, and drive motor-cars, men had not yet learned to become district nurses or feed babies.' At another meeting, in Manchester, he 'appealed to women to volunteer and for attractive service, such as included a smart uniform, pleasant drill, a voyage to France, and a spell of adventure in company with soldiers – (laughter) – with a shell or two close enough to give a little excitement'.[2] Chamberlain was clearly no match for Bairnsfather as a humourist, but the effort to make such jokes in long, serious speeches on war work indicates the perceived value of humour. As the food propagandist Dorothy Peel noted, speakers needed some sense of humour to deal with 'personal chaff with good temper' at public meetings. At one food meeting, it was suggested that

> 'they shouldn't send such a well-fed looking lady as you talking Food Economy!' ...
> 'I don't agree', I remarked smilingly. '... for if I can keep to the rations ... and look, as my friend there remarks, so well fed, I'm a vastly good advertisement for rations!'[3]

With public events exposing propagandists to heckling – which was, at this time, a traditional part of political public speaking – humorous responses could help keep an audience's goodwill.

As noted above, propaganda organizations actively recruited people with humorous reputations. Milne's articles appeared in Dominion papers attributed either to his full name or, sometimes, to 'A. A. M.', to which his pre-war *Punch* articles were attributed. Christchurch's *Press*, which later published some of his MI7b articles, considered his enlistment and the 'interruption of [his] enchantingly funny work for "Punch" ... one of the real hardships of the war'.[4] When Milne later took up propaganda, many pieces were either wholly humorous or contained jokes and quips alongside more serious commentary. His talents as a funny writer were valued alongside his soldierly status. While Milne discussed many of the same topics as other propagandists, his unique style – and existing reputation – were an asset to exploit. Likewise, Bairnsfather was recruited to MI7b based on the success of his Old Bill cartoons and tasked with attempting to produce similar characters for other nations' forces. Before this, his editor, Carter, suggested humourists were neglected:

> 'If only we can get them laughing.' So remarks to himself the individual who has a difficult 'crowd' to manage – a crowd out of humour, critical, peevish, bored and disillusioned. Were the affairs of the Great Nations in the hands of practical men, laughter would be one of the munitions of war, and the recruiting of humorists would be the job of a special department in Whitehall. 'Instead of which' the humorist has been, in our country since the war, perhaps, regarded askance until – well, until the subject of this booklet appeared on the horizon.[5]

Certainly, the war's early years witnessed hostility to leisure, which was treated as inappropriate during such a serious period of war. There were calls for professional sport to stop and for restrictions on what could be shown at cinemas, while everyone was expected to work longer hours and invest in war loans and bonds. However, some comedians were involved in propaganda early on. Harry Lauder, for instance, recalled that, on a US tour in 1915, he 'did a lot of propaganda work on behalf of my country not only from the stage but at meetings arranged in many places'. Lauder believed the United States would eventually enter the war on Britain's side and continued to call for action despite receiving threatening letters and being 'told that I should stick to my legitimate business of the stage without mixing it up with British propaganda'. When officially asked to return to the United States later, Lauder agreed on condition that he should not give lectures but 'go as an artiste, doing my work as I had done for many years, but always accepting any opportunity of putting the British case before the people of the United States'. Lauder found himself particularly popular with US soldiers in training, who 'sang my choruses with lusty glee and vim'. In this case, continuing to entertain let Lauder conduct propaganda indirectly, likely reaching audiences that would have avoided more formal addresses. It also meant he could sometimes avoid accusations of merely being a 'British booster' – he was an entertainer who happened to also mention Britain's war.[6]

It was one thing for individuals to continue their own humorous activities in wartime and even undertake voluntary propaganda from a sense of personal duty, as Lauder did initially. However, official employment of people like Lauder, Bairnsfather and Milne and the NWAC's payment of humorous cartoonists including the *Punch* artists Bateman and Wilmot Lunt, Roland Hill of *Comic Cuts* or the future *Beano* cartoonist Allan Morley shows growing realization that propaganda, like wider wartime culture, needed some room for silliness alongside the serious business at hand.[7]

Chapter 7 has already shown that propagandists used humour to undermine Germany's image as an all-powerful and brutal military force. While audiences could be warned of the dreadful dangers of German victory, they should not be paralyzed by fear. Caricatures of the kaiser, his son and, less frequently, leading generals like Paul von Hindenburg and Erich Ludendorff belittled enemy leadership. Kaiser Wilhelm, almost always depicted in cartoons wearing a *pickelhaube* and with his moustache comedically accentuated, was shown bewildered by German failures. At one point in *Britain's Effort* the early bottling up of the German fleet by Britain's navy and capture of its colonies is shown by the kaiser, in a small tub and bush clothing, being chased around Africa by John Bull, eventually crawling into Kiel harbour, packed with battleships and submarines trapped by the blockade, where he is abandoned by the German eagle.[8] Cartoons, images and discussions of Wilhelm throughout the war also took very serious tones (like the example of him confronted by the ghosts of murdered children, described in Chapter 3), which encouraged calls for him to be tried for war crimes at the end of the war. This did not make mockery inappropriate, however. Rather, ridiculing Germany's head of state added to more sober commentary about German crimes and the problem with German *kultur* (discussed in the next chapter). Germany's militarized culture was both awful and absurd.

Reflecting Bairnsfather's popularity, Hill depicted 'Billhelm' in 1918, instead of Old Bill, squashed into a shell crater with a dishevelled Emperor Karl of Austria, inviting him to go to a 'better 'ole' if he knew one. Published in *Welcome* (The NWAC's newspaper for soldiers on leave) in May 1918, in response to Karl's recent visit to Wilhelm – and presumably referring to earlier peace suggestions by Karl – the joke may have rung hollow, given the German advance under way on the Western Front. Continuing to publish mocking materials even during a challenging period, however, presumably aimed to limit pessimism. Even war savings propaganda, often (as noted previously) somewhat dry, attempted some humour, including a foldout leaflet (Figure 10) showing a grinning, square-headed Hindenburg smiling 'When You *Don't* Buy War Bonds', which switched to 'the Hindenburg frown' when bonds were bought.[9]

Figure 10 'When You *Don't* Buy War Bonds'.
Source: John Johnson Collection, Bodleian Library, University of Oxford (author's photograph).

Germany was undoubtedly the butt of most propaganda jokes, in line with its generally heavier discussion, though NWAC cartoonists did occasionally depict Turkish, Austrian and Bulgarian figures too, usually as clownish allies. A small cartoon by W. F. Blood, for instance, showed a caricatured Turk, wearing a fez and waistcoat and dropping a scimitar labelled 'made in Germany' being stung in the face by a giant bee with union jack wings, wearing a pith helmet – a reference to Edmund Allenby's middle eastern success. Such materials may partly reflect growing confidence later in the war, but also related to the recognized culture of jokes and mockery among soldiers. *Welcome*'s humorous material attempted to tap into this culture, while avoiding the tales of soldierly heroism found elsewhere (and heavily spoofed in the *Wipers Times*). Some jokes were particularly clumsy. Bateman's 'Sport at the Front' cartoons, for instance, showed grinning British soldiers pursuing hapless, chubby and bespectacled Germans. Such scenes lacked any of the scornful wit of Bairnsfather's cartoons, which acknowledged, while making light of, British troops' danger and discomfort. Closer to Bairnsfather's tone was another Hill cartoon, 'The Pessimists', in which a soldier predicted his yet-to-be-conceived son would fight in the war. A further strand of humour in *Welcome* related to soldiers' relationships with women, from Frank Styche's joking cartoon about a soldier's heartbeat increasing each time a nurse approached him to Morley's 'The Advance and the Retreat', showing a soldier approach a seemingly attractive woman before rushing off after seeing her face.[10]

Morley's taste for offensive humour was even more pronounced in another edition of *Welcome* published immediately after the Armistice. Here, he depicted two well-dressed Jewish men, with prominent noses, one with a cigar, the other a jewel-topped cane, discussing a new shop front, which one of them boasts he paid for by putting out a box 'for the blind'. While, for obvious reasons, substantial scholarship addresses anti-Semitism in central Europe during and immediately after the war, this was also a factor in British wartime culture. Sascha Auerbach, for example, notes the strong vein of anti-Semitism and accusations of financial opportunism in assessments of Jewish workers' requests for exemption from military service. Aggressive jokes were also made at the expense of others considered to be failing their duty – 'shirkers', profiteers and 'pacifists' (defined broadly to include the most critical voices). At Keighley a local speaker drew laughs from his audience by asserting that pacifists, already downgraded by a previous speaker to 'defeatists', 'were unfortunate. They were a class of mental defectives, with a mental or moral squint.'[11]

Those criticized did not hold back in their own comments, either. The UDC co-founder, Arthur Ponsonby, described himself at a UDC meeting in Birmingham as 'a Liberal who had lost his party, and he did not see any other party that was particularly inviting. He could not join the Labour Party yet, because he did not want to become a Privy Councillor and a Right Honourable just yet. (Laughter.)' Ponsonby's joke was at the expense of Labour MPs like Arthur Henderson, George Barnes and Will Crooks, who had supported the coalition government and had been made privy councillors. Another UDC member, J. A. Hobson, published a series of pseudonymous satirical articles in the radical newspaper the *Nation* mocking the Defence of the Realm Act (commonly referred to as DORA), propaganda and censorship, skewering both individuals and the public who allowed things to happen. In one piece, Hobson imagined a character, Roxburgh, explaining the government's use of DORA:

> 'When we first took on Dora and her sisters, all of us were subject to the same delusion – how that [sic] Britons stood for personal freedom, every man the arbiter of his own fate, and for something called civil liberty ... Do you know that it took us at least four years to discover that all this was nothing but the rhetoric of sentimental self-esteem – that it had nothing behind it.'
>
> ... 'And how', I asked, 'did this discovery dawn upon you?' ...
>
> 'What was it? Why, what do you think? – the appointment of Sir Edward Carson to the War Cabinet. It was recognized by all of us that if the nation would take that stroke lying down they would take anything.'[12]

Carson, the Irish Unionist who, before the war, threatened to oppose devolved Irish government with armed resistance, if necessary, was brought into Lloyd George's government – in 1917, he briefly oversaw British propaganda. Hobson's joke, like Ponsonby's attack on Labour MPs, accused the government, and Britain generally, of hypocrisy. To their mind, Britons were no more committed to civil liberties, justice and democracy than the Germans they condemned.

If some jokes had sharp, even unpleasant, edges, many more played the role that jokes often did (and do) in public communication – they lightened the mood in a serious discussion. Labour leader Arthur Henderson, speaking on national service in Newcastle in 1917, attempted to deflect criticism of his support for the scheme through both humour and serious argument:

> He had been taken to task for being associated with a scheme which offered a minimum wage of 25s. He was not ashamed of his position ... To-day, in spite of

the cost of living and in spite of high prices, there were a good many agricultural labourers who, if they could get 25s. in cash and 17s. 6d. in addition as subsistence allowance, would begin to think the millennium had come. (Laughter and cheers.) The Government had taken the very first step in fixing a 25s. minimum for agricultural labourers, and he hoped it would soon become a universal minimum throughout agriculture ... Some of the things said in the newspapers were unfair, because, instead of depreciating wages, the National Service scheme would, in his opinion, improve them.[13]

Henderson and other leading Labour politicians were criticized by dissenting socialists in the UDC or Independent Labour Party for supporting the government against workers' interests. Here, Henderson used humour to enliven his argument about wages and support for workers. Despite the heavily asserted seriousness of everything related to the war, propagandists used jokes to weaken opponents, lighten moods and enliven dull material. In some cases, comedic talent was actively employed, but jokes were not only attempted by those who were funny. Undoubtedly, far more propaganda was serious than humorous, but making fun not only added an extra weapon to propagandists' arsenal; it also conveyed some sense of normality in abnormal times. If, as Vivian Carter suggested, Britons were incapable of taking anything completely seriously, a long and punishing war was exactly the moment to make jokes. Joking was a part of British culture to be cherished, even in difficult times – this culture, propagandists regularly assured audiences, was very different from the contemptuous *Kultur* of Britain's main foe, as the next chapter discusses.

Notes

1. See, for example, Edward Madigan, '"Sticking to a Hateful Task": Resilience, Humour, and British Understandings of Combatant Courage', *War in History*, 20, no. 1 (2013); J. G. Fuller, *Troop Morale and Popular Culture in the British and Dominion Armies, 1914–1918* (Oxford: Clarendon Press, 1991), 7–20 (quotation at 14), 143–54.
2. 'Women and National Service', *The Times*, 19 March 1917, 4; 'National Service', *Daily Telegraph*, 28 March 1917, 5.
3. Peel, *Year in Public Life*, 91–2.
4. Untitled editorial, *Press*, 29 January 1916, 8.
5. Vivian Carter, *Bairnsfather: A Few Fragments from His Life* (New York: G.P. Putnam's, 1917), 9.
6. Harry Lauder, *Roamin' in the Gloamin'* (originally Philadelphia and London: J. B. Lippincott, 1928; repr. ed. Wakefield: EP Publishing Limited, 1976), 182–3, 196–201.
7. 'Harry Lauder as Recruiter', *Dundee People's Journal*, 13 February 1915, 1. On Bateman, Lunt, Hill and Morley's payment by the NWAC, see TNA T102/19, NWAC Publicity Department files.
8. Speed, *Britain's Effort* at around 12.28 minutes: https://www.iwm.org.uk/collections/item/object/1060008269.
9. Roland Hill, 'Better 'Ole', *Welcome*, no. 7, 15 May 1918, 79; BLO, John Johnson Collection, Box 8, 'When You Don't Buy War Bonds'.

10 W. F. Blood, 'The Busy Allen-Bee', *Welcome*, 2 October 1918, 3; H. M. Bateman, 'Sport at the Front. No. 1: Cross-Country Running', *Welcome*, 12 June 1918, 127; Bateman, 'Sport at the Front. No. 5: Hurdling'; and Hill, 'The Pessimists', *Welcome*, 17 August 1918, 220, 221; Frank Styche, 'A Critical Case', *Welcome*, 4 September 1918, 268; Allan Morley, 'The Advance and the Retreat', *Welcome*, 31 July 1918, 209.
11 Allan Morley, untitled ('For the Blind' in NWAC publications files, TNA T102/19), *Welcome*, 13 November 1918, 78; Sascha Auerbach, 'Negotiating Nationalism: Jewish Conscription and Russian Repatriation in London's East End, 1916–1918', *Journal of British Studies*, 46, no. 3 (2007), esp. 605–7; H. S. Clough, speaking at a NWAC meeting in Keighley, in 'England's War Policy', *Keighley News*, 30 March 1918, 5.
12 'Union of Democratic Control', *Scotsman*, 4 September 1916, 7; Lucian [J. A. Hobson], 'D.O.R.A. in 1920', *Nation*, 3 November 1917, 155–7. On Hobson's authorship of the series, see Monger, *Patriotism and Propaganda*, 230–1.
13 'National Service', *The Times*, 20 February 1917, 5.

CHAPTER 11
KULTUR

The British eugenicist James Barr's contribution to *King Albert's Book* veered away from the tributes to Belgium for which the 1914 volume was intended, instead offering his views on the nature of Germans, whose *Kultur*, he suggested, represented European barbarism:

> The 'German Kultur' as manifested in Louvain, and by rapine and plunder throughout Belgium, must be exterminated, and this savage breed as far as possible wiped out, but herein arises an insuperable difficulty. [Belgian playwright, Maurice] Maeterlinck truly says the Germans are all guilty, any differentiation is a mere matter of degree, and you cannot wipe out 100 millions. Moreover, any such attempt would degrade the Allies to the low base level of German conduct. We must carry on an honourable warfare which will leave no blot on our escutcheon. We must conquer nobly, we must make the Germans pay to their last stiver for the war which they have so ruthlessly conducted. We must weed out the worst of the barbarians, and utterly destroy the princely looters with the rest of the Prussian military gang who have proved themselves a disgrace to humanity. When the Germans discover that dishonourable conduct does not pay, that it has no survival value, then we may eventually get a newer and truer Germany.[1]

Previous chapters have discussed Germany at length, particularly in commenting on the functions of atrocity propaganda in Chapter 1 and discussing propagandists' use of Germans' own words against them and the habit of mocking Germany, and particularly its ruler, to undermine impressions of the country as a brutal and irresistible force in Chapter 7. Alongside this combined image of Germany as cruel and clumsy, however, an additional intellectual (or quasi-intellectual) strand of propaganda investigated the nature of Germany itself, suggesting its conduct could be understood by assessing its national thought and character. German claims that 'this was a war of *Kultur* against "Asiatic barbarism"' were countered by reference to German wartime barbarity (as in Barr's contribution to *King Albert's Book*), which was traced to underlying attitudes. *Kultur* became a catch-all label, alongside other phrases such as 'Prussian militarism' and 'might makes right' that combined to paint Germans as morally and ethically bankrupt. The Oxford University lecturer Thomas F. A. Smith condemned German academics' defence of their nation after the outbreak of the war, arguing,

> Their activity before the war – in omitting to denounce the glaring injustices … in Germany, and their activity after the war began – in appraising German kultur and denouncing England's perfidious barbarism, shows them to be what they really are – paid, obedient servants of the State.

Smith also argued that Germans 'truly took pleasure in military service, sacrificing their individual will to the love of discipline'.[2] Propagandists like Smith and Barr, very early in the war, suggested there was a fundamental sickness in German culture that needed to be cured before progress could be made. This, however, Barr suggested, must be achieved in civilized fashion by Britain and its allies. Since *Kultur* infected all Germans, no compromise peace agreement was possible – Germany must be completely reformed before it could safely rejoin the ranks of the 'civilized world'.

Smith, who lectured in Germany for twelve years, was one of many British academics who spent time there before the war. Peter Chalmers Mitchell, the head of London Zoo who spent part of the war analysing German propaganda for MI7b before working for Lord Northcliffe's organization producing propaganda for enemy consumption, noted that it was an expected part of a young zoologist's development to read German and visit German institutions, and German academic leadership was more widely recognized before the war. While he wrote in his memoirs that he was always treated well before 1914, he turned heavily against German *Kultur* in wartime, suggesting, in a 1915 work, *Evolution and the War*, that it came from a false, one-dimensional German interpretation of natural selection, taken further by authors without scientific expertise like General Friedrich von Bernhardi or the Anglo-German philosopher Houston Stewart Chamberlain.[3] James Bryce, famously the leading figure behind the 'Bryce Report', which reported on German atrocities in 1914, actually retained affection for the nation early in the war, arguing that there were 'two Germanies' and that *Kultur* was the specific product of autocratic and militaristic Prussia. As noted previously, some propagandists, like H. G. Wells, argued it was possible to appeal to 'good Germans' throughout the war. Bryce, compiling evidence of the Armenian Genocide in 1916, advised his collaborator not to emphasize German responsibility because he hoped Germany would restrain its Ottoman ally, suggesting he retained some belief in German capacity for good. However, Stuart Wallace suggests the 'two Germanies' view was 'effectively destroyed' by the publication of the 'Manifesto of the Intellectuals of Germany' in October 1914, originally signed by 93 leading German academics and eventually by around 4,000, which disavowed any German wrongdoing in the outbreak of war or invasion of Belgium, invoking the desire to protect 'the legacy of a Goethe, a Beethoven, and a Kant' to reassert Germany's civilized *Kultur*. British academics responded with an open letter, published in the *Times*, rejecting many of the manifesto's claims. Further responses followed, particularly a lengthy series of 'Oxford pamphlets' that began by discussing the war's origins and spread to wider considerations. These pamphlets produced a critique of Germany that was, in one scholar's opinion, 'considerably more subtle than much of the more heavy-handed propaganda' that followed. Arguably, however, the earlier and later material are more linked than this suggests: cruder materials that followed, like the NWAC's *Kalendar of Kultur* (listing several German war crimes from 1914–17), was possible because earlier intellectual deconstruction created a particular image of an aggressive, selfish and brutal *Kultur*, driven by German elites and accepted by the masses.[4] By the war's later years, *Kultur* was an understood, negative shorthand – the opposite of civilization.

Gregory Moore notes that British commentary rapidly identified three figures as the intellectual heart of *Kultur* and Prussian militarism – the historian Heinrich von Treitschke, philosopher Friedrich Nietzsche and retired soldier Bernhardi – although earlier minds such as Immanuel Kant, Johann Fichte and Georg Hegel were noted as inspiring these voices. German thought supposedly moved away from a sense of responsibility to God and the need for humility, instead emphasizing self. From there, Nietzsche's idea of the 'Superman' was adopted by less complex thinkers as an image of Germans generally. Treitschke's contribution to the whole was his view that state sovereignty was absolute, and thus international treaties restrained a state only as long as they chose (the 'scrap of paper' idea, discussed previously, obviously connected to this line of thought), and that he believed in the value of wars to cure 'decadent nations':

> German thought seemed retrospectively not only to sanction the pursuit of naked self-interest, but to be itself a symptom of the … self-regard, the overweening arrogance which manifested itself not only in the Reich's colonial ambitions, but also in the work of its historians and writers, in its monumental architecture, and, 'above all', in the 'seven thousand speeches and in the three hundred uniforms of the Kaiser'.[5]

Completing the trio, Bernhardi's interpretation of Darwin suggested an inevitable 'Struggle for Existence' that applied to states as well as species. As Chalmers Mitchell summarized Bernhardi in his 1917 'Report on the Propaganda Library', written for MI7b to help propagandists develop effective counter-propaganda, 'War, therefore, was necessary, right, and admirable, and was beneficent as it brought about the suppression of the weaker and degenerate nations in favour of the rising and progressive nations.' Britain was decadent and in Germany's way, so Germany should prepare for the 'next war' against Britain. These combined ideas, the former home secretary Herbert Samuel said, were 'anti-moral doctrines' that must be resisted.[6] The implications of this triple viewpoint were apparently clear to propagandists: Germans considered themselves superior. Superior beings had a right to prosper at the expense of lesser ones. States were responsible only to themselves, and war was a positive thing to seek. Germans were self-aggrandizing, considered themselves above international law and intended to topple Britain.

Some of this critique of German thought began before the war, but it gained speed, strength and urgency particularly after German intellectuals' supposed subordination to the state's wishes in late 1914. The classical scholar Gilbert Murray (an early recruit to Wellington House) connected these kinds of ideas with *Kultur* in a 1916 lecture published by the Fight for Right Movement:

> The Germans have been fighting, not for loot, but for an idea ... which grips their minds and consciences, which drives them into brutality and frightfulness, but which also makes them endure ...
>
> it has been an intense belief on the part of the dominant and dynamic section of the German people in their own view of life, in their own methods of government and organization, in the benefits which would follow for the whole world if they were made to prevail, and in their own mission as the champions and apostles of a new Kultur. They have contrasted the slovenly methods of democracy, the disunity and disorder of Europe and the world, the poverty and slackness of the rest of mankind, with the order and discipline and efficiency of modern Germany, and they have not the slightest doubt that Germanism was infinitely superior, and consequently must prevail ... The ultimate vision of the neo-Prussians is not so much the universal domination of the existing Germany, as the triumph of the Prussian idea in the minds of men, so that eventually the world will be organized in one vast symmetrical state, to which every individual will owe implicit obedience.

Given such an apocalyptic vision of German aims, any return to the status quo was impossible. There could be no peaceful return to the pre-war balance of power. Instead, 'a combination of civilized Powers to uphold public right' and international law was required.[7] Murray put his energy where his mouth was as a leading advocate of a League of Nations from 1916.

Others saw similar dangers but did not necessarily put their faith in international law. Rather, fundamental regime change was a better bet. *Kultur* and Prussian militarism must be eradicated before the world was safe from Germany. At a recruiting meeting in Twickenham, the chairman of the Urban District Council William Slade noted that he was asked by someone on his way to the meeting why the government did not make peace:

> That man does not know the mind and stamina of the British Empire. Now that we had taken up the sword we were not going to sheath it until victory had been attained. (Applause.) Who was responsible for this convulsion of civilisation, for this disintegration of humanity? ... The answer was Germany and Germany alone. Then, at the instigation of Germany, Turkey, another apostle of kultur and Christianity entered the field. Turkey was a cancer that would have to be cut out of Europe ... The ravagers of Armenia were in very good company with the desolators of Belgium ... Having taken up arms, we must see to it that peace, when it came, was not written on a scrap of paper, but on a scrap of iron.[8]

Such uncompromising sentiments, already evident in 1915, continued throughout the war. They were not only the views of right-wing or nationalistic commentators, however. In 1918, the socialist editor of the *New Age*, A. R. Orage, published a series of questions and answers about the war, which the NWAC reprinted as two pamphlets. Orage acknowledged that 'the cry of "Wolf! Wolf!" has [often] been raised by our governing classes'. Nonetheless, he suggested 'the long falsely threatened Wolf is here at last'. Prussian militarism was a threat unlike those previously faced:

> Prussia looks upon the rest of the world, in the degrees of their amenability to German kultur, as we Europeans have hitherto regarded 'natives' everywhere; that is to say, as objects of mingled pity and contempt whom a superior race must simultaneously exploit and educate. With kultur in one hand and a bomb in the other, Prussia thereupon proceeds to attempt, first, to subject us, and afterwards she would attempt to improve us, the one thing being the means to the other.

Having rejected objections that the 'secret treaties', revealed by Russian Bolsheviks after the revolution, showed Britain and its allies were equally aggressive, Orage suggested the war must end either with total victory for Germany, total defeat of Germany or its voluntary democratization. Since the German people 'lapped militarist suggestion as a cat laps milk', it was unlikely they would bring about a revolution to force democracy themselves, so total defeat of 'Prussianism' was needed.[9]

While Orage, like others quoted above, explained his views of *Kultur* and Prussian militarism at length, the terms were also a well-understood shorthand from relatively early in the war, as in Slade's recruitment speech. When he dismissed Turkey as 'another apostle of kultur', he expected his audience's understanding. Similarly, a 1918 pamphlet promoting investments in war bonds dwelt at length on the material benefits to investors and the security of the government-backed scheme. However, it added a final claim that the investor 'becomes a partner in the enterprise that will succeed in crushing Prussian Militarism'. No explanation of the concept was provided – war bonds investors knew what the term represented.[10]

Another indication of these ideas' perceived impact is their exploitation in critical groups' propaganda. Commentators for organizations including the UDC and ILP highlighted examples of official British conduct that they argued matched 'Prussian' excesses. Norman Angell, one of the UDC's founders, for instance, noted 'a really national expression of opinion … at the beginning of the war' against 'the Nietzschean notion of a super-State entitled to impose its culture on the world'. However, Angell argued Britain had increasingly shown 'a tendency to adopt the methods and morals of the enemy' by arguing that normal standards of civil liberties and international law should be suspended to assist the war effort. As he characterized such arguments,

> We may be fighting for democracy, freedom, parliamentary government, against despotism, government by a military caste, and restraint of free speech; yet, if we are to wage war efficiently, our government must be autocratic, free speech must be suspended, and the military order must have arbitrary power.

Angell's *The Prussian in Our Midst* denounced the rhetoric of high ideals being accompanied by wartime repression. At a UDC event in Finchley in 1915, the pacifist journalist W. N. Ewer condemned 'slang thrown at Germany' since there 'were people here as bad as the worst Prussian', while every European nation had broken treaties when it suited them. Similarly, when the ILP published its MP Philip Snowden's parliamentary speeches criticizing military appeals tribunals for their mistreatment of conscientious objectors and abuse of power in 1916, the pamphlet was entitled *British Prussianism*. Snowden's speeches did not mention Prussia or its militarism at all or make overt comparisons between British and German conduct. The title, therefore, assumed readers would fully understand the implication when reading his examples of unfair treatment.[11] Critical propaganda's exploitation and reversal of these ideas strongly suggest their impact on contemporary audiences.

Extensive discussion of German *Kultur* began with academics and intellectuals deconstructing German thought to demonstrate a fundamental difference in world view between Britain (or broader 'Western' or 'civilized' perspectives) and Germany. Exploring philosophical and other thought from Kant to Nietzsche suggested wartime conduct was not some temporary extreme but an inbuilt consequence of German development. For propagandists, *Kultur* explained both why a nation previously well regarded in European society could commit such awful atrocities and why it was impossible to make peace with the existing regime. *Kultur* had flourished in an anti-democratic and militaristic society – ending the war with that regime intact would only mean future trouble. *Kultur* thus added deeper meaning to anti-German commentary – this was not simply a reactive attack on a present enemy but a higher defence of civilized principles. Over time, *Kultur* and Prussian militarism became familiar enough that propagandists seeking greater contributions to the war effort and those condemning attacks on civil liberties within Britain alike could use them, confident that audiences understood their negative meaning. In an era when much propaganda was conducted locally, as Chapter 12 discusses, establishing simple terms that covered larger issues was particularly useful.

Notes

1. James Barr, 'Some Eugenic Ideals' in Hall Caine (ed.), *King Albert's Book: A Tribute to the Belgian King and People from Representative Men and Women Throughout the World* (London: Hodder & Stoughton, 1914), 177.
2. For the reference to *Kultur* and 'Asiatic barbarism', see Stuart Wallace, *War and the Image of Germany: British Academics, 1914–1918* (Edinburgh: John Donald, 1988), 33; Thomas F. A. Smith, *The Soul of Germany* (London: Hutchinson, 1915), 47, cited in Aoife O'Gorman, 'Wissenschaft at War: British and German Academic Propaganda and the Great War' (unpublished DPhil thesis, University of Oxford, 2016), 69–70, and see O'Gorman's later comment on Smith at 175.
3. On Chalmers Mitchell, see Monger, 'Know Your Enemy', esp. 781–3; Gregory Moore, 'The Super-Hun and the Super-State: Allied Propaganda and German Philosophy during the First World War', *German Life and Letters*, 54, no. 4 (2001), 318, 323.
4. Wallace, 'War and the Image' 31–5; Tomás Irish, 'Petitioning the World: Intellectuals and Cultural Mobilization in the Great War', in Catriona Pennell and Filipe Ribeiro de Meneses (eds), *A World at War, 1911–1949: Explorations in the Cultural History of Warfare* (Leiden: Brill, 2019); John Griffiths, 'Fake News or an Education in War? Communicating

War Aims to the British Public in Its Early Phases: The Oxford Pamphlets, 1914–1915', in John Griffiths (ed.), *Communication and the First World War* (Abingdon: Routledge, 2020), 91; *A Kalendar of Kultur* (London: NWAC leaflet no. 15, [1917]). On Bryce, Germany and Armenia, see Monger, 'Networking against Genocide', 300.

5   Moore, 'Super-Hun and Super-State', quotations at 325, 316 (the final quotation within quotation is from a book by Charles Sarolea written in 1912).
6   P. C. M. [Peter Chalmers Mitchell], *Report on the Propaganda Library* (MI7b, August 1917), 11. Copies are held at TNA CAB 17/196 and in digital form at the British Library; speech of Samuel in *National Liberal Federation. Proceedings in Connection with the Meeting of the General Committee of the National Liberal Federation, Held at Manchester, September 26th and 27th, 1918, with The Resolutions and the Speeches Including That Delivered by the Right Hon. H.H. Asquith, K.C., M.P., in the Free Trade Hall* (London: Liberal Publication Department, 1918), 20.
7   Gilbert Murray, 'Interstate Relations after the War', in *Fight for Right Movement, For the Right*, 142–3, 163.
8   'Recruiting Campaign', *Richmond Herald*, 9 October 1915, 7.
9   Anonymous [Orage], *Shall We GO ON? A Socialist's Answer* (London: W.H. Smith, 1918), reprinted from the *New Age*, 28 February 1918, quotations at 2–4, 18, 19. A shorter version also appeared as *A Socialist Talks It Over* (NWAC *Searchlight* pamphlet no. 5, 1918).
10 *Sound Advice: A Two-Minute Talk on the Wisdom of Investing in National War Bonds* (NWSC, 1918).
11 Norman Angell, *The Prussian in Our Midst* (London, UDC pamphlet no. 15, n.d.), 1, 9; TNA HO45/10741/2632675/60, transcript of speech by Ewer, 4 July 1915, sent to Foreign Office by Anti-German Union; *British Prussianism: The Scandal of the Tribunals* (London: National Labour Press, 1916).

CHAPTER 12
LOCALITY

In January 1918, Herbert Woodger, a Liberal Party staff speaker, was assigned by the NWAC to speak in Bushley, a village of around 250 people in the Malvern Hills of Worcestershire, from which forty-four servicemen had enlisted. A pair of sisters from the village also organized and ran a military hospital in France. Reporting back to the Meeting Department, Woodger noted,

> The attendance here was small [20], there being over 12 inches of snow down, + your speaker had the greatest difficulty to reach there + return.
>   It was necessary for the occupants of the car to get out + push their car out of drifts.

Three days later, Woodger struggled to reach Great Comberton's inhabitants 'owing to floods' but thought speaking to thirty-three out of 167 of them was a success.[1] Woodger's persistence partly reflected his professional interest. With political campaigning suspended during the war, speaking at propaganda meetings provided income for party speakers – those who did not accept or fulfil meetings might not receive future bookings.[2] However, it also reflected the importance attached to conducting propaganda in as many locations as possible. With people's lives lived largely in local contexts, propaganda organizations recognized the need to take their messages to communities large and small. While organizations provided skeleton speeches and notes to touring propagandists, speakers also frequently tailored their discussion to include specific references to the local community. All this recognized that local pride was worth cultivating – adapting general messages and campaigns to particular communities' interests made propaganda more relatable. Alongside centrally produced posters, pamphlets and films, propaganda in the streets and halls of British towns and villages asserted the war's specific relevance to each community. For example, the chairman of a propaganda committee of the Durham County War Savings Committee noted in a circular letter to residents of Bishop Auckland that the tank 'Egbert' would soon visit their town:

> There is now no large town which it has not visited. And now the Tank is to visit Bishop Auckland next week, and thereby a chance will be given to smaller towns and outlying districts so that no tract of land will be left uncovered to contribute to the expense of the war.

Such campaigns acknowledged that British audiences were not an unchanging, uncritical mass. If Bishop Auckland and its surrounds' residents were expected to invest their money, a newspaper advertisement stressed that they should have the same chance to see the war's novel new weapon in '*your* district' as people in larger towns and cities.[3]

While many studies of propaganda (and, indeed, some chapters of this book) focus substantially on central organizations, famous individuals and striking content, much of Britain's wartime propaganda (especially that directed at its own citizens) depended on local, usually voluntary, effort. As the first edition of the NWSC's journal, *War Savings*, noted in September 1916, while a new handbook for speakers would soon be available, there was 'no notion of being fettered by a rigid programme. The brains and enthusiasm of the movement are not all quartered at Salisbury Square.'[4] Organizations in London oversaw (and often funded) the whole effort, but local organizers handled many specific details, including arranging meetings, distributing publications and selecting and displaying posters. Local figures also took active parts in events, adding familiar faces and voices and the credibility of local endorsement to them. Leaving scope for local direction was cheaper and more flexible. Rather than London officials randomly dispatching speakers or publications to towns, regardless of the need or desire for propaganda on particular issues, trusting local agents to judge their community's needs (with occasional prompts to inactive areas) limited wasted effort. While recruitment, national service, war savings, food economy or war aims arguments were relatively predictable and used common themes, selecting particular material or inviting propagandists from a specific organization, alongside local participation, helped to vary what communities received.

Localized propaganda existed from the start of the war. The PRC's meetings sub-department reported that 'Local Joint Parliamentary Committees' were formed in most political constituencies, usually leaning heavily on Conservative, Liberal and Labour party agents, who became local secretaries and 'who were not only experienced in every phase of propaganda work' but had also worked with the national party organizers involved with the central committee. This helped plan 'the campaign best suited to the particular constituencies' and avoid areas where workers on government contracts worked. Though the PRC expected a 'systematic campaign' in each constituency, local agents were trusted to make decisions, and the PRC later responded to feedback that said events ran too long and failed to enrol as many recruits as they might by providing standard instructions for events (partly to restrain local notables from excessive involvement). By the campaign's end, the meetings department reported having organized 21,400 speakers at 12,705 meetings across 422 constituencies and felt that local committees' voluntary work had kept costs down. The experience gained in recruiting propaganda was later reproduced – several members of the PRC's Meetings Department later became organizing secretaries of the NWAC, again using their contacts with agents to establish local War Aims Committees in most English and Welsh constituencies.[5] Likewise, the NWAC leaned heavily on party speaking staffs (alongside fewer MPs, lords and celebrities) for much of their local propaganda.

In early October 1915, as conscription moved closer, a final PRC recruiting effort was made around Dover. At Temple Ewell, north of the town, Fred Finnis congratulated villagers that up to ninety men from a village of less than eight hundred had already volunteered, while further speeches were made at Buckland, on the edge of Dover and two venues within the town. The following day, a larger meeting was held on the seafront, where a PRC speaker, Mr Cronin, noted his personal pride that sixteen relatives had enlisted, including one son who – he asserted in a fiery explanation of German frightfulness – was 'bayonetted while overcome by asphyxiating gas'. Finally, at Northbourne, Lord Northbourne noted, approvingly, that 'there were but scarcely any of military age to join the Services ... Let him remind them, as men and women of Kent, of the motto of the White Horse, "Invicta", and invincible. The men of Kent had never been conquered and never would be'. While centred on Dover, the recruitment effort took in several surrounding villages, and speakers like Finnis and Northbourne encouraged both very local pride, praising existing enlistment levels and wider Kentish spirit, which complemented Cronin's personal experience of family enlistment and condemnation of Germany. Though he did not directly refer to the neighbouring county, Northbourne's references to 'Invicta' and the 'Men of Kent' may also have encouraged his audience to remember their superiority to Sussex, the site of Roman and Norman invasions. While live audiences might only have heard one of these arguments, readers of the *East Kent News* received a mixed tale of local virtue, national urgency, personal tragedy and international outrage.[6]

Localized propaganda organization was a hallmark of many organizations. The NWSC emerged in mid-1916, replacing the earlier Committee on War Loans for Small Investors. In early 1916, this group proposed an extensive scheme to promote investment by 'industrial classes'. The scheme's author, R. T. Jupp, prefaced his proposal by asserting that 'the results of any efforts ... will vary in any locality in strict ratio to the intensity of their individual appeal. More general methods may usefully be employed ... but however excellent these may be ... they will leave untouched a large proportion of the more ignorant and apathetic sections of the public.' The scheme aimed to address all towns of over 10,000 people, dividing England and Wales into thirty-four divisions, each overseen by a superintendent and containing around five districts. Each district (monitored by an inspector) contained one or more 'areas' – towns of 10,000–35,000 people were an area, while larger towns and cities were broken up into more than one, and areas of London were treated separately. Each area housed an office, run by an agent who would 'make himself thoroughly acquainted with all parts of his Area and as far as possible with the chief persons in it likely to be of use in the Scheme, also with the Cinema Theatres, Religious Institutions, Societies, Factories, etc.' Provision was also made for extension to towns and villages below 10,000 people in future, and small towns were listed in a lengthy appendix. The scheme anticipated employing 4,949 local and regional staff – with the costs of maintaining office expenses and the central office, a year's effort would cost a little more than £1.5 million.[7] Beyond these paid staff were the largely voluntary workforce of local committees.

By the end of 1918, the NWSC reported 1,840 Local War Savings Committees across England and Wales, and they had certainly embraced smaller communities. War Weapons Week, run through the summer of 1918, set specific fundraising quotas for individual communities, with those that met their targets across a week entitled to name a tank, plane or artillery piece. The week was specifically targeted at small communities because villagers were considered more likely to participate if their contribution did their own village credit rather than boosting the reputation of a neighbouring town. The NWSC publicized the amounts raised, allowing over-achieving towns and villages a sense of moral superiority over their under-investing neighbours. It was not just that 'we' did well but also that 'they' did poorly. Such instincts were also encouraged for city-dwellers, where residents of the West End were urged to make its contributions to 'Tank Week' 'bigger than that of any other London Borough' (Figure 11). This continued a trend of what one scholar describes as a pre-war 'hot-house of boosterism and place promotion ... [through] civic culture'. The scheme certainly worked, raising nearly £50 million, but it did so substantially on the backs of local activists, who were given instructions on several local events and processes to organize.[8] The committees themselves, prominent local women, the clergy and owners of cinemas and theatres were all expected to help.

Having established such an extensive network of committees, the NWSC also played a role in other areas of propaganda, such as food control. A 1917 circular to the committees identified demand across Britain for better guidance regarding food. The NWSC controller noted, however, that 'it is impossible for this Committee to lay down definite lines of procedure to be followed in every district. The nature of the methods most likely to achieve beneficial results can only be known to those with full knowledge of local circumstances.' Local committees should, thus, survey conditions in their areas and advise communities on the most appropriate local alternative for bread (supplies of which were affected by Germany's submarine campaign). A 'Food Economy Handbook', produced later, added a further warning: that propagandists visiting a local area should always consult the local organizer to learn about the local situation and avoid 'lectur[ing] ... on the need for economy or to accuse them of wasting food' in deprived areas. Activities rapidly got underway. In Wallingford, Oxfordshire, a meeting was called in May at which a speaker from the Ministry of Food, Mrs Philpot, appeared. Speaking directly to women, she suggested economizing in food helped them to 'show in a very real and practical way, their love for their husbands, brothers and sweethearts at the front', adding that if this was not done voluntarily, Britain would face the 'disgrace' of compulsory rationing. She acknowledged that 'children and the very poor' could not eat less bread, but others could forego theirs. Finally, and tellingly, Philpot concluded by appealing 'to Wallingford to do its bit, no matter what other towns might be doing'.[9] Such arguments were common in various forms of propaganda – in some cases (like the recruiting meeting at Temple Ewell discussed above), propagandists noted the already exemplary conduct of a local community; alternatively, as in Wallingford, local pride might encourage residents to exert themselves further, to make themselves exemplary. The same kinds of arguments were made in NWAC talks. One Devon village was encouraged to save food, even though their own community had plenty, out of fellow feeling with industrial communities; residents of Ipswich, by contrast, were praised for not losing time through strikes, like those in Coventry. By no means local rivals, knocking

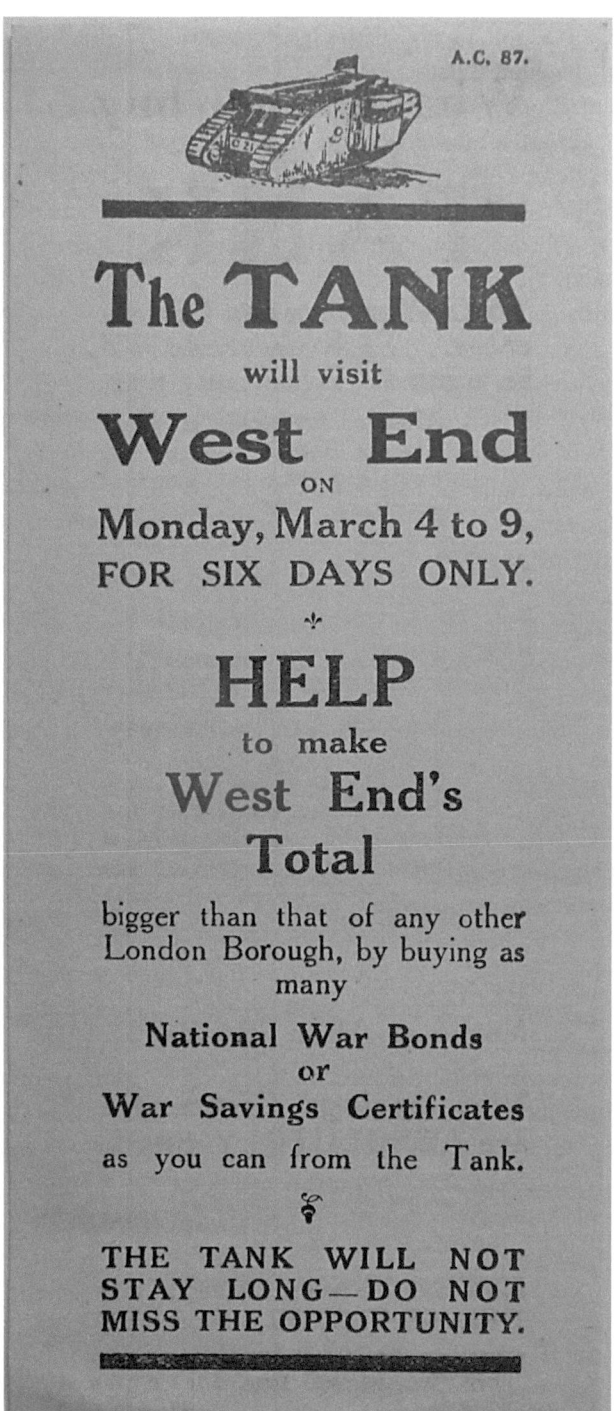

Figure 11 National War Savings Committee leaflet A.C. 87.
Source: John Johnson Collection, Bodleian Library, University of Oxford (author's photograph).

Coventry, here, was simply a way to flatter Ipswich's citizens.[10] Either way, propagandists often realized that national issues needed to be addressed in local contexts.

While organizations clearly recognized the need for local action to handle propaganda's logistics, local voices were also important. The main attraction at a propaganda event might be a visiting MP, soldier or other novel figure, but these people benefitted from local endorsement. Platform propaganda retained many of the rituals and expectations of pre-war politics. Meetings were usually chaired by an important local figure – often the mayor or lord mayor for major events and a local councillor or clergyman for smaller occasions. After the guest speakers, other locals often moved and seconded a vote of thanks. Each of these local notables might also speak for a few minutes themselves. All this added a sense of order and familiarity to propaganda events.[11] At Wells, Somerset, the national service scheme was launched at a large event, featuring the 'Wells detachment of the Somerset Volunteer Regiment … and the Wells Patrol of Boy Scouts', while the mayor, dean and chancellor of Wells Cathedral and a local labour representative put the national scheme into local context. Introducing the main speaker, the mayor stated

> that in all questions of national importance Wells had always been to the fore. They were proud of the great response to Lord Kitchener's call, and the amount subscribed from Wells for the War Loan had placed them well to the front. The Government was now asking for something else, national service, and he felt the citizens would respond in as patriotic a manner as before.

The main speaker, T. W. Hemsley from the Directorate of National Service, then spoke at length about manpower needs and the fact that Britain was seeking volunteers, whereas Germany used compulsion. He outlined terms of pay, acknowledging 'it was not unduly generous, but he thought it was just' and called for sacrifice before answering questions. The dean, moving a vote of thanks, suggested tougher times were likely to come and that 'sufferings at home, not felt here in Wells, would probably be more keenly felt yet'. Citizens of Wells could thus afford to make this effort because they were more comfortably off than others. The chancellor declared himself ready to guard German prisoners if necessary to overcome the 'barbarism of Prussia'. Finally, a motion of support was put, and J. Roberts of the local labour bureau praised the mayor and town clerk's previous efforts, noting that 'through their efforts they had more men join the labour battalion from Wells than from Weston-super-Mare'. Again, Roberts's words suggested it was not enough that people from Wells felt a sense of duty to serve because of national need or German awfulness – they also had the chance to outshine less patriotic neighbours! The meeting concluded with the national anthem.[12]

Such propaganda events as the Wells national service meeting acknowledged both national and local loyalties and identities. People from Wells should accept national service, even if the pay was modest, not only because the nation needed it but also because Wells had established a reputation for loyal service, because their city was more comfortable than some and because it gave them moral superiority over

Weston-super-Mare. Incorporating locality into propaganda thus added several possible extra motivations for those unconvinced by the central issue.

Playing up to local identity was not universally positive. The well-known decision to allow the enlistment of 'Pals' battalions from particular communities was useful to recruitment, allowing people some control over who they fought (and did not fight) alongside, but could be devastating to a local community when a battalion was caught in a severe fight such as, most famously, the Accrington Pals on the first day of the Battle of the Somme.[13] However, localizing national messages, both through referring specifically to a local community's needs and virtues, and through incorporating the work and voices of local figures, made calls for recruitment, investment, service or restraint less abstract. Trusting local knowledge and addressing local pride embedded the war's national and transnational stakes in familiar soil.

Notes

1 TNA T102/23, NWAC Speakers' Daily Reports: Herbert Woodger – Bushley, 16 January 1918; Great Comberton, 19 January 1918. For Bushley's population and its inhabitants' wartime service, see Richard Webb (ed.), *Bushley Through the Great War* (online, n.d.): http://www.bushleyparisharchive.co.uk/Filename.ashx?systemFileName=BPCBDOC000005.pdf&origFilename=BPCBDOC000005.pdf (accessed 23 January 2024).
2 For fuller discussion, see Monger, *Patriotism and Propaganda*, 49–51, 251–3.
3 IWM, MS Women, War and Society 1914–1918: Women at Work Collection, LR47-2, circular letter from J. J. Aubin re. S. W. Durham Tank Campaign, April 1918; 'Durham County Tank Fortnight' advertisement, *North Star*, 1 April 1918, 3 (original emphasis).
4 'The Journal', *War Savings*, no. 1 (September 1916), 1.
5 TNA WO106/367, PRC Meetings Sub-Department Report (March 1916). For further discussion of the connections between PRC and NWAC organization, see Monger, *Patriotism and Propaganda*, 30–1.
6 'The Recruiting Rally', *East Kent News*, 8 October 1915, 2. On 'Men of Kent' and county rivalry in an earlier period, see Kathryn Beresford, '"Men of Kent": Gender and Nationhood in Regional Perspective, 1815–1837' (unpublished PhD thesis, University College London, 2007), 18.
7 TNA NSC7/35, R.T. Jupp, *A Scheme for Largely Increasing the Sale of War Loan Stock Amongst Members of the Industrial Classes and Small Investors Generally*, 24 February 1916, quotations at preface, 12, staff numbers at 36.
8 TNA NSC2/3, National War Savings Committee, *Third Annual Report*, 2 June 1919, 7; on War Weapons Week, see Monger, 'Familiarity Breeds Consent?', 519–24; on boosterism, see Jon Stobart, 'Identity, Competition and Place Promotion in the Five Towns', *Urban History*, 30, no. 2 (2003), 182.
9 TNA NSC 7/37, circular letter on 'Food Control Campaign', 10 April 1917; IWM, MS Women, War and Society, 1914–18: The Women at Work Collection, FOOD 3.2.6, *Food Economy Handbook* (n.d.), 2; 'Food Control Campaign', *Berks and Oxon Advertiser*, 4 May 1917, 5.
10 Monger, *Patriotism and Propaganda*, 179, 182.
11 For full discussion, see Monger, 'Familiarity Breeds Consent?'. For the importance of platform speaking, see Jon Lawrence, *Speaking for the People: Party, Language and Popular Politics in England, 1867–1914* (Cambridge: Cambridge University Press, 1996), esp. 164, 178–88;

Jon Lawrence, *Electing Our Masters: The Hustings from Hogarth to Blair* (Oxford: Oxford University Press, 2009), 25.
12 'National Service. Scheme Explained at Wells', *Wells Journal*, 23 March 1917, 3.
13 On the Pals Battalions, see Peter Simkins, *Kitchener's Army: The Raising of the New Armies, 1914–16* (Manchester: Manchester University Press, 1988), 79–100; Ian F. W. Beckett, 'Nations in Arms: Enlistment and Conscription', in Strachan (ed.), *British Home Front*, esp. 282–7; Gregory, *Last Great War*, 78–80, 127–8.

CHAPTER 13
MOTHER OR MUNITION WORKER

A young woman strides towards the viewer, so far in the foreground that she steps out of the frame. Behind her, to the left, a soldier waves goodbye, rifle over his shoulder, about to join his comrades outside. The woman pulls a long coat on with one clenched hand – is she waving goodbye with the other or simply putting on her uniform? Behind her, to the right, two lines of women work at clean, orderly benches, the comrades *she* is about to join. The cleanliness seemingly recreates an ideal kitchen, except for the cluster of shells, 'as if they were practising a neat domestic craft rather than a deadly domestic process'. The tidiness was actually necessary to avoid lethal accidental sparks. No one is in sharp focus but her, stepping out of her old life and into munitions work, a uniformed equivalent of the departing soldier.[1]

Septimus Scott's poster for the Ministry of Munitions (Figure 12) captures much of the wartime propaganda representation of British women, particularly once initial resistance to women's war work was overcome. Propagandists celebrated women's willingness to come forward and their success in unfamiliar roles. Women were appealed to as individuals making active choices and, increasingly, those choices were portrayed as those of citizens. There was often a sense of the war as a new departure for women, even while such service was treated by some as merely extending existing effort.[2] Yet, behind propaganda to and about women was the soldier. He was why women should act; to be an active female part of the war effort was to be equivalent to a soldier; and when soldiers returned (soldiers, especially, were reassured), things would return to normality. Alternatively, mothers – either of soldiers or of their children – were the outright image of continuity, depicted as aiding the war effort by keeping home as it always was. Women already played many roles before 1914 and added new ones during the war, but munition workers and mothers were the positive poles of propaganda representations. This masked a reality in which many women undertook both war work and domestic management and could be sharply criticized for 'failing' to fulfil either role appropriately.

The war's outbreak saw a suspension of most political campaigning, including the campaign for women's suffrage. Millicent Garrett Fawcett, head of the National Union of Women's Suffrage Societies, and her executive committee urged their 500 local societies to suspend their campaigns and offer their services to local authorities for relief work. Fawcett noted that committees involved themselves in providing workshops for out-of-work women, 'life-saving activities by the formation of maternity centres, baby clinics, schools for mothers, and other similar associations' and Red Cross centres. She added that the NUWSS was 'first in the field, afterwards so well tilled by the war savings committees, to call attention to the great national importance of personal and

Figure 12 Septimus Scott, *These Women Are Doing Their Bit*.
Source: (Ministry of Munitions, 1916), TNA EXT1/315/17.

household economy', mounting war savings events. Women of the NUWSS, then, accustomed to activism, added their expertise to the local voluntarism discussed in Chapter 12, including through propaganda work. However, they were also frustrated by the government's initial intention to maintain 'business as usual' in organizing home affairs. Fawcett noted,

> I well remember the resentment and melancholy of some able young women in our employment when they saw the advertisements everywhere displayed calling upon young men to join the colours, announcing in huge letters YOUR COUNTRY WANTS YOU, and reflected that their country did not want them.[3]

Such frustrations were publicly aired during a march organized by Emmeline Pankhurst, founder of the militant Women's Social and Political Union (WSPU), in July 1915. An enormous procession marched through London, echoing earlier suffrage marches, demanding women be given war work. Pankhurst declared that 'women are going to work. They are going to save the men in the trenches.' As above, Pankhurst explicitly tied women's war work to armed service. Far from spontaneous, however, this demonstration was funded by the then Minister of Munitions Lloyd George to show that men in industry could join the army and be replaced by women. Nonetheless, Gullace notes, the event had the effect of making women's war work a national priority, while also catapulting Pankhurst and her daughter Christabel, so recently scourges of the British government, into positions as 'the organizers of patriotic British womanhood' and 'an undeserved status as representatives of female munitions workers'.[4] Pankhurst subsequently undertook propaganda tours of Russia and the United States on the government's behalf.

Fawcett and Pankhurst were not the only female activists who contributed to wartime propaganda. The journalist Dorothy Peel and social investigator Maud Pember Reeves, as already noted, played significant roles in organizing food propaganda, while May Tennant and Violet Markham, and later Viscountess Rhondda, took leading roles regarding women's national service. The anti-suffragist and novelist Mary Humphry Ward wrote propaganda for US consumption, apparently encouraged by former president Theodore Roosevelt. Beneath these prominent figures, industrious women like Grace Curnock organized press releases for the National Service Women's Section, and the journalist E. M. Goodman (editor of the feminist paper *The Englishwoman*) produced regular articles for the NWAC, making very clear that she expected to be employed and paid professionally.[5] Finally, many women served on local committees or spoke at meetings, sometimes specially arranged for female audiences, continuing pre-war habits, promoted by organizations like the Conservative Primrose League and Women's Liberal Federation, of separating women's events from the rough and tumble of platform politics.

While mothers and munition workers featured prominently in propaganda, women's wider roles were also acknowledged. A mass of posters encouraged women into wartime occupations. H. G. Hawthorn's national service poster depicted a Woman's Land Army figure steering a horse-drawn plough towards the sunset with the motto 'God Speed the Plough – and the Woman Driving It'. *More Aeroplanes Are Needed* showed a woman in work clothes, but with carefully styled hair, lipstick and eye makeup, gesturing to a military plane flying overhead – implicitly, one that she helped make – while providing information about training and allowances. Another poster seeking Scottish fruit pickers pictured a young woman imagining men in the trenches eating jam from the fruit she picked, while the accompanying text reassured applicants they could be employed amongst 'parties of friends'. Such posters aimed to inspire and reassure – in all three, the images of work are placid; the aeroplane mechanic maintains her appearance despite her labour; and in two images, servicemen (pilots and soldiers) remind women who their work benefitted. At the same time, they featured the kind of informational content discussed in Chapter 9. Women were informed of financial opportunities and did not have to venture into this work alone. Goodman, discussing women in aeroplane manufacturing in an article for a weekly war supplement for provincial papers, noted the 'flying man can do nothing without a good machine. His life depends on the reliability of his engine.' Women only learnt part of the manufacturing process and may not retain the jobs post-war but should be glad to get good money and training, which increased their skills and future prospects: 'It is better to be a jeweller or dressmaker or housemaid who can make aeroplane parts than just a housemaid or dressmaker or jeweller.'[6] This was clearly an appeal to existing woman workers, not those unused to earning a living.

Nursing – a long-accepted woman's role – allowed propagandists to enhance two angles. One further emphasized women's care and nurturing of servicemen – in some cases, particularly in propaganda to soldiers, to the point of romance. Along with victims of air raids, meanwhile, nurses provided an opportunity to depict British women as victims of atrocities. The Cavell execution discussed in Chapter 1 was the most enduring (if questionable) source, but German sinking of hospital ships with nurses on board was also regularly condemned. At a remembrance event organized by Evesham's War Aims Committee in August 1918, the main speaker, A. H. Coulter, asked the audience to remember

> those splendid nurses in all the hospitals, and when they thought of how many of the nurses had met a cruel death at the hand of murderous German airmen, and many more who on hospital ships had found a watery grave at the hands of enemy submarines their hearts were torn with anguish.[7]

Attacks on British nurses heightened the stakes for Britain – what was currently a small number of nursing casualties could become wider British women's suffering if Germany was not stopped.

While women's work – frequently framed as service, as Gullace and Janet Watson have discussed – was celebrated in all forms, two types of women arguably dominated discussion: mothers and munition workers. From the outset, propaganda targeted mothers, anticipating that fearfulness for sons' lives might impede recruitment. As the London correspondent of the *Western Morning News* asserted in September 1914,

War is a woman's cause as well as a man's. Women do not fight, but many of them fight a hard battle with themselves when they surrender their sons to the God of War … For a mother to give up her husband or sons for the country is no light thing … Let homage be paid to her who tearfully bids her sons go forth to fight … Therefore, when asking for fresh recruits, make the appeal reach the wife and mother, with whom often the decision of the spirited and dutiful son rests.[8]

The PRC's poster, *Go! It's Your Duty Lad*, showed a well-dressed man being shown the right path by his mother, while *Women of Britain Say – "Go!"* showed two women, a boy clinging to the clothes of one of them, anxiously watching a line of soldiers march away. Another PRC publication, by Henrietta Boas, imagined a young villager seeking to persuade his parents to let him enlist. Here the father needed most persuasion, and the mother's bravery overcame his reluctance. Not only, Boas suggested, should mothers bravely bear their child's enlistment but also comfort anguished husbands. In fact, as Boas's tale suggested, and as historians such as Paul Ward and Gullace indicate, those concerned 'need not have been afraid'.[9] The outbreak of war saw an outbreak of 'patriotic motherhood' among many women, although Gullace notes some recruiters' discomfort with women's enthusiasm – 'noble sacrifice of a mother or the erotic sweetness of a lover' was appropriate, 'the militant energy and independence of a suffragette or lady reformer' was not. Even less palatable were critiques by women on the left who attacked the idea of a war in defence of women by noting the particular harm caused to mothers by loss of their children or arguing that women, as natural caregivers, had a special duty to promote peace.[10]

From the beginning, mothers were expected to demonstrate dutiful, self-sacrificing care. Whatever their own difficulties, they should support their sons at the front or maintain the soldier's family at home. NWAC propaganda for soldiers featured numerous cartoons of soldiers returning to wives and children, as well as 'Mother!', depicting a filial reunion. As the war progressed, so did appeals to (and demands on) mothers. Because women were increasingly needed for war work, changes were made to workplaces such as adjusting work tasks as pregnancy progressed and providing space for nursing mothers. Goodman, late in the war, suggested efforts to create healthier working environments recognized women's importance as workers, mothers and citizens, using this to call for yet more exertion on women's part. Other propagandists, like Peel and Reeves, placed more emphasis on the need to recognize working women's limited resources of income and time, noting exhausted mothers attending food economy demonstrations with children in tow.[11]

Goodman's articles varied between discussing women's war work and domestic topics like spring cleaning and jam-making. Her overall interpretation was captured by that late piece merging child-rearing, factory work and citizenship – women, she argued, whether running a household, doing war work, or both, were fulfilling citizens' responsibilities. This chimed with wider propaganda suggestions that *everything* contributed to the war effort and that the key was to stick to a role and do it thoroughly. Others, however, depicted things separately. Munitions workers, mostly younger women, were the subject of much admiring propaganda. The former prime minister Asquith, at a 1917 meeting at which he was heckled by women in Liverpool, singled out 8,000 women in a local munitions factory as an example of women's 'adaptability and flexibility that have made them largely responsible for the success of the war (cheers)'. He later credited such work with convincing him to abandon opposition to women's suffrage, adding to Fawcett's view that war work 'revolutionized the industrial position of women. It found them serfs and left them free.'[12] The novelist Hall Caine was commissioned by the Ministry of Munitions to write about munitions workers in 1916. *Our Girls* remarked on the strangeness of seeing women in dangerous industrial settings but praised their adaptability, albeit in dubiously sexualized terms:

> The machines themselves seem almost human ... and, if you show a proper respect for their impetuous organisms, they are not generally cruel. So the women get along very well with them, learning all their ways, their whims, their needs and their limitations. It is surprising how speedily the women have wooed and won this new kind of male monster.

Continuing to idealize their work, Caine noted, despite their drab uniforms:

> If there is any man in London who can pass through the workshops of Woolwich without thinking he has been looking at some thousands of the best-looking young women in the world, it is certainly not the present writer. Their hard work does not seem to be doing much harm to their health, for their eyes are bright, their cheeks are fresh, and there is hardly any evidence of fatigue among them.

Caine's commentary pointed to a tension surrounding war work. Women's work was needed, but he evidently aimed to dispel any suggestion it might dilute their femininity. Caine, at least, seemed incapable of seeing women as workers, without also thinking of them in relation to men. Even their capacity to work machines came from long experience of romantic game-playing. Likewise, the famous poster, *On Her Their Lives Depend*, portrayed a munitions worker staring into the camera and smiling as she puts on her cap, an artilleryman at the front kneeling by shells in the background.[13]

Such enthusiasm was ironic, however. Although propaganda regularly positioned women's roles and responsibilities in relation to men – to the point of suggestiveness in some cases – women walked a tightrope of acceptable behaviour throughout the war. Though called upon to admire soldiers above all else, young women were accused of 'khaki fever'. Young women workers, who often entered war industries from domestic service, where they were closely supervised and constrained within the house they worked, were condemned for demonstrating too much independence and risking disgrace through drink and illegitimate relationships. Mothers were lectured on wastefulness, yet Goodman suggested cutting corners on housewifery was unpatriotic. Soldiers' wives could have their separation allowances (paid to cover the loss of a husband's wages) stopped upon accusations of 'unchastity [seen as an appalling betrayal of the soldier and nation], drunkenness, neglect of children or conviction ... Soldiers' wives and relatives', Sylvia Pankhurst later observed, 'were thus to be subject to a penalty in excess of that imposed by the ordinary law'. Regulation 40D of the Defence of the Realm Act, meanwhile, permitted women to be imprisoned for passing sexually transmitted infections to a serviceman, echoing the repressive, previously overturned, sexual double standard of the 1860s Contagious Diseases Acts.[14]

To some extent, double-dealing was part of all propaganda. Men and women alike were simultaneously praised for stoicism and service and called on for yet more; men who did not meet expected standards (by not enlisting, 'shirking', profiteering) could expect fierce criticism. Yet, propaganda to women encouraged them to embrace new opportunities and challenges. Wartime working hours meant many worked lengthy shifts before tending to the home (towards war's end, often via long food queues). While doing so, however, they should avoid getting above themselves. For all the emphasis on munition workers' part in persuading Parliament to grant votes for women, finally, many of those young women were excluded by a franchise limited to women over thirty.

Notes

1. TNA EXT1/315/17, Septimus Scott, 'These Women Are Doing Their Bit' (Ministry of Munitions poster, 1916); quotation from Rebecca West, 'Hands That War: The Cordite Makers', in Jane Marcus (ed.), *The Young Rebecca: Writings of Rebecca West, 1911–17* (London: Virago, 1982), 381 (originally published in the *Daily Chronicle*, February 1916).
2. For some discussion of the representation of citizenship, see Gullace, *Blood of Our Sons*; Monger, 'Nothing Special?'
3. Millicent Garrett Fawcett, *The Women's Victory – and After: Personal Reminiscences, 1911–1918* (London: Sidgwick & Jackson, 1920), 87–93.
4. Gullace, *Blood of Our Sons*, 126–8.
5. Some of this information draws from ongoing research into female propagandists by my PhD student, Kate Pickworth; for extended discussion of Goodman and her propaganda, see Monger, 'Nothing Special?', 526–36.
6. H. G. Hawthorn, 'National Service: Women's Land Army' (National Service poster Series W9, n.d. [1917]); 'More Aeroplanes Are Needed' (Ministry of Munitions poster, 1918); TNA NATS1/109, '4,000 Women Wanted for Fruit Picking'; 'Margaret Osborne' [Goodman], 'The Woman's Part: Housemaids for Aeroplane Making', *Droitwich Guardian War Supplement*, week ending 17 August 1918, 2.
7. On nurses' portrayal as romantic and sexual opportunity in propaganda to soldiers, see Monger, 'Soldiers, Propaganda and Ideas of Home', 341–2; Monger, 'Nothing Special?', 521–3. 'Evesham. Remembrance Day at Evesham', *Evesham Journal and Four Shires Advertiser*, 10 August 1918, 6.
8. 'From Our London Correspondent', *Western Morning News*, 2 September 1914, 4.
9. 'Go! It's Your Duty Lad' (PRC poster no. 109, n.d. [1915]); 'Women of Britain Say – "Go!"' (PRC poster no. 75, 1915); Mrs F. S. Boas, *Our Village and the War* (PRC leaflet no. 33), quotation at 6.
10. Paul Ward, '"Women of Britain Say – Go!" Women's Patriotism in the First World War', *Twentieth Century British History*, 12, no. 1 (2001); Gullace, *Blood of Our Sons*, 66; Sabine

Grimshaw, 'The Responsibility of Women: Women's Anti-War Writing in the Press, 1914–1916', *Women's Writing*, 24, no. 1 (2017).

11 On care towards soldiers at the front, see Michael Roper, *The Secret Battle: Emotional Survival in the Great War* (Manchester: Manchester University Press, 2009), esp. chs. 1–2. For propaganda to soldiers, see Monger, 'Soldiers, Propaganda and Ideas of Home', 342–5; Wilmot Lunt and W. F. Blood, 'Mother!', *Welcome*, no. 27, 2 October 1918, 1. On workplace improvements, see Susan R. Grayzel, *Women's Identities at War: Gender, Motherhood, and Politics in Britain and France during the First World War* (Chapel Hill: University of North Carolina Press, 1997), ch. 3, esp. 114–19; Goodman, 'The Woman's Part: After the War', *Nuneaton Observer War Supplement*, week ending 2 November 1918, 2 and see Monger, 'Nothing Special?', 534–5; Peel, *Year in Public Life*, 26–7.

12 'Picton Hall. 'Mr. Asquith & Unruly Women. Tribute to Navy and Munition Workers', *Liverpool Daily Post and Mercury*, 12 October 1917, 6; Fawcett, *Women's Victory*, 106, and see 133 for Asquith's citation of munitions work as a factor in his conversion.

13 Hall Caine, *Our Girls: Their Work for the War* (London: Hutchinson, 1916), 23–4, 45; *On Her Their Lives Depend* (Ministry of Munitions poster, 1916). For a summary of working conditions in Woolwich Arsenal, see Deborah Thom, *Nice Girls and Rude Girls: Women Workers in World War I* (London: I.B. Tauris, 1998), 144–60.

14 See, for example, Angela Woollacott, '"Khaki Fever" and Its Control: Gender, Class, Age and Sexual Morality on the British Homefront in the First World War', *Journal of Contemporary History*, 29, no. 2 (1994); Grayzel, *Women's Identities*, 129–40; Stella Moss, '"Wartime Hysterics"?: Alcohol, Women and the Politics of Wartime Social Purity' in Jessica Meyer (ed.), *British Popular Culture and the First World War* (Leiden: Brill, 2008); E. Sylvia Pankhurst, *The Home Front* (London: Cresset Library, [1932] 1987), 99; Laura Lammasniemi, 'Regulation 40D: Punishing Promiscuity on the Home Front during the First World War', *Women's History Review*, 26, no. 4 (2017).

CHAPTER 14
NEUTRALS

Although British mothers were targeted by recruitment propaganda from the war's first days, encouraged to support their sons' enlistment regardless of their own qualms, most formal British domestic propaganda took a long time to get underway. The NWAC only emerged in 1917 as an organization specifically focused on British public morale, while other focused groups like the NWSC and Directorate of National Service also developed as the war progressed. Meanwhile, unofficial groups like the Victoria League, Fight for Right Movement and CCNPO addressed British audiences. By contrast, propaganda to neutral nations (alongside Britain's imperial Dominions) was prioritized from day one. British officials and propagandists hoped to attract new allies to its side. Hall Caine specifically wrote that he had hoped *King Albert's Book*, published in December 1914, would entice the United States to enter the war. It featured fifty contributors from then-neutral nations, ostensibly paying tribute to Belgium but also endorsing Britain's intervention by inference. By 1918, the NWAC handbook crowed that twenty-six nations, up to Costa Rica in May, had declared war on Britain's side. Not only did this supposedly show the righteousness of Britain's cause, but it also increasingly cut off the Central Powers from raw materials. Brazil's redirection of coffee and rubber from Germany to Britain and the United States (even before declaring war) likely had more impact than the small number of troops and paramedics sent to France or the eight warships that joined the British fleet on 10 November 1918.[1] Nations that remained neutral might at least be dissuaded from assisting German efforts by propaganda.

Efforts were led by Masterman's War Propaganda Bureau at Wellington House. As already noted, literary figures, such as John Galsworthy, wrote propaganda for consumption abroad – his 'Diagnosis of the Englishman', discussed in Chapter 8, appeared first in the Netherlands, for instance. Wellington House established four departments for the Netherlands; Scandinavia; Italy and Switzerland; and Spain, Portugal and South America. A separate approach was taken in the United States, where the novelist and former MP Gilbert Parker gathered a list of 13,000 influential US men to contact indirectly on behalf of Wellington House, trusting that enough would take interest in the propaganda to spread it wider. Masterman explained the principles behind Wellington House's methods in its first report in June 1915. The departments analysed the neutral press, wrote and translated material expected to be useful and directly contacted individuals from neutral places who might influence opinion but imposed its own limits:

> Anything in the nature of a promiscuous dumping of unwanted literature has … been scrupulously avoided. Germany is flooding the world with enormous

quantities of literature at vast expense, and irritating those whom she wishes to win over …

In dissemination of books and pamphlets we have largely endeavoured (except in the case of the U.S.A.) to place our literature on sale and induce people to buy it …

Anything in the nature of an appeal to neutral countries has been rigidly ruled out. We have determined rather to present facts and general arguments based upon those facts. Strict secrecy has been observed as to any connection of the Government with the work.

Masterman felt that this discreet approach worked, although discretion sometimes went too far. When the popular novelists J. M. Barrie (author of *Peter Pan*) and A. E. W. Mason (*The Four Feathers*) arrived in New York for a propaganda tour in September 1914, for instance, nobody had informed the British Ambassador, Sir Cecil Spring-Rice. He immediately forbade them to give talks, prompting Mason to return home.[2]

While the United States was Britain's most important neutral propaganda target, substantial efforts were made elsewhere. In Argentina, María Inés Tato notes, Wellington House supplied translated copies of works by many of its authors, as well as Ambassador Lichnowksy's condemnation of Germany's pre-war diplomacy. Additionally, a *Comisión de Propaganda Aliados* was formed by local British voluntary associations, which funded three million copies of over eighty works. Unsurprisingly, given the scale of translation, Tato suggests the propaganda arguments were similar to those used elsewhere: Germany's responsibility for the war, the necessary defence of Belgium and Germany's brutal methods. Wider emphases on duty that featured in much domestic propaganda were less appropriate for neutrals, even if some material (like *King Albert's Book*) addressed world opinion and the duty of wider action. A further vehicle was Wellington House's illustrated Spanish language newspaper, *América-Latina*, which Tato notes 'defined itself as a "work of propaganda"' and put across pro-Entente material. Its December 1915 edition, for instance, featured 'English pages' including articles on the Post Office in wartime, 'The Success of Lord Derby' and the work of the PRC; a cartoon from *Punch*; 'French pages' featuring an article on Parisian lawyers, a 'Credo' by the writer Henri Lavedan and pictures of the destruction of Arras; and 'Belgian pages' discussing refugees in England and Belgium's second grey book, documenting the outbreak of war.

Wellington House's efforts were supplemented by local pro-Entente Argentinian commentators, who linked German conduct to earlier Latin American suffering under Spanish imperial rule. Just as national lines of argument were adapted to local communities' interests at home, volunteers abroad related Britain's broad propaganda to more meaningful contexts for their communities. While Argentina had substantial trade connections with both Britain and Germany, Tato argues public sympathy was ultimately more with the Entente because of existing French cultural influence. In the same issue of *América-Latina*, an article by the Mexican author Armado Nervo, 'Something about Kultur and Culture', dismissed *Kultur* while celebrating French, English and Italian influences on 'our intellectuals'.³ The articles listed above and this comment suggest a mass audience for the paper was unlikely.

América-Latina also circulated in Spain. Britain only slowly moved into propaganda here, believing Spain's dependence on the Entente made friendly neutrality secure. When it got underway, however, the British embassy and consulates gave support by providing propaganda materials to Spaniards and Britons in Spain, hoping that these individuals would disseminate them more widely. Again, this seemingly targeted a more elite audience. Over time, greater interest in press propaganda beyond *América-Latina* emerged and both translated articles and those by sympathetic Spanish writers were funded. Propaganda content skewed towards Spanish concerns, identified by Marta García Cabrera as including commerce, religion and post-war prospects. The Catholic Bishop of Southwark undertook an extensive tour of Spain, meeting the royal family, visiting colleagues in several cities and speaking to influential writers, which provided access to the religious press. He was advised that propaganda should not attack Germany but rather emphasize religious liberty in Britain. However, Germany's 1917 U-boat campaign was particularly highlighted as harming Spain – Spanish ships were sunk by Germany, not Britain. Film propaganda was also supplied to Spain (as discussed in Chapter 6), although the estimated 15,000 people who watched *Britain Prepared* and *Battle of the Somme* was tiny compared to the millions of British and US viewers.⁴

Despite the apparently narrow content, Masterman considered *América-Latina* and other foreign-language illustrated papers particularly effective, claiming they 'attract the mass of readers much more readily' than other publications, while the head of the Spanish Department Percy Koppel claimed 38,000 readers and growing by early 1916. However, it was heavily criticized by the newspaper editor, Robert Donald, whose 1917 report on propaganda considered its production expensive and wasteful. He suggested the original Spanish content had some value but could have been produced more cheaply, while the rest of the paper, consisting of 'belated speeches, stale news, descriptions of events several weeks old … cannot be a success'. Although the circulation grew to over 160,000 by late December 1917, Donald suggested the bulk was sent indiscriminately in Spain to hotels, barber shops, clubs and railway companies as well as specific individuals, meaning many copies 'may be lying idle'. Here was a conflict between Masterman's original principles of allowing propaganda to circulate discreetly and increasing calls for more efficient methods by the war's later years.

Donald, who fundamentally believed propaganda should have been entrusted to experienced pressmen, was hardly a sympathetic assessor. Building on his critique in January 1918, he wrote that

> Mr. Masterman makes the grotesque claim that as the result of propaganda 'nineteen countries have declared war against Germany, and ten have broken off relations with her'. One could say with more reason that, but for our defective propaganda, America would have been in the war sooner, when its help would have been more timely, and Russia would not have deserted the Allies.⁵

However, Donald's jibe about the United States was both empirically suspect – US entry was delayed until German provocations became too much to ignore and until British purchasing for itself and its Allies put it in a position of what Kathleen Burk describes as financial 'servitude' – and narrow.[6] His critique primarily focused on clumsy reactions to negative US press commentary and the expenses incurred in providing books and pamphlets there. By contrast, Parker, working on Wellington House's behalf, happily claimed credit for propaganda there, even as the war continued, suggesting that in monitoring the press, arranging interviews with prominent Britons, distributing films and news material and personally corresponding with influential US figures, Britain's case had been effectively made. However, he shared Masterman's preference for discretion:

> We asked our friends and correspondents to arrange for speeches, debates, and lectures by American citizens, but we did not encourage Britishers to go to America and preach the doctrine of entrance into the war …
>
> I believed that the American people could not be driven, preached to, or chivied [sic] into the war, and that when they did enter it would be the result of their own judgment and not the result of exhortation, eloquence, or fanatical pressure of Britishers.[7]

In fact, British efforts to attract US sympathy were wide-ranging, with some pre-dating the war. As noted in Chapter 10, the comedian Harry Lauder toured the United States on his own initiative in 1915, calling for the United States to prepare for war, returning later by official request. Parker, as a former executive committee member, was also familiar with the Pilgrims Society, which organized personal propaganda (or what Stephen Bowman labels 'cultural diplomacy') between Anglo-US elites before the war. While its US section was restrained in public sympathy for Britain out of respect for neutrality, it had laid some groundwork for wartime efforts and resumed larger activities after US entry, as Parker acknowledged.[8]

Propagandists seeking US sympathy gained from the efforts of the Pilgrims and others, since the turn of the century, to foster a shared 'Anglo-Saxon' identity between the United States and Britain. Putting aside the awkward reality that some such advocates previously aimed for wider 'Teutonic' fellowship, including Germany, wartime propaganda to the United States played up 'universal virtues' such as 'justice, honour, humanity and civilization', which were 'often Anglicized to emphasize the commonalities between Britain and the United States'. Jessica Bennett and Mark Hampton suggest that emphasis on the 'humane' was particularly important. Britons were compelled to fight the war in justice to 'little' Belgium (whose plight attracted US sympathy even before propaganda was underway), while their opponents paid little attention to established rules of international conduct. Emphasizing humanitarian concern enabled British propagandists to seek US sympathy, despite the irritations Britain's war caused. Its blockade interfered with US free enterprise (not to mention severely harming German domestic health), but it did not see civilians – particularly US civilians, as in the sinking of the passenger liner *Lusitania* in 1915 – killed by explosions or drowning in the icy Atlantic as Germany's U-boat campaigns did.[9]

The recently retired Ambassador to the United States, Lord Bryce's well-known leadership of the inquiry into German atrocities in Belgium has already been discussed. It was condemned in much twentieth-century history as an example of sensationalism, the compilers all too ready to accept sketchy accounts of German brutality, though Horne and Kramer's work establishes the reality of many crimes. Bryce's appointment tied very substantially to his US popularity. A better example of Bryce's work in neutral propaganda, however, was the subsequent report on the Armenian Genocide that he edited alongside Arnold Toynbee (then working at Wellington House). Not only did this project intend to provoke neutral hostility to the Central Powers, but it also involved active participation from many individuals in neutral countries. Its documents included accounts from United States, Swiss, Scandinavian and even German missionaries, businessmen, doctors and nurses, often supplied to Bryce or Toynbee by the prominent US missionary organizer, James Barton or others including the Swiss humanitarian Léopold Favre and the German missionary, Johannes Lepsius, then in the Netherlands. The latter provided information to Bryce but asked for it to be excluded from Bryce and Toynbee's parliamentary report because his country was currently at war. Both Bryce and Masterman accepted this, demonstrating, again, that lazy assumptions of cynical, vindictive and opportunist propaganda are inappropriate. However, collaboration with Barton involved more than just shared knowledge. Barton had access to the US president and influential figures like John D. Rockefeller and advised Bryce and Toynbee on the release and dissemination of the report in the United States. Bruno Cabanes notes that 'humanitarianism became increasingly organized around international networks' during the war, and, in this case, humanitarianism and British propaganda were mutually supportive. Meanwhile, managing the Armenian report to garner maximum US impact suggests a growing sense that international moral authority (alongside Burk's financial strength) was passing across the Atlantic during the war.[10]

Such networking did not mean neutrals were open conduits of British propaganda, however. At different times, Toynbee was warned by collaborators to avoid intruding with British material that might induce suspicion rather than sympathy. Criticizing the British issue of a pamphlet containing the evidence of a German witness to the genocide, Martin Niepage, Favre suggested his Armenian relief organization had already

> undertaken, in order to come to the aid of Armenians, a large propaganda in our country; it continues and does not demand this more active propaganda by means of this booklet; ... propaganda conducted in our country on behalf of a belligerent country is not only inappropriate but presents serious disadvantages. Switzerland has been so invaded by so many tendentious publications which ... plead only the cause of one party or the other, that it has become entirely mistrustful, and often with good reason. It will seem extraordinary that a booklet already published in Switzerland will be spread and published in England.

This may risk giving the impression that this booklet has an English and not an Armenian goal.

Replying, Toynbee accepted Favre's rationale and tried to have the British pamphlet stopped.[11]

Similarly, British appeals to US fellow feeling were not guaranteed success. Even after the United States entered the war, the historian Geoffrey Butler, who undertook a speaking tour in 1917 before returning to oversee a British Bureau of Information in New York, reported to the Minister of Information, Beaverbrook, that he thought 'We are rapidly removing the "slacker" taunt but one still comes up against the attitude "Yes, you aren't slackers, but you are shits."' Butler largely put this down, at least in New England, to residual hatred of Revolutionary War redcoats. Some authors, like Parker, acknowledged continued 'hostility' towards Britain but attempted to distance Britain from the revolution by arguing that the colonists fought for British principles against redcoats who were often 'German mercenaries'.[12] As Chapter 25 argues further, propagandists bent over backwards to accommodate US sentiment, again suggesting the passage of presumed authority across the Atlantic. Propaganda to neutrals (and those who joined the war) continued throughout. Propagandists recognized the war's scale from its inception and that Britain's efforts, alone, would not win it.

Notes

1. Monger, 'Speaking to or for the World', 86, 92; *Aims and Effort*, 52–3; Phillip Dehne, 'How Important Was Latin America to the First World War', *Iberoamericana*, 14, no. 53 (2014), esp. 155–60; Frederik Schulze, 'Brazil' in Ute Daniel, Peter Gatrell, Oliver Janz, Heather Jones, Jennifer Keene, Alan Kramer and Bill Nasson (eds), *1914–1918 Online: International Encyclopedia of the First World War* (Berlin: Freie Universität Berlin, 2015).
2. TNA INF4/5, Charles Masterman, 'Report of the Work of the Bureau Established for the Purpose of Laying before Neutral Nations and the Dominions the Case of Great Britain and Her Allies', 7 June 1915, 2, for the US number, see 6; Buitenhuis, *Great War of Words*, 55–6.
3. María Inés Tato, 'Luring Neutrals. Allied and German Propaganda in Argentina during the First World War', in Paddock, *Propaganda and World War One*, quotation at 329; Amado Nervo, 'Algo sobre la Kultur y la Cultura', *América-Latina*, 10, 15 December 1915, 29–30. Digitized copies of *América-Latina* are accessible via the 'municipal newspaper archive' section of the *Memoria de Madrid* website: www.memoriademadrid.es.
4. Marta García Cabrera, 'International Propaganda in Spain during the First World War: State of the Art and New Contributions', in Griffiths, *Communication and the First World War*, 199–204; TNA INF4/5, 'Second Report on the Work Conducted at Wellington House', 1 February 1916, 43.
5. TNA INF4/5, 'Second Report on the Work Conducted at Wellington House', 7, 43; INF4/4B, Robert Donald, 'Reports on Various Branches of Propaganda Work and Recommendations', 14 December 1917, 17; 'Comments on Reports by Colonel Buchan and Mr. Masterman', 6 January 1918, 5, 6.
6. Kathleen Burk, *Britain, America and the Sinews of War, 1914–1918* (London: George Allen & Unwin, 1985), 10.

7   Gilbert Parker, 'The United States and the War', *Harper's Monthly Magazine*, 136, no. 814, March 1918, 521–2.
8   Bowman, *Pilgrims Society*, 49, 118–47; Parker, 'United States', 528.
9   Jessica Bennett and Mark Hampton, 'World War I and the Anglo-American Imagined Community: Civilization vs. Barbarism in British Propaganda and American Newspapers', in Joel H. Wiener and Mark Hampton (eds), *Anglo-American Media Interactions, 1850–2000* (Basingstoke: Palgrave Macmillan, 2007), at 157–8. On Belgium and US opinion see May, *World War and American Isolation*, 36–8, and see also his comments on the blockade and Germany's antagonization of the United States through its U-boat campaigns at 62–6, 113–36. On the blockade's effects in Germany, see Mary Elisabeth Cox, *Hunger in War and Peace: Women and Children in Germany, 1914–1924* (Oxford: Oxford University Press, 2019) and C. Paul Vincent, *The Politics of Hunger: The Allied Blockade of Germany, 1915–1919* (Athens: Ohio University Press, 1985).
10 For fuller discussion of Bryce and Toynbee's Armenian report network, see Monger, 'Networking against Genocide'. Bruno Cabanes, *The Great War and the Origins of Humanitarianism, 1918–1924* (Cambridge: Cambridge University Press, 2014), p. 4.
11 TNA FO96/207, Léopold Favre to Arnold Toynbee, 28 January 1917; Toynbee to Favre, 8 February 1917. For another example of Toynbee being warned about British propaganda, see FO96/205, William Walker Rockwell to Toynbee, 15 May 1916.
12 PA, Beaverbrook Papers, BBK/E/3/9, Geoffrey Butler to Beaverbrook, 9 July 1918. A typed transcript suggests Butler wrote 'skits' and 'skittish'. His handwritten 'h' and 'k' are somewhat similar, but the tone of his discussion suggests 'shits' is more likely accurate; Parker, 'United States', 52–8.

CHAPTER 15
ORGANIZATIONS

Wellington House, discussed at length in Chapter 14, was one of the first dedicated propaganda organizations established in the war and continued its work, promoting Britain's cause to neutral and Dominion audiences, to the Armistice, despite being absorbed within the Department of Information in 1917. However, it was only one among many official and unofficial organizations producing propaganda. Other official groups – many of which have featured in previous chapters – existed to promote military and worker recruitment (PRC and Directorate of National Service), public investment in war savings, loans and bonds (NWSC), food economy and other forms of reduced consumption (NWSC and Ministry of Food), to oversee press censorship (Press Bureau), boost civilian morale at home (NWAC) or overseas (MI7b) or undermine enemy morale (Directorate of Secret Intelligence, then Lord Northcliffe's Department of Enemy Propaganda at Crewe House). Efforts to consolidate official propaganda efforts in 1917 and 1918 only partly succeeded in uniting these groups – the NWAC and MI7b remained outside the Ministry of Information's control in 1918, for instance. The war's early years saw competition between the Foreign Office, which saw the promotion of British interests abroad as its task, and the War Office, with its close oversight of army representation. Some groups overlapped with unofficial groups like the FRM or CCNPO. Other ministries – among them the Admiralty, Ministries of Munitions and Food and, latterly, the Air Ministry – also produced propaganda. Sanders and Taylor's standard analysis of the evolving shape of British propaganda administration notes that various Departments 'were determined to retain control over their own publicity needs' even if they lacked dedicated expertise. More cuttingly, the author G. K. Chesterton, remembering propaganda organization in his 1930s autobiography, criticized 'the small and spinsterish vanities and jealousies that seemed to divide those Departments', while Chapter 7 noted the NWAC and Ministry of Information's squabble about publishing Prince Lichnowsky's memorandum.[1]

Despite this evolution and awkwardness, scholarly and other accounts often suggest the existence or creation of a British 'propaganda machine' during the war. Sanders and Taylor refer at various points to central 'machinery'; Buitenhuis's second chapter is subtitled 'Setting up the Propaganda Machine', while Wallace (inaccurately) suggests Lords Northcliffe and Beaverbrook 'took over the propaganda machine in 1918 after two years of upheaval' and that Bryce was 'caught up in the atrocity propaganda machine'.[2] Describing the varied and sometimes competing organizations as a machine is doubly misleading. First, for a machine to function effectively, all its parts need to work together – depicting something as a machine implies order and precision, which was simply not the case with British propaganda, which developed incrementally through trial and error. Second, as Wallace's comment on Bryce implies, depicting something as a machine can imply it is unstoppable and its force irresistible. This is inaccurate both in relation to propaganda's practitioners and its audience. As noted in Chapter 7, propagandists like Wells sometimes quit propaganda work when they disagreed with their organization's approach, while Butler's comments about US reactions in Chapter 14 are a reminder that propagandists did not have everything their own way. Audiences could heckle as well as cheer while opposing propaganda groups also challenged official lines. Resisting the 'machine' interpretation helps to understand the variety of propaganda attempted during the war. It also reduces unwarranted implications of a population powerless to resist propaganda's claims.

Early official propaganda and censorship work rested mainly with three groups, each tied to a different government department. The PRC, responsible to the War Office, was formed with cross-party support. Its task was clear and well understood: to recruit volunteers for Britain's armed forces. As the only major European power without peacetime conscription, this was imperative. The Press Bureau, responsible to the Home Office, was rapidly established to oversee censorship of news, building on less substantial organizations such as the Admiralty, War Office and Press Committee that had liaised between the press and armed forces. Finally, Wellington House, responsible to the Foreign Office, focused primarily on neutral and imperial Dominion audiences. From the start, therefore, official propaganda served differing government priorities.

Brock Millman, generally suspicious of British propaganda (particularly that of the NWAC) as an underhanded attack on dissent, suggests the PRC's organization of propaganda was 'not provocative' and 'less an innovative attempt to influence British minds, than a necessary recourse to time-honoured methods' – in-person appeals, leaflets and pamphlets and posters. As discussed in Chapter 12, the PRC set the blueprint for much domestic propaganda – it established local committees and trusted local figures, mainly volunteers, to judge the best times and locations for meetings. It used party political organizers for its central administration, several of whom later worked for the NWAC (a continuity that Millman misses). And it was clear and forthright in its messages. It wanted to recruit men for armed service. Despite the notoriety of posters like 'Daddy, What Did *You* Do in the War', scholars including Nicholas Hiley, Jim Aulich and John Hewitt have long since shown that more common and popular messages focused on participation and camaraderie.[3] While stressing duty, it did so openly, with methods imitated by other apparently 'single issue' organizations like the NWSC.

While the PRC attempted open persuasion, the Press Bureau (discussed in greater detail in Chapter 24) limited some public knowledge, while, as previously noted, Wellington House attempted persuasion through interpreted facts but often masked its involvement. The Bureau, formed in August 1914, initially took a very restrictive line (demanded by government departments) about publishable information. With the appointment of the experienced pressman, Sir Edward Cook (also a wartime propagandist via the Victoria League), to co-direct the Bureau in 1915, however, better relations were formed with the press. Information that risked security for the armed forces, industrial infrastructure or prominent figures continued to be restricted by D notices, but Cook avoided censoring opinion, was prepared to negotiate with editors and press advisory groups around limits and appointed other journalists to roles in the 300-strong Bureau. Editors sometimes chafed at restrictions. Sir George Riddell, owner of the *News of the World*, took particular issue with a D notice chiding newspapers for overly optimistic reports, arguing that the lack of information forced them to speculate, but he also suggested the Bureau sometimes did not do enough to rein in newspapers, particularly outside London. Tolerable cooperation developed, based significantly on the Bureau trusting editors to exercise patriotic self-restraint.[4] Nonetheless, as discussed in Chapter 6, haggling was required before journalists, photographers and film-makers were permitted close to the front, eventually resulting in the establishment of Beaverbrook's WOCC, among other things – again a sign of the differing priorities of the War Office.

While wider official domestic propaganda took longer to emerge, other groups added to the PRC, PB and Wellington House's efforts. Peterson pointed to ten 'groups' that supplemented Wellington House's output, including the PRC; Oxford academics and a 'nameless group of Anglican clerics'; existing groups like the Cobden Club (which promoted free trade), the pro-empire Victoria League and elite Anglo-US society, the Atlantic Union; the Council of Loyal British Subjects of German, Austrian, or Hungarian Birth; the CCNPO, set up in the war to coordinate patriotic propaganda (and eventually absorbed into the NWAC) and the critical, dissenting organization, the UDC. The last of these groups was a further reminder that the official line was not unchallenged – the UDC and other critical groups continued to speak and publish throughout the war, albeit increasingly harassed by prosecutions and counter-propaganda.[5] Other groups like the FRM also soon appeared, promising (as previously discussed) to fill a gap in government attention through propaganda to the public.

Government hopes to maintain 'business as usual' as far as possible, including limited involvement in propaganda, were slowly eroded by total war's demands. Organizations like the NWSC (Figure 13) emerged by 1916 to address specific needs such as wartime fundraising although, as previously noted, once it established its network of local associations it took on additional tasks like food control campaigns. In line with his wider demands for more vigorous and efficient prosecution of the war, one of Lloyd George's first acts upon becoming prime minister in December 1916 was to commission an investigation into propaganda operations by the *Daily Chronicle*'s editor. Robert Donald criticized a lack of direction and obstructions caused by the 'traditional atmosphere of the Foreign Office':

When one leaves the top one meets with a diffusion of responsibility and a confusion of method. There is no clear-cut organisation, no system of efficient delegation, no definite line of distinction between the work of one branch and that of another … This lack of cohesion leads to overlapping, delay, and much wasted labour …

Another weakness, also due to the amateurish way propaganda work has developed, is the absence of harmony between one branch and another and the existence of inter-departmental jealousies.

Figure 13 A selection of National War Savings Committee publicity material, including its use of the swastika as its organizational logo.
Source: TNA NSC6/105 (author's photograph).

Donald's proposed solution was the appointment of a director of propaganda, which eventually led to the creation of the Department of Information, headed by the novelist John Buchan. Wellington House was brought within this new organization with a reduced literary remit. However, Donald specifically suggested the new organization should not address 'publicity at home', with the result, according to Sanders and Taylor, that the new department remained an 'annex of the Foreign Office', while the NWAC had to be formed in mid-1917 to address growing concerns about domestic morale. It followed the PRC's lead in structure, organization and even some of its personnel, while informing the CCNPO that its work should be taken over – the NWAC adopted the CCNPO's standard resolution for its own public meetings.[6]

Donald believed propaganda was the expert domain of journalists, hence his critique of 'amateurish' work. However, his suggestion that domestic work should be done by people within various relevant ministries encouraged further difficulties. The NWAC, for instance, sometimes found it difficult to arrange meetings because propaganda by other groups including the NWSC, food control committees and the Ministry of Munitions had exhausted local demand. Exhaustion could also overtake local organizers, such as the Conservative and Liberal agents in Bradford, J. H. Walker and F. J. Smith, each holding multiple honorary secretaryships of local propaganda and charity committees, spreading themselves very thinly:

> Messrs. Smith and Walker ... are the joint honorary secretaries of (1) Bradford Local Central Committee for War Savings and War Loan Campaigns; (2) Bradford Food Economy Campaign; (3) Bradford National War Aims; (4) Lord Mayor's Comforts Fund for Soldiers in Bradford units serving abroad; (5) City of Bradford Sailors and Soldiers' Christmas Fund; (6) Bradford Flag Day Organization; (7) Bradford Citizens' Army League (Bradford Recruiting Committee).

Every new organization that emerged, therefore, further burdened local organizers – not only party agents but also mayors, councillors, JPs and other paid or voluntary members of civic society. Bradford's agents were not the secretaries of the Bradford National Service Committee, however. H. B. Ratcliffe played that role in one of the 951 English and Welsh committees listed in July 1917. It seems unlikely that the Hastings Secretary Percy Idle lived up to his name.[7]

With Buchan unable to unify propaganda operations, hamstrung by the omission of domestic matters, the Foreign Office's continued forcefulness and his lack of formal government title and access to Lloyd George, a further restructuring in early 1918 created the Ministry of Information, led by Beaverbrook and involving more experienced press figures, such as the head of Reuters Sir Roderick Jones. Yet propaganda remained competitive. Badsey suggests others disliked Beaverbrook's overbearing attempts to control all decision-making. The NWAC continued to operate independently (though Beaverbrook sometimes spoke for it in Lords debates), as did MI7b. Beaverbrook was selected partly to tie him to the government, and his appointment of Northcliffe to lead an enemy propaganda office also aimed to shackle his critical press voice. However, it added a further layer of competition and jealousy, as Brigadier-General George Cockerill's Directorate of Secret Intelligence had previously driven enemy propaganda. Cockerill believed it had done so more effectively through its reliance on simple, truthful statements than Northcliffe's department's subsequent efforts.[8]

Cockerill was one of several leading propaganda organizers who contributed a report in late 1917 to a specially formed Committee on Overlapping in Production and Distribution of Propaganda. Chaired by the Irish Unionist Edward Carson (then the minister responsible for propaganda), its first meeting involved Donald and the owner of the *Daily Telegraph*, Lord Burnham, as well as Buchan, Masterman, Jones, Lord Onslow representing the War Office and others. Some of the discussion indicates the continuing improvisation at the heart of most British propaganda. Onslow explained MI7b activities in producing propaganda for overseas newspapers, for instance. He noted that the War Office employed 'officer journalists' to produce articles for the foreign press, that this work had little connection with the Department of Information and that a 'general written order' had asked 'anybody serving on light duty in England ... to contribute'. He added,

> Long before the Dept. of Information began, the [Royal] Colonial Institute agreed to send articles for publication under the censorship. We went to the Colonial Institute because I happened to be a member, and I did not know much about Colonial papers at the time.

The RCI became the standard conveyor of MI7b articles to the Dominion press, therefore, largely because a senior War Office figure happened to request its help rather than consulting the Empire Press Union, as Burnham suggested. The remaining discussion focused on how far the War Office collaborated with the Department of Information, with Onslow largely sticking to the line that the War Office's work began before the department existed, although a diffident resolution stated Onslow 'should see if it were not worth while to get into touch with the Empire Press Union'.[9] Despite calls for efficiency and professionalization, propaganda depended largely on informal networks of politicians, writers, press figures and others who leaned on social connections.

For all the effort to systematize and regiment propaganda in the war's later years, it continued to be undertaken by a wide variety of official and unofficial organizations, sometimes collaborating, sometimes competing. Tammy Proctor notes a general wartime culture of demand for 'expert' intervention – a move away from pre-war, gentlemanly leadership. Propaganda sought experts too, from the established writers swiftly recruited to assist Wellington House and professional staff speakers used at many NWAC events to those with logistical skills. A draft Ministry of Information memorandum, prepared close to the end of the war, asserted that propaganda

> is essentially expert work, but it is the work of different kinds of experts. All varieties of talents are needed – the skilled journalist and the expert in publicity for the actual business of propaganda, the experienced business man for the control of expenditure and machinery, and the student of public affairs for intelligence and policy. The Ministry of Information has been fortunate enough to secure ... representatives of all three classes.

Nonetheless, on the same page, the memorandum accepted that

> propaganda can never be made a matter of hard and fast routine. It has to be often revised, both in material and method ... Moreover, there must inevitably be some wastage of effort. Propaganda work, indeed, resembles an election campaign, where seed must be sown broadcast, regardless of the fact that much will fall on unsuitable ground.[10]

Propaganda never became a 'machine', certain to generate predetermined results. Even in 1918, Beaverbrook's organization depicted it in ways similar to the Vatican's seventeenth-century *Congregatio de Propaganda Fide* (Congregation for the Propagation of the Faith) from which modern propaganda derived its name. Propagandists scattered seeds, some of which took root. Were results wholly predictable, propaganda would not have been necessary in the first place. It was always, fundamentally, a human endeavour, depending (as Chapter 16 discusses further) on thousands of individuals acting as organizers, creators or deliverers of its messages and goals and subject to very human frailties – unclearly expressed or misunderstood ideas; anxieties about status and desires to compete; ignorance of the efforts made by others. By 1918, there was certainly no shortage of British propaganda in Britain and abroad – how much hit its intended mark is harder to identify.

Notes

1 Sanders and Taylor, *British Propaganda*, 80; G. K. Chesterton, *Autobiography* (London: Hutchinson, 1936), 248, cited in Monger, 'A "Not Uncongenial Task"', 9.
2 Sanders and Taylor, *British Propaganda*, 31, 55, 65, 67, 70, 162, 246; Buitenhuis, *Great War of Words*, ch. 2; Wallace, *War and the Image*, 173, 185.
3 Brock Millman, *Managing Domestic Dissent in First World War Britain* (London: Frank Cass, 2000), 34; Hiley, 'Kitchener Wants You'; Jim Aulich and John Hewitt, *Seduction or Instruction? First World War Posters in Britain and Europe* (Manchester: Manchester University Press, 2008), ch. 2.
4 Sanders and Taylor, *British Propaganda*, 18–32; Monger, *Press Bureau*.
5 Peterson, *Propaganda for War*, 19–20; on the Victoria League's wartime propaganda, see Hendley, *Organized Patriotism*, ch. 3; on the Atlantic Union, see Bowman, *Pilgrims Society*, 54, 124, 128. On the harassment of the UDC and wider dissenting voices, cf. the interpretations of Millman, *Managing Domestic Dissent* and Monger, *Patriotism and Propaganda*.
6 TNA INF4/4B, Robert Donald, *Report on Propaganda Arrangements*, 9 January 1917, quotations at 6, 14; Sanders and Taylor, *British Propaganda*, 63; for details of the NWAC's creation, see Monger, *Patriotism and Propaganda*, esp. 18–24, 26–33, 37–40.
7 Monger, *Patriotism and Propaganda*, 248; 'Personal Notes', *Conservative Agents' Journal*, 47 (January 1918), 14; TNA NATS1/70, list of National Service Committees.
8 Badsey, *German Corpse Factory*, 193–8; Hew Strachan, 'John Buchan and the First World War: Fact into Fiction', *War in History*, 16 (2009), no. 3, 303–4; Monger 'A "Not Uncongenial Task"', 8, 12.
9 TNA CAB27/17, draft minutes of meeting of Committee on Overlapping in Production and Distribution of Propaganda, 8 November 1917, 2–3, 8 (pencilled numbers).
10 Tammy M. Proctor, *Civilians in a World at War, 1914–1918* (New York: New York University Press, 2010), esp. ch. 6; PA, Beaverbrook Papers, BBK/E/3/1, draft memorandum, 'The Ministry of Information', 8.

CHAPTER 16
PROPAGANDISTS

As should already be obvious (particularly from Chapters 12 and 15), wartime propaganda was not a small endeavour involving a few famous press magnates, artists and writers. Though organizations developed piecemeal throughout the war, it was a mass undertaking by thousands of paid and voluntary organizers and producers working locally, nationally or abroad. Existing profiles of individual propagandists tend to relate to eminent, seemingly 'expert', figures or distinct communities such as academics, but many of the wartime propaganda workforce are recorded only as names on a staff or local committee list or speakers mentioned in a local newspaper article.[1] Just as assessing propaganda content by its most obvious or dramatic examples gives a false impression of its breadth (and ignores the plainness of much of it), focusing on the most famous names overlooks the much wider organizational and creative workforce who produced it.

The poster, pamphlet, film or speech aiming to motivate an audience was the final element of a larger process. Propagandists thought in terms of 'campaigns' – not single publications or meetings but series reaching wider audiences. Such approaches often reflected organizations' political backgrounds – propaganda activities at constituency level were organized similarly to electoral campaigns, where face-to-face communication remained important, hence the determination to hold midwinter meetings in tiny country villages, discussed in Chapter 12. Additionally, 'campaign's military tone evoked growing commitment to total war and made propaganda work an alternative outlet for those incapable of military service. In the war's early days, established creative (and male) talents like Galsworthy (almost 47 at the war's outbreak), Anthony Hope Hawkins (51), Rudyard Kipling (53) or the painter John Lavery (58) were invited by Wellington House to produce propaganda. Some younger talents like Milne, Bairnsfather or the novelist Keble Howard initially joined the armed forces before taking up propaganda work later. In other cases, younger men took up propaganda as a form of war work short of armed service, such as the historian Arnold Toynbee, who obtained exemptions based on a generous medical report and then his importance to Wellington House. Propagandists like Dorothy Peel (a pre-war journalist and one of many women somewhat belatedly brought into propaganda work) sometimes stressed their voluntarism, and the hard work involved, to show their active part in the war effort, as did the biographer Charles Mallet when recounting Hope Hawkins' work. For those unable to fight, propaganda proved their determination to serve Britain, whether openly or discreetly. The Classical scholar Gilbert Murray (also Toynbee's father-in-law), who wrote propaganda and undertook tours of Sweden and the United States, declined a 1917 honour, ostensibly, because his 'war-work has been mostly propaganda ... therefore better not to accept reward from

Govt'. In fact, he told his daughter, his refusal reflected his strong dislike of Lloyd George and fear that, in accepting a Companion of Honour, 'I might find other companions besides Honour'. Nonetheless, his propaganda efforts continued.[2]

Others, however, took a firm view of their professional expectations. The journalist E. M. Goodman, for example, wrote to the NWAC more than once demanding promised rates of payments for her articles. She was undertaking a job and expected prompt and accurate payment. Central organizations, meanwhile, recruited and often paid staff believed to have special talents for propaganda. Masterman oversaw Wellington House because of previous experience with propaganda campaigns related to the Liberal Government's introduction of National Insurance. As well as recruiting eminent writers' voluntary services, Masterman's organization also required paid staff. In August 1915, for example, the civil servant Ernest Gowers, Wellington House's chief executive officer, wrote to the Treasury seeking an increased salary for the historian Lewis Namier, citing his Oxford education, 'journalistic and literary experience' and 'responsible work for which [his] present remuneration is manifestly inadequate'. Gowers noted that Masterman feared he would lose Namier's services without an increase. The same letter requested employment of the former editor of the *Lucknow Daily Telegraph* E. E. Long on a salary 'not exceeding £400':

> His knowledge of the Moslem world, combined with his experience of practical journalism, renders him peculiarly well fitted to undertake the task of editing and producing a fortnightly illustrated newspaper which this Department is about to produce at the request of the Foreign Office and India Office for propaganda purposes in the Middle East.

Both requests were granted by the Treasury soon afterwards.[3] Despite continual emphasis on wartime voluntarism, government propaganda was seen to need expert contributions, even if this often relied on personal connections (while critics like Donald argued only press personnel were really useful). Long's salary was matched, in 1917 at least, by two women involved with Ministry of Food propaganda: Maud Pember Reeves, serving as 'Principal of the Education Propaganda and Cookery Branch of the Local Authorities and Rationing Division' and Margaret Bryant, a publicity assistant in the Wheat Commission.[4]

Attempts to benefit from expertise in other fields were regularly used by propaganda organizations. The NWSC was headed by the banker Sir Robert Kindersley, who not only oversaw the financial side of things but also regularly wrote and spoke about war savings and loans, while its propaganda efforts were particularly influenced by advertising expert Sir Hedley Le Bas. Leaving aside Beaverbrook and Northcliffe, experienced press organizers also brought knowledge of their trade to assist propagandists. Roderick Jones, general manager of the wire news service Reuters, oversaw cable and wireless propaganda for the Department of Information. Gerard Fiennes, formerly assistant editor of the *Pall Mall Gazette* and *Evening Standard*, headed the NWAC's Publications Department, and the *Times* journalist Henry Wickham Steed played a leading role at Northcliffe's Crewe

House. Perhaps one step down the hierarchy from these figures, Grace Curnock, a *Daily Mail* journalist, was press representative of the Women's Section of the National Service Department during 1917. Part of her role (noted in Chapters 4 and 6) involved preparing and distributing releases for the press as well as wider administrative work related to publicity. A series of notices seeking female clerks for service in France across April and May, for instance, required Curnock's approval to pay the substantial sum of just over £625 to national, regional, religious and women's papers.[5]

Nicholas Hiley notes that the advertising specialist Le Bas began propaganda work for the government in January 1914 by organizing a promotional campaign for the army but found Kitchener's War Office surprisingly restrictive about what could be done once war commenced. He thus organized a voluntary committee with other advertisers to encourage enlistments. A series of 'questions' – to employers, unenlisted men and women – published in the press in late 1914 sought to encourage volunteers through guilt. Their apparent success (despite Hiley's argument elsewhere that shame was less effective than material stressing comradeship and taking part) persuaded the War Office that Le Bas was useful, and he was asked to assist Irish recruitment. By mid-1915, he turned his attention to the first War Loan, obtaining funds from the Treasury to run a campaign on similar lines to recruitment, stressing the need for national unity and 'practical patriotism'. Hiley suggests these activities meant, despite the lack of formal organization, that domestic propaganda was well under way by mid-1915. Another advertiser was recruited to promote the Ministry of Munitions, while Le Bas began advising on film propaganda before being appointed to the National Organizing Society for War Savings (the NWSC's precursor) and producing films and posters (such as Figure 14) promoting thrift. Messages about unpatriotically flamboyant dress did not attack specific people, but his campaign apparently shocked sensitivities about interfering with women's activities (previously considered part of 'private' life) and angered businessmen who feared lost profits. However, it promoted a restrained atmosphere in keeping with the emerging total war. Le Bas's influence waned, Hiley suggests, because he supported Asquith, while Lloyd George also preferred press expertise to inform propaganda.[6]

Le Bas's shift between different formal and informal propaganda organizations over time was common. Those considered useful often shuffled from group to group – as previously noted, many party organizers and speaking staffs who aided the PRC's campaigns reappeared working for the NWAC later on. Toynbee, Namier and other Wellington House academics shifted more formally to the Foreign Office's Political Intelligence Department in 1918, while MI7b's analyst of German propaganda, the zoologist Peter Chalmers Mitchell, was seconded to Crewe House. Much of the work at Crewe House, meanwhile, was overseen by the Canadian Campbell Stuart, who had come to Northcliffe's attention after assisting his 1917 'mission' to the United States.[7]

At local levels, propaganda organizations often sought eminent local figures to assist with propaganda in their areas. In Liverpool, for instance, the NWAC benefited from the influence of Archibald Salvidge, a leading political organizer within the city and beyond, who had boosted workers' support for Conservatism. As a city alderman, Salvidge appeared on propaganda stages from the war's early days, calling for recruits and national

Figure 14 *To Dress Extravagantly in War Time Is Worse than Bad Form, It Is Unpatriotic.*
Source: NWSC poster no. 7 (1916). © Imperial War Museum (Art.IWM PST 10122).

subsidization of Belgian refugees while chairing a meeting as part of a propaganda tour by the actor Martin Harvey. By 1915 he was chair of Liverpool's Recruiting Committee. In 1917 he urged Liverpudlians to economize in food consumption and display the purple ribbon indicating that citizens ate less bread and was a principal speaker for the War Savings 'Tank Week'. At a conference to set up local War Aims Committees in Southwest Lancashire in October 1917, Salvidge particularly emphasized monitoring 'opposition propaganda' and counteracting the 'insidious underground policy' of critics by holding counter-meetings wherever they spoke. He was supported by the ILP founder–member, general secretary of the National Union of Dock Labourers and Liverpool city councillor, James Sexton, at the conference and later endorsed by the local Conservative newspaper, which demanded 'Vigilance Committees in every town, in every ward of every large town'. It speculated, 'What a force, for example, would the Workingmen's Conservative Association [Salvidge's political power-base] be in Liverpool if it could concentrate its energy on war aims propaganda with the same zeal as it infuses into an election campaign'. Though an obscure name today, obtaining help from influential local figures like Salvidge brought not only their own energies and skills but also their networks of influence to propaganda's cause.[8]

Street propaganda also required a small army of 'ordinary' speakers, alongside more notable figures like MPs, senior clerics, sailors or soldiers and allied and imperial visitors. The NWAC recorded nearly 400 individual speakers, including over 100 MPs, in its incomplete register of meetings between August 1917 and October 1918. However, much of each meeting involved introductions, votes of thanks and speeches accompanying the NWAC's standard resolution, all of which were usually done by what the register records only as 'local speakers'. For example, a large meeting at Bognor Regis was introduced by the Chairman of the Council H. H. Gibbs before Lord Edmund Talbot, the local Conservative MP, gave the main address. He was supported by Lewis Haslam, Liberal MP for Monmouth, while the local Liberal candidate Dove Keighley gave a vote of thanks, seconded by W. H. B. Fletcher, J.P. None of these men formally worked for a government organization but all contributed to NWAC propaganda. A fortnight's campaign in neighbouring towns in September, meanwhile, saw a rotating line-up of staff speakers introduced and supported by locals. A report of these small meetings took more interest in the visitors' home towns (variously Bristol, London, Southend and Southport) than what they had to say.[9] Out-of-towners brought novelty, backed up by local endorsements.

Travelling for propaganda was not only an occupational requirement for speakers. Keble Howard (originally John Keble Bell) was a pre-war journalist and novelist, specializing in light comic stories. His first book reprinted some of his pieces as assistant editor of the *Sketch* in 1901, and he later worked as the *Daily Mail*'s drama critic but antagonized Northcliffe with his 1913 novel, *Lord London*, which fictionalized Northcliffe's career. Howard's 1919 memoir, focused on his war years, listed eighteen novels, eleven 'papers and sketches' and thirteen plays to his name. The book's front matter also specified two examples of his propaganda, *The Glory of Zeebrugge*, about the 1918 Zeebrugge Raid, and *The Quality of Mercy* (regarding German treatment of prisoners). *An Author in Wonderland* also included other examples he wrote about civilian war work, covering shipyards, mines, fishing and women's farm work, as well as explaining how he became a propagandist.[10] Howard volunteered for armed service but, thirty-nine in 1914, was too old for combat, instead largely filling administrative roles. He noted that over-age men wanted 'to serve their country to their utmost ability' but were prevented by obstructive systems. Despite offering to write or edit national service propaganda, for example, he received no reply, only to later be asked informally by a different official in the department to contribute. He hoped

> posterity may understand that patriotism and experience are not sufficient to get a man an unpaid job at a time of national crisis. If you want to work for your country at such a time, you must keep pointing to your breast and assuring all and sundry that you are a very exceptional fellow. As for being a hero, if you are ineligible for the Army or Navy, and long to die for your country, you must have excellent introductions.

Sure enough, when Howard was finally asked by Masterman to write for the Ministry of Information in 1918, it was due to a more eminent writer's introduction. Once established, Howard set to work writing *The Quality of Mercy* from official reports before his successful account of Zeebrugge. However, he continued to describe his experiences, despite pride, with an emphasis on the ridiculous and uncomfortable:

> When I went north for the Admiralty Propaganda Department I left London about one and arrived in Newcastle about eight-thirty ... I had neither bite nor sup till I arrive in Newcastle. Even then I had to carry my suit-case to the hotel ...
> So these journeys were no joy-rides.

Further, unlike journalism, Howard endured tortuous bureaucratic processes before being allowed to tour war work sites: 'A fortnight has elapsed since you opened the negotiations, but it is a long war, and there is no particular hurry.' However, the delays meant he completed only four of an intended twelve studies of war work by the Armistice![11] Once again, if British propaganda was a 'machine' it remained in dubious working order.

Howard's war-work sketches included short, light character studies of British workers. In one, he described a Wearside shipworker: 'Clear-eyed, clean-skinned, strong-lunged – the very pink of a first-rate Britisher.' Howard wrote admiringly about his skill and dexterity before reporting that the worker had only once been to sea, on a holiday to London and the Isle of Wight:

> That was the extent of his travels. The ships he builds ransack the oceans of the world and come again, please God, to port. The winds rage round them and the great seas buffet them; but the honest work holds firm and true. The British sailorman knows what he owes to the shipyard workers of Great Britain, and the

men who build the ship may righteously exult when she goes gliding from the slips into her natural element.[12]

Such propaganda celebrated each Briton's potential patriotic contribution. Quality ship construction was equally as important as excellent sailing and gunnery in ensuring the British Navy's greatness and power, while the humble shipworker, Howard claimed, was satisfied with his unexciting lot (Howard's memoir, meanwhile, asked readers to realize that 'humble' writers like himself also served). This quotidian propaganda – the celebration and elevation of everyday, routine service – was a core wartime message used by multiple organizations and individual propagandists. With so many individuals undertaking propaganda for varied purposes, common themes like this, as Chapter 17 discusses further, helped create familiar, inclusive and repeated messages for British audiences.

Notes

1 For works that closely discuss individual propagandists or groups, see Messinger, *British Propaganda*; Wallace, *War and the Image*; Trevor Wilson, 'Lord Bryce's Investigation into Alleged German Atrocities in Belgium, 1914-1915', *Journal of Contemporary History*, 14, no. 3 (1979); Nicholas Hiley, 'Sir Hedley Le Bas and the Origins of Domestic Propaganda in Britain, 1914-17', *European Journal of Marketing*, 21, no. 8 (1987); McKernan, 'Propaganda, Patriotism and Profit'; Cook, 'Documenting War'; Strachan, 'John Buchan'; Monger, 'Networking Against Genocide' and 'Know Your Enemy'.
2 See Messinger, *British Propaganda*, 41-2; Monger, 'A "Not Uncongenial Task"', 6-7, 13-14; William H. McNeill, *Arnold J. Toynbee: A Life* (Oxford: Oxford University Press, 1989), 68-74; BLO, Murray Papers, MS 463, Murray to Mary Murray, 4 July 1917; MS 568, Murray to Rosalind Toynbee, 6 July 1917.
3 Monger, 'Nothing Special?', 526-7; TNA T1/11992, E. A. Gowers to T. L. Heath, 24 January 1916; Heath to Gowers, 3 February 1916.
4 IWM, MS Women, War and Society, 1914-1918: The Women at Work Collection, EMP 51/1/16-18, Ministry of Food, 'Employment of University Women in Government Offices'.
5 TNA NATS1/1320, 'Women's Army Auxiliary Service: Publicity Matters', minutes to Curnock, 11 April to 11 May 1917.
6 Hiley, 'Hedley Le Bas', quotation at 39; see also Hiley, 'Kitchener Wants *You*' for his views on shame vs participation.
7 Wallace, *War and the Image*, 173; Monger, 'Know Your Enemy', 795; Hamilton Fyfe, *Northcliffe: An Intimate Biography* (London: George Allen & Unwin, 1930), 207-9, 236-8.
8 'Statues to Belgian Gallantry?', *Liverpool Daily Post*, 26 October 1914, 4; 'Getting the Men', *Liverpool Echo*, 28 October 1915, 8; 'Give Your Pledge', *Echo*, 23 May 1917, 3 (on the purple ribbon, see Monger, 'Tangible Patriotism', 251-4); 'To Liverpool', *Echo*, 8 December 1917, 2; 'Allies' War Aims. Conference in Liverpool', *Liverpool Courier*, 12 October 1917, 4; 'Vigilance Committees Wanted', *Courier*, 13 October 1917, 4. On Salvidge's growing influence, see Paul A. Nuttall, 'Sir Archibald Salvidge and the Failed Realignment of British Politics, 1918-1922', *Northern History*, 60, no. 1 (2023).
9 'War Aims Meeting', *Bognor Regis Observer*, 27 November 1917, 3; 'National War Aims. Meetings at the Seaside', *Chichester Observer*, 12 September 1917, 4.

10 Waller, *Writers, Readers and Reputations*, 31, 122, 351–2; Keble Howard, *An Author in Wonderland* (London: Chatto & Windus, 1919), see front matter for his listed publications, including 'propaganda'.
11 Howard, *Author in Wonderland*, 23–4, 91, 96–102; Keble Howard, *The Quality of Mercy: How British Prisoners of War Were Taken to Germany in 1914* (n.p.d., 1918); Keble Howard, *The Zeebrugge Affair* (New York: George H. Doran, 1918), listed in *Author in Wonderland* as *The Glory of Zeebrugge*.
12 Howard, 'The Spirit of the Yard', in *Author in Wonderland*, 124–6.

CHAPTER 17
QUOTIDIAN PROPAGANDA

Among a collection of national service posters in a National Archives file – some intact, some in scraps and fragments – are several partially developed pieces of poster art, survivors of a wider cull of propaganda files after the war. Some targeted Irish recruitment. One asks, 'Do you Understand Horses?', with letter-press to be added beneath. Another shows John Bull, bedecked in a Union Jack waistcoat, holding out a 'National Service' sledgehammer. Figure 15 shows a middle-aged man rolling up his sleeves. Beneath him, a soldier talks to civilians, while, alongside, the question 'Can you use a *Spade*?' is written on the tool itself. The message's blunt dullness requires a straightforward answer – of course I can. Therefore, there is no excuse to avoid national service. The soldier reminds the viewer why they should bother – others bear greater burdens – and the message depends on an assumption (stated by propagandists of all stripes) that all Britons wanted to serve. Wielding a spade aided the war effort and met the soldier's example.[1] The artist drew on a persistent strand of propaganda that identified wartime service with everyday activity. Everything related to the war and everything people did, therefore, counted towards its conclusion, the unspectacular as much as the dramatic and violent.

Early in the war, the phrase 'business as usual' was used to suggest that, despite the war, Britain could continue to function as in peacetime. Moving from initial, seemingly spontaneous, statements of resolve by shop owners, it evoked assurance that British business, trade, government and everyday life could largely proceed. Cabinet government continued with full discussions involving more than twenty ministers, which was eventually pointed to as evidence of inefficiency and lack of urgency. Maintaining trade thanks to naval dominance would allow Britain to supply its allies with their larger conscript armies. However, business as usual 'was in truth the best of a bad job' – a statement of faith more than reality. As contributors to a recent survey of Britain's home front note, despite the rhetoric, government intervention in the economy, affecting people's everyday existence, began immediately. Exports of cereals, feed, fertilizer and dozens of resources essential to military needs were prohibited and, by 1915, calls for urgent expansion of agricultural production were made. To prevent a financial crisis, the stock exchange was closed for some time, prompting Lloyd George to use the phrase to reassure investors.[2] Restrictions on the right to strike or even, for workers in war industries, take a new job without permission from their existing employer followed as increasing recognition of a 'total' war, requiring full commitment of Britain's resources, emerged. Nonetheless, the sentiment of 'business as usual' continued in other forms throughout the war. War was an everyday reality for Britons, felt in increasing work

Figure 15 Draft National Service poster artwork.
Source: TNA NATS1/109.

hours, prices, expectations and anxiety for loved ones, as well as coastal bombardments, air raids and U-boat attacks on passenger and merchant ships.

Propagandists harnessed the 'new normal' of wartime expectations, using inclusive language to suggest all civilians had important parts in the war through the everyday tasks they performed. Someone did not need to carry a rifle or walk a deck to do war service; anything they did – paid or domestic work, economizing on food and essential materials, investing in war funds, volunteering their time – was a small but tangible contribution to the overall 'war effort' (a term first recorded by the *Oxford English Dictionary* in a 1914 *Manchester Guardian* headline). Such arguments were, depending on each audience member's perspective, an antidote or complement to the discussion of broad ideals and principles (addressed at various previous points, but especially in Chapters 4 and 11) that featured strongly in propaganda appeals. Elaborate outlines of international law, justice, duty and honour, though important, could easily seem too grand, abstract or overwhelming, and endless accounts of German barbarity too frightening. Also identifying smaller, achievable actions offered everyone an individual stake in the nation's success. Small businessmen investing in wartime schemes, mothers mending clothes and cooking unfamiliar ingredients and labourers volunteering for national service were all assured their day-to-day wartime activities were crucial to eventual victory. Such claims were assisted by using local figures, familiar to their audiences, as propagandists, as Chapter 12 noted. Positive reinforcement could also easily become a negative motivation, however. Those who failed to play their part, refused to economize or, worse, hoarded resources or profited from others' sacrifices were open to accusations of selfishness at best, if not treachery.

Quotidian propaganda – material addressing everyday experience – is readily found, particularly directed at domestic audiences. As Gregory notes, wartime attitudes revolved heavily around 'the ethic of doing one's bit'. By early September 1914, the *Runcorn Guardian*, discussing a recent public meeting, claimed most people already understood the war's key issues and were looking for opportunities to serve:

> At a time like this the business instinct, which is a feature of the British temperament, is a most valuable possession. On Monday evening there was a general realization that the moment is one for doing things and not for shouting more or less bombastic threats. 'Do your bit' was the note behind all of them …
>
> In every ward in the town meetings are to be called to arrange for the systematization of the work to be done. The aid of every man and woman is asked and will be wanted …
>
> Those who want to help – and every man, woman and child in the town comes within that category – have no need to wait till the ward meetings are called … Every one cannot go to the front or even perform garrison or special police duty, but all can do something at home.[3]

In practice, it took time before all parts of the community were encouraged to undertake war work, with women demanding more access to work in 1915, as Chapter 13 noted.

However, as the war continued, more and more aspects of people's lives were tied to wartime service. Savings and domestic economy were equated with combat, with women in Ministry of Food posters encouraged to 'save two thick slices [of bread] every day and defeat the "U" Boat'. Pushing the point further, a woman in her kitchen in the foreground (or, in another version, a mother with her daughter) cuts bread while a ship clashes with a submarine in the background.[4] The message was clear and simple – foregoing two slices of bread a day to make supplies go further was a manageable sacrifice. It was also more modest than broader demands to 'Eat Less Bread', which propagandists like Peel and Pember Reeves pointed out was not necessarily possible for poorer people. This manageable act was no small thing, however: it directly affected merchant sailors' safety.

Other appeals, similarly, encouraged people that things they would not miss were essential to the war effort. A war savings leaflet made a double appeal to national duty and parental concern for children. Parents should invest in war savings certificates to save for their children's education: 'The kind of schooling you would wish to provide for your little ones, costs money ... The money you save in this way will amount up [sic] surprisingly. You will never miss it.' On the leaflet's reverse, however, readers were reminded of 'national duty': 'Every penny spent in non-essentials is hampering the efforts of our gallant Army and Navy ... Our fighting men are *giving* their lives. You are only asked to *lend* your money.'[5] Here, the message differed a little from requests to reduce bread consumption – war savings not only fulfilled national duty and aided the war now but also would benefit someone's own family later. Likewise, a campaign seeking recycled cotton and paper pulp asked every woman to 'turn out her box-room and her paper-cupboard', noting 'she is asked to give only those things which she does not want and not what she really requires. She is not asked to give money, but only time and good-will.' After a successful trial in London, the Women's Section of the Directorate of National Service was expanding the scheme nationwide, with collection centres listed not only in major cities like Bristol but also in small villages like Winchelsea (East Sussex), Shere (Surrey) and Egloskerry (Cornwall). An article drawing on the notice in the *Illustrated War News* added,

> Here is a chance for those Englishwomen who from one cause or another, are not able to help their country as actively as they would like. If they cannot work, they can at least help to clothe our soldiers and sailors ... The only sacrifice involved [in helping organize collections] is the expenditure of a little time and trouble.

Both the original notice and its adaptation, and organizing collection centres in small communities, emphasized that even small-scale voluntary contributions aided the war. Likewise, E. M. Goodman, writing her regular column for women for the NWAC, encouraged housewives to recycle redundant sheets, old clothes, metal, jars, corks and paper as part of their spring-cleaning, rather than 'hoard' them and 'waste the nation's resources'. Household detritus thus became a national priority, and domestic chores patriotic war work.[6]

While propaganda often stressed choice and opportunity, it also embraced stricter tones. In Plymouth, soon after becoming Minister of National Service, Sir Auckland Geddes explained why a 'comb-out' of fit men in other occupations for military service would soon begin. The nation, despite previous economy and national service campaigns, had failed adequately to connect personal choices and global consequences: 'We have done well in the big things; we have not done well in the small. We have, I fear, woefully lacked imagination.' People did not realize that woollen clothes came from Australian wool, expensively transported to Britain. Reaching his peak of indignation, Geddes assured his audience,

> Ladies' clothing is the grave of an enormous amount of human energy. New hats alone absorb the work of millions of fingers, and whatever effect they may have that effect certainly does not include helping beat the enemy.
>
> If we are to make the effort which we should make, if we really are going to make the greatest effort in our history, our imaginations must be quickened to understand the effects of our smallest actions.

People should stop buying new clothes, and makers of those items should find more valuable work. All able men and women should take their skills to national service – civil occupations should be suspended until the war was won. Britons were at war with profligate millinery as well as Prussian militarism.[7]

In line with these quotidian tones, even some soldiers' propaganda conveyed less exciting and dramatic elements of military service. MI7b authors discussed the routine but important work of those whose primary army task was not combat. Milne, previously a signals officer himself, wrote more than one article for Dominion papers explaining that role. 'A Specialist', for example, noted the responsibility involved, since there was only one officer per battalion who understood signalling, and itemized signal officers' day-to-day tasks of telephone-line maintenance within the trenches:

> Every civilian knows what it is to ring up somebody on the telephone, to be kept waiting ten minutes, and then to be given the wrong number. If you are merely asking your friend to dine with you one night next week, the delay may be annoying, but it will not be serious. If, however, you are the officer commanding B Company, and an attack has suddenly been made on your part of the line, and you want immediate artillery support... .

K. N. Colvile, meanwhile, devoted an article to the work of an army farrier, stressing his pride in the quality of his shoeing and prevention of colic in his horses: 'There cannot be many more valuable soldiers in the British Army than Farrier-Sergeant H—.'[8] Such pieces (both published in several Australian and New Zealand papers) acknowledged the valuable military service of those not primarily charged with fighting, which might satisfy both the pride of such soldiers' relatives and the curiosity of readers. The pieces also stressed individuals' personal pride in their work, however, conveying the broader message that service – civilian or military – need not be glamorous to make a difference.

Propaganda was also literally quotidian. The many organizations competing for public attention by the war's later years made propaganda itself an everyday feature of wartime Britain. The NWAC claimed that its free newspaper, *Reality*, was distributed to over one million readers, primarily in industrial areas, and thanked W. H. Smith, more widely, for circulating one hundred million propaganda publications on the government's behalf. Arrangements to distribute one pamphlet quoting Lloyd George amounted to over 2.5 million copies. Millions, too, Chapter 6 noted, crowded into cinemas to watch *Battle of the Somme* in the autumn of 1916. Passers-by in 1917–18 might expect to come across a meeting in support of not only the NWAC – the official organization responsible for domestic propaganda – but also appeals from war savings, food economy, national service, Ministry of Munitions and other propagandists, not to mention unofficial and critical voices. Indeed, competition was not always amicable, with critical propagandists sometimes facing counter-meetings (and violent disruption) from official and unofficial groups that rejected their right to speak. 'Factory gate' meetings were held at shift change times, while national service propagandists targeted women shopping in department stores or visiting holiday resorts in 1917. Multiple posters for various organizations, with more or less impact depending on billposters' skills, also adorned railway station and other public hoardings.[9]

By its nature, street propaganda targeted a passing audience. Creating familiar formats for events thus helped normalize and standardize them, allowing someone to fall into step regardless of when they arrived. As noted in Chapter 12, meetings commonly involved a notable local figure as chair, one or more prominent local or visiting speakers as the main attractions, and further local figures who gave votes of thanks or moved the organization's resolution. Events frequently ended with the national anthem. Such conventions continued even where new media were employed, as with local tours projecting patriotic films. Arguably, these conventions created legitimacy for the events. Both local endorsement and rituals familiar from pre-war elections suggested 'business as usual' on Britain's streets (provided a particular event was not disrupted by a counter-meeting, though even violent disruption was familiar in pre-war public politics).[10] Despite regular comments by propagandists on the unprecedented nature of the war and its demands, emphasizing everyday contributions and recycling pre-war conventions kept things manageable. Elevating everyday tasks to national wartime priorities made everyone part of the war effort, for better or worse.

Notes

1 TNA NATS1/109, 'Can you use a *Spade*?', draft National Service poster artwork; on assumptions of a desire to volunteer, see Monger, 'Press and Propaganda'.
2 DeGroot, *Blighty*, 54–64, quotation at 55; Hew Strachan, 'Introduction', 11–12, George Peden, 'The Growth of Cabinet Government', 63–7, 71–2; G. R. Rubin, 'The Defence of the Realm Act and Other Emergency Laws', 89–90; Keith Grieves, 'Agriculture', 205–7, all in Strachan, *British Home Front*.
3 Gregory, *Last Great War*, 95; 'Jottings', *Runcorn Guardian* 4 September 1914, 4.

4 'Don't Waste Bread' (Ministry of Food poster F.C. 18, n.d.) IWM catalogue number PST 13368, and see the alternative version, dated 1917, catalogue number PST13354.
5 IWM, MS Women, War and Society, 1914–18: The Women at Work Collection, EMP 53/24 NWSC leaflet A.C. 59, original emphasis. For further comments on war savings propaganda and this dual message, see Simon Hancock, 'Duty and Personal Advantage Combined: The War Savings Movement in Pembrokeshire during the First World War', *Welsh History Review*, 31, no. 3 (2023).
6 TNA NATS 1/1286, 'More Collectors Needed', draft notice for press, 18 July 1917; 'Women and the War', *Illustrated War News*, 1 August 1917, 40; 'Margaret Osborne' [Goodman], 'The Woman's Part. How to Tackle Spring-Cleaning in War-Time', *Nuneaton Observer War Supplement*, 11 May 1918, 2. For further discussion, see Monger, 'Nothing Special?'; Paul Ward, 'Empire and the Everyday: Britishers and Imperialism in Women's Everyday Lives in the Great War', in Philip Buckner and R. Douglas Francis (eds), *Rediscovering the British World* (Calgary: University of Calgary Press, 2005).
7 TNA NATS 1/97, 'Sir Auckland Geddes at Plymouth', *Weekly Bulletin of the Ministry of National Service*, 15 November 1917, 37. For a local newspaper's record of his speech, differing from the Ministry's version, see 'Call to Service', *Western Morning News*, 13 November 1917, 5. For another angle on wasteful clothing, see Figure 14.
8 A. A. Milne, 'A Specialist. The Battalion Signalling Officer', *Newcastle Morning Herald and Miners' Advocate* (Australia), 1 April 1918, 6 (also published in the *Ballarat Courier, Launceston Examiner, Launceston Daily Telegraph* and *Lyttelton Times*), original ellipses; Lieutenant K. N. Colville, 'The Farrier. A Character Sketch', *Taranaki Herald*, 4 April 1918, 7 (also published in the *Rangitikei Advocate and Manawatu Argus* and *Ashburton Guardian*).
9 Monger, *Patriotism and Propaganda*, 11, 42–4, 55–8; on W. H. Smith, see also Stephen Colclough, '"No Such Bookselling Has Ever Before Taken Place in This Country": Propaganda and the Wartime Distribution Practices of W.H. Smith & Son', in Mary Hammond and Shafquat Towheed (eds), *Publishing in the First World War: Essays in Book History* (Basingstoke: Palgrave Macmillan, 2007). On rival meetings and violence, compare Millman, *Managing Domestic Dissent*, esp. ch. 6; Jon Lawrence, 'Public Space, Political Space', in Jay Winter and Jean-Louis Robert (eds), *Capital Cities at War: Paris, London, Berlin 1914-1919*, vol. 2, *A Cultural History* (Cambridge: Cambridge University Press, 2007) and David Monger, 'Transcending the Nation: Domestic Propaganda and Supranational Patriotism in Britain, 1917–18', in Paddock, *World War I and Propaganda*. On department stores, see Monger, 'Tangible Patriotism', 258 and on the holiday resort campaign, see TNA NATS1/1286, circular letters from Arthur Collins on Women's Army Auxiliary Corps Holiday Resorts Campaign, 26 and 28 June 1917. For posters and their variable display, see Aulich and Hewitt, *Seduction or Instruction?*, esp. 44–5, 87–91.
10 For a full discussion of the importance of ritual and familiarity, see Monger, 'Familiarity Breeds Consent?'; for violence's place in public politics, see Lawrence's various comments in *Speaking for the People*; *Electing Our Masters*; and 'The Transformation of British Public Politics after the First World War', *Past and Present*, 190, no. 1 (2006).

CHAPTER 18
RELIGION

Clerics no longer lead the masses; they are led by them.

Therefore it is not so curious that religion almost invariably lent its weight to augment war fervour. The Churches are on the side of the big guns. All forms of Christianity favoured the Great War. Only an infinitesimal number of professed Christians dissented ...

Clerics went out of their way to abjure peace and in its place to cherish and fortify war obsession.

The general complete failure of clerics to walk the way of Life and the enthusiasm with which they adopted the aberrations of belligerent madness are very strange. These perversities mark the completeness with which Society became infected by war psychosis.[1]

For the Christian pacifist Caroline Playne, revisiting the war in a lengthy chapter on the 'Failure of the Clerics', Britain's religious leaders, nationally and locally, betrayed the public by readily endorsing the war. Despite some general clerical statements favouring peace and opposing force, she condemned the willingness to add religious sanction to wider justifications of Britain's war. Her book appeared in 1931, during a peak of disillusioned commentary on the war, but Playne was no post-war rewriter of her views – she was an active pacifist and committee member of the critical UDC and her critique reflects severe disappointment at organized religion's support for war.[2] Religious commentary had a strong presence in wartime propaganda. Senior and local clerics alike actively contributed to propaganda, speaking and writing for various organizations, while wider commentary was tinged with religious and quasi-religious ideas. While Playne bemoaned this, another wartime commentator, Edward Heron-Allen (by 1918, editing a propaganda newspaper for MI7b, to be dropped over occupied France and Belgium), recorded attending a 'War Anniversary' service in August 1918. Many of these events were organized as propaganda by the NWAC, as discussed later. Despite the service, Heron-Allen sardonically noted 'a widely growing impression that if God could stop the war he is – like the Americans – putting off the moment of his intervention somewhat unduly'. Nonetheless, incorporating religious perspectives not only associated Britain's war with higher ideals, alongside the everyday messages discussed in Chapter 17, but also aimed to benefit from organized religion's ongoing cultural authority. Despite declining pre-war religious attendance, clerics retained cultural influence.[3]

Religious references were common among regular claims of British defence of civilization from enemy barbarism. As discussed in Chapter 11, propagandists particularly identified the German philosopher Nietzsche as representing a *Kultur* that disavowed decency and restraint in favour of necessity. The Oxford historian C. R. L. Fletcher writing one of the early, propagandist 'Oxford pamphlets' in 1914, noted that Nietzsche 'spent his life railing against the "superstition", as he called it, of Christianity, and against the virtues of pity, mercy and love'. By inference, British intervention was the reverse of German godlessness. A later propagandist, Liberal MP Charles McCurdy, writing for the NWAC in 1918, did not leave readers to infer virtue:

> We regard war as evil. The Germans regard war as a good and wholesome thing, a 'biological necessity', a 'divine institution. ...
>
> the Germans stand alone among the civilised nations to-day as a people who have been taught to regard as right what other peoples regard as wrong ... The whole people are trained to observe ... a new set of Commandments – the Commandments, not of God, but of the devil ...
>
> We must disarm Germany, substitute Right for Might in the settlement of any questions that may arise between Germany and her smaller nations, bury the Law of the Jungle, and restore the Ten Commandments as rules of civilised life in Europe.[4]

McCurdy's pamphlet, countering suggestions of a compromise peace with Germany, not only rejected German conduct but also superficially elevated Britain's war effort to a bid to recentre international relations in line with Biblical precepts.

McCurdy was particularly explicit in connecting the war and the Bible, but many secular propagandists either invoked it directly or spoke in broader religious terms. Contributors to the unofficial propaganda work *King Albert's Book* certainly freely invoked God – The former First Sea Lord, Baron Fisher, provided two sparse quotations as his contribution. A line from a *Times* report, asserting the rape and murder of a young woman during the invasion, followed a line from Jeremiah (51.56): 'The Lord God of recompences shall surely requite.' The following lines, not quoted by Fisher, who evidently expected his audience to understand the allusion, refer to 'that God to whom vengeance belongs, and will recompense it; who is a God of justice and of equity'. Britain, therefore, intervening on Belgium's behalf, enacted God's vengeance. Even less subtle, the *Observer* editor J. L. Garvin declared,

> We in England would rather be blotted out of the book of nations than that Belgium should not be lifted up from ruin and gloriously restored. To that cause we have pledged our all, and until our pledge is redeemed in such sort that the justice of an overruling God shall be made manifest through us, never can we know soul's comfort in our own land spared by war nor cease our efforts.

Garvin's conversion of his country into an avenging angel chimed with wider contemporary condemnation of German contempt for religion and civilization, apparently exemplified by shelling Reims Cathedral in September 1914. Bryce (later considered a chief purveyor of atrocity propaganda) wrote to the President of Harvard, noting the damage and suggesting a 'protest, influentially signed, from the U.S. against such acts would tell in Germany as nothing else would. People here are wondering when bombs will be dropped on Westminster Abbey.' Bryce feared British civilians already believed too easily in Germany's unlimited cruelty and that an independent inquiry was needed. Nonetheless, his note about Westminster Abbey further stressed the significance of religious symbols as markers of identity. Damaging a church that was also a national landmark was unthinkable. Despite Bryce's suggestion about US independence, meanwhile, Alan Kramer notes the damage at Reims poisoned US opinion considerably, even though the reasons for shelling were disputed between Germany and France.[5]

As noted by multiple scholars, wartime appeals were frequently couched in terms of sacrifice – soldiers willingly made the 'ultimate' sacrifice; civilians should, thus, uncomplainingly accept lesser ones. While not always used in a religious sense, it often was, as with the Amalgamated Society of Engineers member F. H. Rose's call in a NWAC pamphlet for members to recognize a 'holy and righteous impulse' to avoid industrial strife and increase output. At a war savings meeting in Tiverton, Devon, meanwhile, local MP Charles Carew insisted everybody

> must economise in spending money and in food ... [E]verybody should have brought home to them that the war was not merely being fought on the field of battle, but also by the support given to them from the homeland. No sacrifice of those who remained at home should be reckoned too great to give them encouragement in the righteous cause for which they were hourly risking their lives.

National and local savings activists then outlined their schemes. Both Rose's call to trade unionists and a 'social meeting' of war savings activists, while relatively prosaic and businesslike messages, leaned on religious terms to elevate their demands. Again, tolerating tougher working conditions and investing in war funds was, implicitly, not only good citizenship but also 'righteous'.[6]

Philip Jenkins suggests occasional 'pious rhetorical flourishes' are not enough to justify a definition of 'holy war'. Instead, 'repeatedly and centrally, official statements and propaganda [must] declare that the war is being fought for God's cause', the armed forces are 'sanctified' and the enemy is ungodly. Nonetheless, with all these criteria, he detects 'a powerful and consistent strain of holy war ideology'. The Press Bureau actively attempted to prevent references to a holy war between Britain and the Ottoman Empire:

> The attention of the Press is again drawn to the undesirability of publishing any article paragraph or picture suggesting that military operations against Turkey are in any sense a Holy War, a modern Crusade, or have anything whatever to do with religious questions. The British Empire is said to contain a hundred million Mohammodan [sic] subjects of the King and it is obviously mischievous to suggest that our quarrel with Turkey is one between Christianity and Islam.

This restriction did not, of course, apply to Britain's main enemy, Germany, whose kaiser was sometimes portrayed with horns and a tail. Further, Germany – a supposedly more 'civilized' Christian nation – was also condemned for allowing its Ottoman ally to conduct genocide against Armenian Christians. Propagandists failed to fully accept restrictions regarding a 'holy war' in the Middle East. The NWAC, for instance, celebrated Jerusalem's capture by reproducing a *Punch* cartoon (Figure 16) depicting Richard the Lionheart looking down on the city, declaring, 'My dream comes true!' Similarly, a lantern lecture prepared by the NWSC, entitled 'The Deliverance of the Holy Land', noted that the day the Turks left Jerusalem was 'the same date over 2,000 years before that Judas Maccabaeus drove out the heathen Seleucids in 165 B.C.' and that 'the Holy City [was] won back by heroic modern crusaders'. However, Eitan Bar-Yosef suggests that, despite careful attempts to stage-manage Jerusalem's capture for propaganda value, the Cabinet was disappointed to find it had not been used enough at home due to censorship restrictions.[7] Once again, the 'machine' did not function smoothly.

If the press was partly discouraged from mentioning holy war, many clerics felt less restraint. Albert Marrin suggests Germany's use of poison gas in April 1915, followed by the sinking of the *Lusitania* and publication of the Bryce Report on German atrocities in May, encouraged 'crusading-apocalyptic war hysteria'. Rev. Basil Bourchier, who Marrin considers typical, disliked Germany after humiliating treatment while working with the Red Cross in 1914. He wrote,

> Not only is this a Holy War, it is the holiest war that has ever been waged. The cause is the most sacred that man has been asked to defend ... The Christian man never has had less cause for misgiving for being a soldier ... Odin is ranged against Christ, and Berlin is seeking to prove its supremacy over Bethlehem. Every shot that is fired, every bayonet thrust that gets home, every life that is sacrificed, is in very truth 'for His Name's sake'.[8]

Though not formal propaganda, Bourchier's assertions chimed with those by laymen like McCurdy and Garvin, above. Britons could again rest assured their cause was not only just but righteous. Such statements illustrate why pacifists like Playne condemned clerics' wartime 'failure'. However, other scholars note more complex examples of clerical behaviour. Robert Beaken recently reconsidered Arthur Winnington-Ingram, the wartime Bishop of London – a figure notorious for his apparent enthusiasm for the war and Playne's exemplar of 'the blood-lust of ecclesiastics'. Despite his reputation, genuine belief in the war as just and enthusiasm for recruitment, Beaken notes that, both early and later in the war, Winnington-Ingram called for kindness towards Germans and disavowed air raid reprisals, a point also noted by Alan Wilkinson. Similarly, Wilkinson records that the Archbishop of York Cosmo Lang attracted severe hostility after generosity towards the kaiser in a speech, the stress apparently turning his hair prematurely white.[9] Despite this, Lang, with the Archbishop of Canterbury, affirmed the war's justice. As noted in Chapter 2, he later took a prominent part in propaganda, touring the United States and promoting Anglo-US ties.

Religion

Figure 16 Reproduction of Bernard Partridge cartoon, 'The Last Crusade'.
Source: *Reality*, 26 December 1917, 1.

While claiming his tour, apparently involving eighty-five speeches to over 100,000 people, was 'unconnected with any official propaganda', Lang's recollections were published and distributed by the NWAC, drawing on a speech in London it organized, while his tour was aided by Geoffrey Butler's Bureau of Information in New York. The US press was aware that, though 'sent to us by the Church', he had really 'come to us at the request of the British Government, and with the approval of the whole English people'. At Harvard, Lang told his audience that, in joining Britain, the United States had 'found her soul', but its impact 'depends upon how far you will throw your whole moral force toward carrying through this sacrifice'. Lang feared US remoteness would undermine its urgency, since it would not see its cities' inhabitants 'flee into Winter nights ... to escape falling bombs from German airplanes'. Despite this, doubts about Lang remained in Britain, where a *Globe* article noted his call to 'think kindly' towards Germany and condemned (via abstract references to German crimes) his 'misplaced soft-heartedness towards a ruthless enemy, who only despises us'.[10]

Lang was one of the most eminent religious propagandists, but many more contributed. Four years before his US visit, Rev. Dugald MacFadyen was credited as Britain's first propagandist there, touring north-eastern cities as a precursor to wider religious propaganda. Macfadyen declared that he undertook 'four distinct projects' with endorsement by Bryce, former ambassador to the United States:

> He went to the U.S. intending to speak on the war, fixing the responsibility on Germany, to counteract German misstatements in the Press as to our motives, to sound American opinion on certain points, and to write letters to the Press as to our motives, and fourthly to appeal to Americans on behalf of Belgian refugees.

MacFadyen reported back on US opinion, noting the 'hidden dread and suspicion of British maritime power', which was 'only partially allayed' by stressing Britain's enthusiasm for free trade. One US critic noted wider efforts to reach all religious sects, as part of which propagandists 'popularized and almost canonized Cardinal Mercier', a Belgian Catholic priest imprisoned by Germany.[11] As noted in Chapter 14, others like the Bishop of Southwark made similar efforts elsewhere.

At home, meanwhile, clerics assisted by writing, speaking, chairing events or serving on committees. In Ramsgate, in March 1917, the previous local recruiting committee was converted into a national service committee following a national appeal, with five reverends among the members, while, from Birmingham, Rev. R. J. Campbell demanded 'every pulpit in the land ring with this message: Go and do something if you have any time to spare at all. It is urgent; it is your plain duty.' Campbell, here, added his position's weight to the kinds of quotidian propaganda discussed in Chapter 17. Doing any little thing was thus sanctified. Similarly, in Edinburgh, the Church of Scotland's Moderator told its Commission of Assembly that ministers must do all they could to support the call for national service, setting 25 March as a day for ministers to promote the cause, while members of the Aberdeen Presbytery were reminded that, if other national service was beyond them, they could at least contribute by organizing war savings. In Wales a poster, in English and Welsh, appealed to Welsh free churches to make similar efforts.[12]

As the national service discussion among different denominations made clear, clerics felt the need not only to do patriotic service but also to do and promote it publicly. This was also the case in a nationwide set piece in August 1918, the War Anniversary, often organized by the NWAC (which inherited the idea from the CCNPO), featuring multi-denominational processions and services attended by various civic groups. In Sheffield Cathedral, 1,800 people attended, with another 500 unable to find places. If Heron-Allen was right that many wondered what was taking a sympathetic God so long, many were, at least, still keen to know. Participants, including members of the Corporation, University, Church Burgesses, Board of Guardians, members of 'various regiments' and two groups representing discharged servicemen, as well as the US Consul and soldiers, heard Rev. F. T. Cooper, chaplain to the Base Hospital, discuss

> a struggle between the religion of revelation and a materialistic creed, the worship of the State. In fighting for righteousness and freedom, he said, we were fighting in the very spirit of Christ ... If the cause was to triumph, it would not do so by mere lip service ... The sooner we realised that we were fighting for spiritual redemption, the better it would be for us in progress through this war. We must be true to our sacred dead, and pray to be worthy of the sacrifices which had been made for us.

Cooper's sermon reiterated many stock lines of religious-infused propaganda, emphasizing sacrifice and an existential contest between Christ-like righteousness and materialism. The newspaper noted further services at the Cathedral as well as others for Methodists, Baptists, Catholics and Jews, where a rabbi, Barnet J. Cohen, told an audience including Jewish soldiers that 'their prayers were for a universal and lasting peace ... [which] could only be brought about by the destruction of the forces of militarism'. Nonetheless, Cohen disavowed any desire for 'crushing the enemy'; peace was the ultimate goal, not victory.[13]

Religious ideas remained meaningful in British propaganda – not only were they invoked, comfortably, by lay propagandists, but religious leaders, nationally and locally, willingly involved themselves in propaganda activities. Despite suggestions of the war as a modernist departure, religious language and voices were evidently still expected to resonate. Playne expressed honest revulsion for clerics' willing participation in propaganda, but later scholarship has, sometimes, too lazily dismissed such efforts as surrendering to nationalism. Such critiques, like many of propaganda more generally, often seem rooted in assumptions that people were duped by non-existent atrocities, which modern research shows is a false assumption. Also, similarly to condemnations of atrocity propagandists, criticism of excessive religious propaganda tends to identify the most extreme rhetoric. This ignores those, like Lang or Cohen, who believed the war was just and must be won, but also believed, and said, that this was necessary to restore decent conduct, not to kill for the sake of killing.

Notes

1. Caroline E. Playne, *Society at War, 1914–1916* (Boston: Houghton Mifflin, 1931), 188, 219.
2. See Richard Epsler, 'Caroline Playne: The Activities and Absences of a Campaigning Author in First World War London', *London Journal*, 41, no. 3 (2016); for disillusionment and reshaped memories of wartime, see Watson, *Fighting Different Wars*, ch. 6.
3. Heron-Allen's diary, 5 August 1918, in Brian W. Harvey and Carol Fitzgerald (eds), *Edward Heron-Allen's Journal of the Great War: From Sussex Shore to Flanders Fields* (Lewes: Sussex Record Society, 2002), 205. For the Church's enhanced cultural authority, alongside reduced social authority, see Arthur Burns, 'The Authority of the Church', in Peter Mandler (ed.), *Liberty and Authority in Victorian Britain* (Oxford: Oxford University Press, 2006).
4. C. L. R. Fletcher, *The Germans: What They Covet* (Oxford pamphlet no. 7, 1914), cited in Wallace, *War and the Image*, 50; Charles A. McCurdy, *To Restore the Ten Commandments: The Basis of a Permanent Peace for Europe* (London: Hodder & Stoughton, n.d. [1918]), 2, 4–5, 13.
5. Fisher and Garvin contributions in Caine, *King Albert's Book*, 48, 74; Gregory, *Last Great War*, 52; BLO, Bryce Papers, MS Bryce USA 23, Bryce to A. L. Lowell, 2 October 1914; Kramer, *Dynamic of Destruction*, 18–19. For Reims in French and German propaganda, see Lambourne, 'First World War Propaganda'.
6. On sacrifice and religion, see, for example, Gregory, *Last Great War*, ch. 5; Monger, *Patriotism and Propaganda*, esp. 174–80, quotation from Rose at 175; 'War Savings in Tiverton District', *Tiverton Gazette*, 30 October 1917, 2.
7. Philip Jenkins, *The Great and Holy War: How World War I Changed Religion For Ever* (Oxford: Lion, 2014), 6–7; TNA HO139/45, Press Bureau D Notice 607, 15 November 1917; see also the earlier request for restraint in HO139/44, D363, 21 February 1916; 'The Deliverance of the Holy Land, or, the Modern Crusaders' (NWSC Lantern Lecture A.C. 102), 7; Eitan Bar-Yosef, 'The Last Crusade? British Propaganda and the Palestine Campaign, 1917–18, *Journal of Contemporary History*, 36, no. 1 (2001), 102–3.
8. Basil Bourchier, *"For All We Have and Are"* (London: Skeffington & Son, 1915), 2–3, cited in Albert Marrin, *The Last Crusade: The Church of England in the First World War* (Durham, NC: Duke University Press, 1974), 140 and see 141 for Marrin's wider description; for Bourchier's early-war experience, see *For All We Have*, xi–xv. For similar comments on clerics' excessive zeal, see A. J. Hoover, *God, Germany, and Britain in the Great War: A Study in Clerical Nationalism* (New York: Praeger, 1989).
9. Robert Beaken, *The Church of England and the Home Front, 1914–1918: Civilians, Soldiers and Religion in Wartime Colchester* (Woodbridge: Boydell Press, 2015), 201–5; Playne, *Society at War*, 210; Alan Wilkinson, *The Church of England and the First World War*, 2nd edn (London: SCM Press, 1996), 217–19.
10. York, *Hands Across the Atlantic*, 5–6; TNA T102/17, NWAC Meetings Register entry no. 3114; W. G. Lyddon, *British War Missions to the United States, 1914–1918* (Oxford: Oxford University Press, 1938), 139, 186; Lambeth Palace Library, London, Cosmo Gordon Lang Papers, Lang 280, clipping by James Walter Smith in unidentified Boston newspaper, n.d; 'Bishop Lang Warns Boston of War Trials', unidentified newspaper, n.d.; '"Slop" About Germans', *Globe*, 24 May 1918, 6.
11. Lyddon, *British War Missions*, 185; 'Rev. Dugald MacFadyen', *The Citizen* (Letchworth), 12 February 1915, 2; 'Declares German Raid Aided British', *Evening Star* (Washington, DC), 21 December 1914, 4; D. MacFadyen (letter), 'American Opinion on the War', *Manchester Guardian*, 25 January 1914, 4; Peterson, *Propaganda for War*, 28.
12. 'National Service', *Thanet Advertiser*, 10 March 1917, 5; 'National Service. Appeal by Rev. R.J. Campbell' (letter), *Western Morning News*, 19 March 1917, 5; 'National Service. Church

of Scotland Takes Action', *Aberdeen Evening Express*, 7 March 1918, 3; 'National Service for Ministers', *Aberdeen Press and Journal*, 28 March 1917, 2; TNA NATS1/1091, 'National Service. To the Free Churches of Wales and Monmouthshire' (poster, n.d.).
13 'Solemn Intercessions in Sheffield', *Sheffield Daily Telegraph*, 5 August 1918, 2. For wider discussion of the War Anniversary, see Monger, 'Familiarity Breeds Consent?', 524–7.

CHAPTER 19
SOLDIERS

While, as Chapter 18 discussed, propaganda was often tinged with religious language and imagery, unquestionably its true First World War icon was the soldier. Domestic propaganda, particularly, used soldiers to justify nearly all demands for civilian actions. However hard civilians' lives might be, however much they had already sacrificed, soldiers did more. If possible, soldiers themselves delivered messages and demands to the public; if not, other propagandists happily spoke for them. In propaganda coverage, soldiers – willing, if necessary, to make the 'ultimate sacrifice' – were largely infallible, embodying everything good and virtuous. Further, praising soldiers was often localized, with acknowledgements of a local regiment potentially reminding audiences of relatives in uniform and making broader points relatable. As the war progressed, propagandists also addressed soldiers themselves, but such efforts veered away from the wider representation of soldiers, instead focusing on humour, leisure and future opportunities.

Other servicemen – sailors and airmen – were also discussed by propagandists, but coverage was substantially lighter. Dual Ministry of Food posters, calling on people to save food, showed a soldier and sailor, respectively, with the implied message that food economy was a step towards matching servicemen's equally important efforts. However, after the war's early naval battles, the navy largely (besides 1916's Battle of Jutland) remained on important but unspectacular blockade and patrol duty. By 1918, the NWAC felt the need to publish two pamphlets reminding the public of the navy's role. Both reproduced a parliamentary speech by Lloyd George, suggesting the navy was taken for granted. He noted that it kept international trade routes open and enabled the transportation of US troops through its destruction of German submarines and that Germany attempted victory at sea (by resuming unrestricted submarine warfare) before their 1918 military offensive because they knew naval success would end the war. Thus, simply by existing, 'the British Navy wins a great victory every day, and … upon that Navy and its mastery of the sea all the effective power of all the Allies does actually in the last resort depend'. The pamphlets suggested propagandists' recognition that naval contributions were underappreciated – a concern similarly seen in the belated despatch of a British naval officer to speak on the subject in the United States.[1] This neglect was evident compared to much more common praise of soldiers' endurance and patriotism.

Airmen also received limited attention. Flyers were a new part of the armed forces, with 'only 66 aeroplanes and 100 men belonging to the Royal Flying Corps, and 64 aeroplanes and 800 men in the Royal Naval Air Service' in 1914. By 1918, these numbers stood at 10,000 planes and 100,000 men, with reportedly '30,000 miles a week … covered by the flying patrols' at sea, and more planes constructed each week than in the whole of 1914, according to a propaganda handbook. MI7b propagandists like Frederick Sleath thus began publicizing airmen's exploits in ways that stressed daring, risks and bravery. One article, published in New Zealand, described a 'thrilling duel' between two 'sportsmanlike' British and German pilots, romanticizing lethal combat as an entertaining and somehow nobler spectacle than industrial military conflict. Another described the near misses and skilful safe return of a pilot blinded by fog. Here, the airman battled climate and technology rather than an armed opponent. A third, published the same day, explicitly evoked the renowned heroic sacrifice of the Antarctic adventurer Captain Oates in describing the experience of an unnamed pilot and mechanic who grounded their plane in the African desert. Low on water, the pilot (an officer) 'had gone out into the desert and blown his brains out' to give the mechanic more chance of survival. 'It was his privilege to do so', Sleath wrote, because 'wherever the sacrifice is demanded Britons will lay down their lives for the sake of their kin'. The pilot's decision 'added to the glorious wreath of self-sacrifice which the years have woven to the honour of the British soldier'.[2] The exoticism of new aerial technology mixed here with longer-standing conventions of heroism – not only did Sleath invoke Oates; his article's title invoked a famous Biblical passage, sanctifying the pilot's sacrifice in another example of the casual propaganda use of religion. Further, as Sleath's final comment noted, airmen still had an uncertain place in public understanding – while their deeds offered exciting new angles for describing combat, the unnamed officer's act added to soldiers' overall credit. Despite some attention to wartime aviation 'aces', hinted at by Sleath's first article, here the pilot was an airborne soldier.

An obvious reason to spend more time discussing soldiers was the greater likely connection with audiences. If there were 450,000 sailors and 100,000 airmen by 1918, as the NWAC's handbook suggested, 7,500,000 soldiers were enlisted. Propagandists were thus far more likely to find audiences with connections to soldiers. The once prominent assumption that civilians and soldiers were estranged because of the war – that civilians did not understand (or even care about) soldiers' experiences and that soldiers withdrew from contact as a result – has been thoroughly disproved. Civilians remained eager to learn about soldiers' experiences, helped in the war's early years by letters published in local newspapers, as McCartney notes. Soldiers, Michael Roper shows, remained keen to keep contact with home, while ideas of soldiers' sacrifice on behalf of home were relevant to both communities.[3] Unsurprisingly, therefore, such references in propaganda were widespread.

Associating soldiers with sacrifice was not a justification found by propagandists after years of heavy casualties; it featured in early recruiting propaganda too. Reflecting both the reverence for Antarctic self-sacrifice shown by Sleath and the religious validation of soldiers' service noted in Chapter 18, speakers at a recruitment meeting in Burton, Staffordshire, in September 1914 emphasized sacrifice strongly, tying it to national identity. The Conservative MP and Staffordshire Territorial Colonel John Gretton took a simultaneously immodest and morbid approach to inspiring his audience:

> I suppose our ideal of Englishmen, English freedom, English justice, and English truth, and English religion has been the most inspiring thing in the history of the

past three or four centuries which has fired every human race on the face of the earth – (applause). There is nowhere that you may go where you will not find the grave of an Englishman who has died for England – (applause). The sea is sown with English dead, who will rise again at the trumpet sound ... What sent Captain Scott to the North Pole [*sic*] – and Captain Oates – to die gloriously in the dreary desert of snow and ice, except the love of England? That is our great inheritance.

Following Gretton, Baptist pastor James Porteous added that, despite his preference for peace, Britain had to fight and, therefore, he was bound to help recruit soldiers:

If we believe – as the great mass of the people of this country believe – that our cause is a righteous one, we are justified in asking God to prosper it ... It is because our soldiers are men who have, of their own free will, given themselves to the defence of their country, that they prove the most stalwart and most reliable of all warriors ... The love of one's country is a noble and an ennobling passion. It is almost religious in its power to expel self-seeking propensities. It is a force to lift men above party, above personal aims and pursuits, and to beget in them a spirit of self-sacrifice and contempt for pain and loss.[4]

Gretton and Porteous could hardly be accused of understatement, and it is perhaps easy to see how a soldier like Wilfred Owen might condemn 'the old lie' of patriotic sacrifice, but their (seemingly popular) rhetoric was echoed in official PRC messages. A reproduced handwritten and signed appeal by PRC presidents (and party leaders) Herbert Asquith, Andrew Bonar Law and Arthur Henderson in November concluded that while the 'difficulties and dangers' were great, they awaited further enlistments 'with confidence, relying on the spirit and self-sacrifice of our fellow country men'. A PRC pamphlet quoting Asquith and Lloyd George in 1915, meanwhile, noted that soldiers, sailors, workers and employers were all 'partners and co-operators in one great exercise'. Everyone had a part to play.[5] Such appeals recognized the need for industrial workers as well as soldiers.

Where recruiters led, others followed. The classicist Gilbert Murray, speaking for the FRM at King's College London in 1916, declared himself proud of not only soldiers and sailors, whose 'violated and nameless graves' on European battlefields equalled those of eminent Britons in Westminster Abbey. He was also proud of workers, foregoing usual working conditions to accept overtime and work on holidays, and of the government's and civil servants' patriotic leadership despite unmerited press criticism. He concluded by depicting ranks of exhausted soldiers filing into trenches. The country was 'worth that sacrifice', he claimed, because its cause was just and its effort united. War savings propaganda, meanwhile, distinguished soldiers and investors: 'The fighter makes sacrifices when he fights. The lender makes no sacrifice' – investors would profit from their investment: it was the least they could do.[6]

Critical voices, too, addressed servicemen's sacrifice. UDC Secretary E. D. Morel denied hostile suggestions of a lack of sensibility towards the courage and suffering of the brave men in the battle line ... Our movement is entirely reconcilable with the most fervent admiration for our brave soldiers and sailors ... It is on behalf of these men ... that our efforts are directed, efforts which are calculated to give the greatest permanent value to all their sacrifices.

A further leaflet quoted several soldiers' approving comments on the UDC and its campaign.[7] No matter the cause, reference to soldiers supposedly validated it.

Widespread sympathy meant soldiers' own voices were particularly welcome in propaganda. MI7b's writers, drawn from experienced authors serving in the army, produced articles for the Dominion press – a 1918 War Office report suggested 400–500 articles a week were sent to 200 papers; another report claimed 7,500 articles between September 1916 and the Armistice.[8] Generally, the author's full name and rank were provided, sometimes meaning a potential double impact – readers identified both a soldier's voice and that of a noted author like Milne, discussed previously, or the Irish poet and novelist Patrick MacGill. MI7b pieces took many forms – critiques of Germany, factual descriptions of army life, humorous pieces, poetry and fictional stories all appeared. MacGill's contributions included the light-hearted fictional exploits of a trio of trench comrades, who appeared in several articles, exemplifying soldiers' humorous endurance of their situation. However, his pieces also sometimes took a more serious tone. 'Mud' described winter conditions on the Western Front:

> The plain of Northern France and Flanders is one sea of slush and slime, with trenches that are ditches and shell-holes that are mere cesspools ...
>
> Over all this dreary waste of country an ardent, energetic life is stirring. Brave soldiers, apparently unconscious of their own worth, knowing not self-glory or self-pity, live a life, heavy in physical suffering, doing the duties soberly and steadily, and endure, despite all the worry and trouble of their existence.

The article asserted the equal heroism of infantrymen, artillerymen, pioneers, cooks, drivers, signallers, stretcher-bearers and others, all playing their parts in awful conditions. A conventional tribute to soldierly heroism, the piece nonetheless conveyed at least part of trench life's misery. 'Mud' was one of at least eleven MacGill articles in which the cold felt by soldiers featured prominently. Some, like 'The Samaritan in Khaki', played the topic for laughs, with his recurring character, Spudhole Bubb, reviving comrades' spirits with a bottle of rum. Another, however, noted that 'winter is never a nice period for a man to find himself alone in a sap, looking out on the dead men in front, and thinking of things that come to the mind of a man who is in close touch with death'.[9] If MI7b propaganda did not confront Dominion civilians with every horror of the trenches, neither did it always romanticize soldiers' experiences. Soldier propagandists found ways to bring home some of their comrades' suffering.

Soldiers could also sometimes demand more than civilian propagandists. By 1918, propaganda often trod carefully around civilian morale, recognizing increasing war weariness. Requests or demands were generally balanced by praise and thanks. Soldiers, however, could be blunter. Captain Robert Gee told Leicester residents 'they heard too much about people being sick and tired of the war'; soldiers had things much worse. The war was not about 'Glory', as every soldier knew. Civilians should stop complaining and invest in war savings. Gee grew up in Leicester's cottage homes orphanage before winning a Victoria Cross during the 1917 Battle of Cambrai. He was a genuine local hero, doubly empowered to demand greater efforts: 'In soldierly ruggedness the Cottage Houses V.C. gave the people of Leicester a straight talk on duty and discipline', wrote a local editor, who endorsed his message but felt Gee judged the public too harshly.[10] Bairnsfather's cartoon, 'A Parcel Worth Holding on For' (Figure 17), made similar points less severely. His famous soldier-character, Old Bill, by then serving MI7b (and, here, the NWAC) stands atop a ladder, labelled 'patience', reaching for a large parcel at the top of a Christmas tree ('the sort of peace we want') rather than the smaller and easier reached 'peace of a sort'. To reach the best parcel 'the man in the street' needed to hold the ladder steady a little longer: soldiers would get the job done properly, if civilians supported them long enough.

While soldier propagandists might tell uncomfortable truths, propaganda to soldiers themselves generally avoided demands or statements of high ideals in favour of more concrete present or future concerns. As Chapter 3 noted, images of soldiers with children were regularly provided in a propaganda newspaper for soldiers on leave as a comforting image. Organizations interested in providing 'improving' books for soldiers at the front soon recognized their much greater desire for adventure and detective novels than 'useful' reading. Similarly, soldiers' enthusiasm for sport and gambling was not only confined to sporting contests close at hand – copies of newspapers like the *Athletic News* were eagerly sought as a means for soldiers to keep up with sporting news from home. The NWAC responded by including a regular column of sports and leisure news in its newspaper for soldiers on leave, *Welcome*. The column, paid for as propaganda, offered no patriotic or motivational interpretation of the sport and entertainment discussed. It simply gave an undemanding, hopefully comforting, reminder of British civilian life. Likewise, *Welcome* provided varied visual depictions of an idealized home. Young soldiers were portrayed – often in leafy, rural settings (an antidote to MacGill's cold cesspools) – with young women, offering promises of future romance, while married soldiers were catered to by images of wives and domestic bliss. Finally, as noted in Chapter 10, recognizing soldiers' embrace of humour, propagandists included jokes and cartoons, while humourists like Bairnsfather and Milne were incorporated into propaganda activity. NWAC efforts to foster affection for home, while avoiding high-minded or bloodthirsty content, in propaganda to soldiers again undermines common misconceptions about propaganda's one-dimensional tone and approach.[11]

Soldiers' life-risking service granted them nearly absolute authority. While politicians and civilian propagandists might be treated sceptically, propagandists of all stripes leaned on soldiers' authority when seeking greater domestic contributions. Soldiers themselves wrote and spoke propaganda with a conviction rooted in certainty about their importance and rightful expectations of audiences. While, as previously seen, propagandists also

Figure 17 Reproduction of Bruce Bairnsfather cartoon, 'A Parcel Worth Holding on For'.
Source: *Reality*, 17 November 1917, 1. National Archives Library (author's photograph).

Soldiers

invoked divine sanction, there was arguably no higher truth in wartime propaganda than that provided by soldiers. Nonetheless, as Chapter 20 discusses further, truthfulness – not a trait commonly associated with the medium – was an important feature of wider propaganda.

Notes

1. 'Do Your Bit! Save Food' (Food Control poster no. 54 – soldier edition, n.d. [1917]); 'Do Your Bit. Save Food' (Food Control poster no. 56 – sailor edition, 1917); David Lloyd George, *The British Navy's Part* (NWAC *Searchlight* series, no. 24, 1918); *What Is the Navy Doing?* (London: W.H. Smith, n.d. [1918]) – quotation from the latter pamphlet; Lyddon, *British War Missions*, 190–1.
2. *Aims and Effort*, 70–3; Second Lieutenant F. J. Sleath, 'The Challenge from the Sky', *Dominion*, 26 November 1917, 7; Second-Lieutenant E. J. [*sic*] Sleath, 'Fogged. An Airman's Adventure', *Lyttelton Times*, 9 January 1918, 9; Second Lieutenant F. J. Sleath, '"That a Man Should Lay Down His Life". A Sacrifice in the Desert', *Dominion*, 9 January 1918, 4. This article appeared in several other New Zealand papers. On the fame and wide repetition of Oates's sacrifice, see Max Jones, *The Last Great Quest: Captain Scott's Antarctic Sacrifice* (Oxford: Oxford University Press, 2003), 202–18, 255, 270.
3. *Aims and Effort*, 65, 71; McCartney, *Citizen Soldiers*; Roper, *Secret Battle*, esp. chs. 1–2; Gregory, *Last Great War*, 131–6; Helen B. McCartney, 'The First World War Soldier and His Contemporary Image in Britain', *International Affairs*, 90, no. 2 (2014); Alexander Watson and Patrick Porter, 'Bereaved and Aggrieved: Combat Motivation and the Ideology of Sacrifice in the First World War', *Historical Research*, 83, no. 219 (2010); Monger, 'Soldiers, Propaganda and Ideas of Home'.
4. 'Burton's Patriotic Meeting', *Burton Chronicle*, 1 October 1914, 5.
5. BLO, John Johnson Collection, Box 3, Untitled reproduced handwritten appeal from PRC presidents, November 1914; *"Partners in One Great Enterprise"*.
6. Gilbert Murray, 'How We Stand Now', in *For The Right*, 98–100; *Keep It Up!* (NWSC leaflet no. 302, 1918).
7. E. D. Morel, *War and Diplomacy* (UDC leaflet no. 11, 1915), 3–4; *Our Soldiers and the Union of Democratic Control* (UDC leaflet no. 8, n.d. [1915]).
8. TNA INF4/4B, 'Letter from War Office to Treasury: April 1918'; INF4/1B, 'Military Press Control: A History of the Work of MI7, 1914–1919' (1920), 20.
9. Rifleman Patrick MacGill (all), 'Mud', *The Mercury* (Hobart), 3 April 1918, 6; 'The Samaritan in Khaki', *The Queenslander* (Brisbane), 2 March 1918, 43; 'The Give and Take of War', *The Telegraph* (Brisbane), 30 May 1918, 5.
10. Gee, quoted in Monger, *Patriotism and Propaganda*, 190; see also Monger, 'Soldiers, Propaganda and Ideas of Home', 347–9; for the second quotation, see 'V.C.'s Straight Talk' (editorial), *Leicester Daily Post*, 13 July 1918, 2.
11. Marcella P. Sutcliffe, 'Reading at the Front: Books and Soldiers in the First World War', *Paedagogica Historica*, 52, nos. 1–2 (2016), 111; Fuller, *Troop Morale*, 85–94; Eliza Riedi and Tony Mason, '"Leather" and the Fighting Spirit: Sport in the British Army in World War I', *Canadian Journal of History*, 41, no. 3 (2006), 500; David Monger, 'Sporting Journalism and the Maintenance of British Servicemen's Ties to Civilian Society in First World War Propaganda', *Sport in History*, 30, no. 3 (2010); Monger, 'Soldiers, Propaganda and Ideas of Home'.

CHAPTER 20
TRUTH

One of the most enduring – and lazy – assumptions about British First World War propaganda, still indulged by some professional historians of the war, let alone non-specialists, is that it was fundamentally dishonest and deceptive. As the propaganda discussed in numerous previous chapters shows, much of it involved open efforts to persuade audiences to act and think in particular ways. If the PRC, NWSC, NWAC and other groups did not include 'propaganda' in their names, their involvement with it was evident, understood and sometimes directly declared. More material than might be expected was bland and straightforward, as Chapter 9 discussed. Most propaganda drew from a basis of fact, which propagandists interpreted for audiences in ways that helped their cause.

Even the heads of organizations that concealed their role, like Masterman at Wellington House or Cockerill at the Directorate of Secret Intelligence, stressed that their propaganda relied on truthful material. Cockerill 'attached the greatest importance to ensuring the factual truth of all we published abroad, not the whole truth, but so much of it as was likely to be helpful to our cause'. This comment did not admit deception but rather described the persuasive use of truthful material to serve his organization's purposes. Expecting propagandists (or, indeed, almost anybody attempting a persuasive argument) to fully discuss every angle and perspective, including those contradicting their own, to qualify as honest and truthful, and assuming that failure to do so is immoral, is unreasonable both intellectually and practically. While some propaganda speeches and pamphlets were long-winded or complex, most material conveyed clear, straightforward messages. Truthful content was valuable for propaganda – it was difficult to contradict the facts behind interpretations, even if the interpretation itself was rejected. Providing dishonest or deceptive material, meanwhile, would be all very well provided nobody noticed. However, it was very risky. People, generally, dislike being lied to: if lies were discovered, a propagandist or organization's credibility would be severely undermined. Anticipating Cockerill's comment about useful truth less positively, the US interwar analyst Peterson claimed British propagandists used 'only that part of the truth which benefited their cause': 'Falsehoods were used, but they were comparatively unimportant. It was much easier and much safer to give warped interpretations.'[1] Most British propaganda provided interpretations of truthful material that favoured their cause and discredited their enemies. This was not dishonest.

Research over the past twenty-five years shows that propaganda's negative reputation was largely a post-war development. As discussed in Chapter 1, a combination of wartime critics like Ponsonby, German nationalists explaining away defeat and US analysts lamenting unnecessary intervention established an image of dishonest British propaganda. Recent analyses, partly exploring shifting dictionary definitions, note the largely neutral definition of propaganda before 1914 and the truthful roots of even exaggerated and 'mythic' material. They also stress limited connections of propaganda with political purposes and the surprising rarity of negative definitions – despite the post-war backlash – until the mid-1970s, when reactions against the Cold War, and particularly the Vietnam War, developed this perspective more strongly. 'Modern propaganda is not the same entity as it was one hundred years ago', concludes Fiona Houston:

> What many authors wrote during the First World War *was* propaganda; it was produced with the intention of influencing public opinion and supporting official aims ... yet at the actual time of their writing the act of producing propaganda was a far more innocent undertaking than it eventually became.[2]

This does not mean there was no wartime criticism of propaganda, of course. Dissenting parliamentary voices protested state funding for the NWAC in 1918, for example, while the UDC member Hobson challenged the notion of wartime 'truth' in a satire in the *Nation*. Here, an imaginary former Oxford philosophy student 'revealed' supposed government methods:

> Truth is a raw material, infinitely malleable and adaptable to the purposes of the State ... This idea of the relativity and adaptability of knowledge is then generalized and applied in the processes of our laboratory, for producing out of the same raw material the separate truths which war requires for the home consumer, the Ally, the neutral, and the enemy. The crude fact is the same for all; everything depends on the treatment ...
>
> The public mind must not be allowed to be confused or depressed by information which, however accurate and even interesting, is not nutritious.

Hobson, clearly, did not consider a basis of truth enough, disliking the creative interpretations that followed. His hostility expanded in a post-war foreword to an analysis of 'Press Propaganda', where he suggested 'politicians, journalists and other literary gentlemen ... deemed it to be their duty to suspend the ordinary canons of truth in the interests of victory, and to allow their inventive imagination a license fitted to the needs of the situation'.[3] By 1928 (in line with late-twenties critiques of propaganda), Hobson moved from satirizing the interpretation of truthful content to asserting that propagandists simply lied. Nonetheless, both the openness of much British propaganda and its usually truthful roots show that assumptions of fundamental dishonesty, often the starting point for casual thinking about propaganda in this period, should be abandoned.

Hobson was certainly right that propaganda was consumed by different audiences. Thus, while Wellington House propaganda circulated indirectly, with the novelist and

MP Sir Gilbert Parker sending supposedly personal letters accompanying propaganda materials to influential US figures, domestic propaganda was much more open about its origins. PRC recruiting posters clearly identified their source – there was no suggestion these were spontaneous calls to enlist – and the local press openly discussed the PRC's propaganda work. In St Austell, Cornwall, an editor noted that, after local efforts, the 'work of recruiting propaganda now devolves upon the Mid Cornwall "Parliamentary" Recruiting Committee ... and we commend to them the idea of a more personal approach to prospective candidates', which he hoped would appeal to a generation untouched by previous wars. In Guildford, Surrey, party organizers informed the existing local recruiting committee that new PRC measures would add to their existing 'excellent work' through meetings 'in every large village and town ... as to the cost of the propaganda or campaign if that were not met locally the committee in London would bear the expense'.[4] Both examples treated references to propaganda as uncontroversial; indeed, the Cornish editor suggested an improvement.

This continued through the war, with similar references to propaganda arrangements undertaken for war savings, national service and (as noted in Chapter 9) NWAC work. A 1917 report in Lincoln asserted that national service 'propaganda offers some reassurance' to white-collar workers, concerned about losing income or status, and praised the 'stirring propaganda speech' of the former mining union official Barnet Kenyon, MP, who 'urged the national as against the individual point of view. This was everyone's war. From Buckingham Palace to the humble thatched cottage, we were all in it.' Other speakers labelled their own efforts, explicitly, as propaganda, suggesting little concern that this invalidated their arguments. Launching a War Loan in London in June 1915, the Prime Minister Asquith declared:

> This meeting was called not only to advertise the merits and advantages of the War Loan, but to initiate a concerted movement for what may be called war economy. My text, and the text of all those who will take part in this propaganda, is a very simple one ... Waste on the part either of individuals or of classes, which is always foolish and short-sighted, is in these times nothing short of a national danger.

In Wigan in late 1917, meanwhile, the Conservative MP R. J. Neville explicitly distinguished his own open work for the NWAC from supposedly false German propaganda:

> Some people liked propaganda. He hated it unless it came out into the open – (applause) – and they knew where it came from – (hear, hear) – honest propaganda was a fine thing, but treacherous, lying, and dishonest propaganda should be dealt with as some damned serpent.[5]

Such statements as Asquith's and Neville's showed continuing belief that audiences would accept openly acknowledged propaganda. There was nothing inherently disgraceful about the word or act. Meetings hosted by Britain's domestic propaganda groups did not mask their purposes and were widely reported. This, in many ways, extended pre-war political communication, where politicians proved themselves by open communication with the public, accepting heckling and even violent reactions as part of the process.[6] These were open attempts at persuasion that continued pre-war methods.

Neville's separation of his own efforts from the 'German insinuation, German falsehood, German cunning' that supposedly weakened morale in Russia and Italy did not make the obvious point that British propagandists similarly attempted to undermine enemy morale. Nor did his preference for 'open' propaganda acknowledge that organizations like Wellington House concealed their involvement with overseas propaganda or even that, despite state funding, the NWAC remained officially unofficial, keeping its connection to government at arm's length because of political concerns about government-linked propaganda. However, while Masterman's organization operated in the shadows, it also worked on the assumption that 'lies are the least effective propaganda. The effect of a lie diminishes and the effect of a square fact increases' over time. Wellington House thus worked in a contradictory way – it produced truthful, fact-based propaganda while obscuring its own presence, believing materials produced by eminent British authors and others carried more weight without an official stamp. As noted in Chapter 14, Masterman reported in 1915 that Wellington House dealt in fact-based content but obscured its government connection because 'the intrusion of a Government ... invariably excites suspicion and resentment'. US opinion-formers received materials via 'personal' messages from the well-regarded Parker (or, really, his increasingly large staff), who suggested the facts presented may interest them. Having established links, Parker facilitated requests for interviews with other prominent Britons. Thus, he believed, he allowed Americans to make up their own minds. Once the United States entered the war, however, he wrote a candid article for *Harper's Magazine*, outlining his 'publicity' efforts and asserting that if 'the United States had not believed in Great Britain's *bona fides*, she would not have committed herself to this stupendous effort'.[7]

Put cynically, Wellington House could afford to emphasize facts because its opponents provided so much useful material. Germany's war crimes during the 1914 invasion were not 'the usual barbarous aspects of war', as Peterson falsely suggested. Rather, modern research demonstrates (as discussed in Chapter 1) that they resulted from deliberate policy. The Bryce Report, 'almost a byword for propagandistic deception ... turned out to be substantially correct', Nick Milne notes, its flaws tied to the willingness to publish exaggerated alongside proven personal accounts. Gleeful exploitation (discussed in Chapter 7) of the former German ambassador Lichnowsky's memoir criticizing pre-war German diplomacy did not invent his arguments; German U-boats really sank merchant ships, passenger liners and hospital vessels, despite US protests. British propagandists knew Britain's own blockade had vicious effects on civilian health and took steps to prevent discussion of the topic. This omission, however, did not alter the shocking impact of the deaths in one day of over 1,000 people, including over 100 US citizens, on the *Lusitania*. The German Chancellor really did dismiss the treaty guaranteeing Belgian neutrality as a 'scrap of paper' (Figure 18) and declare that 'necessity knows no law', a line

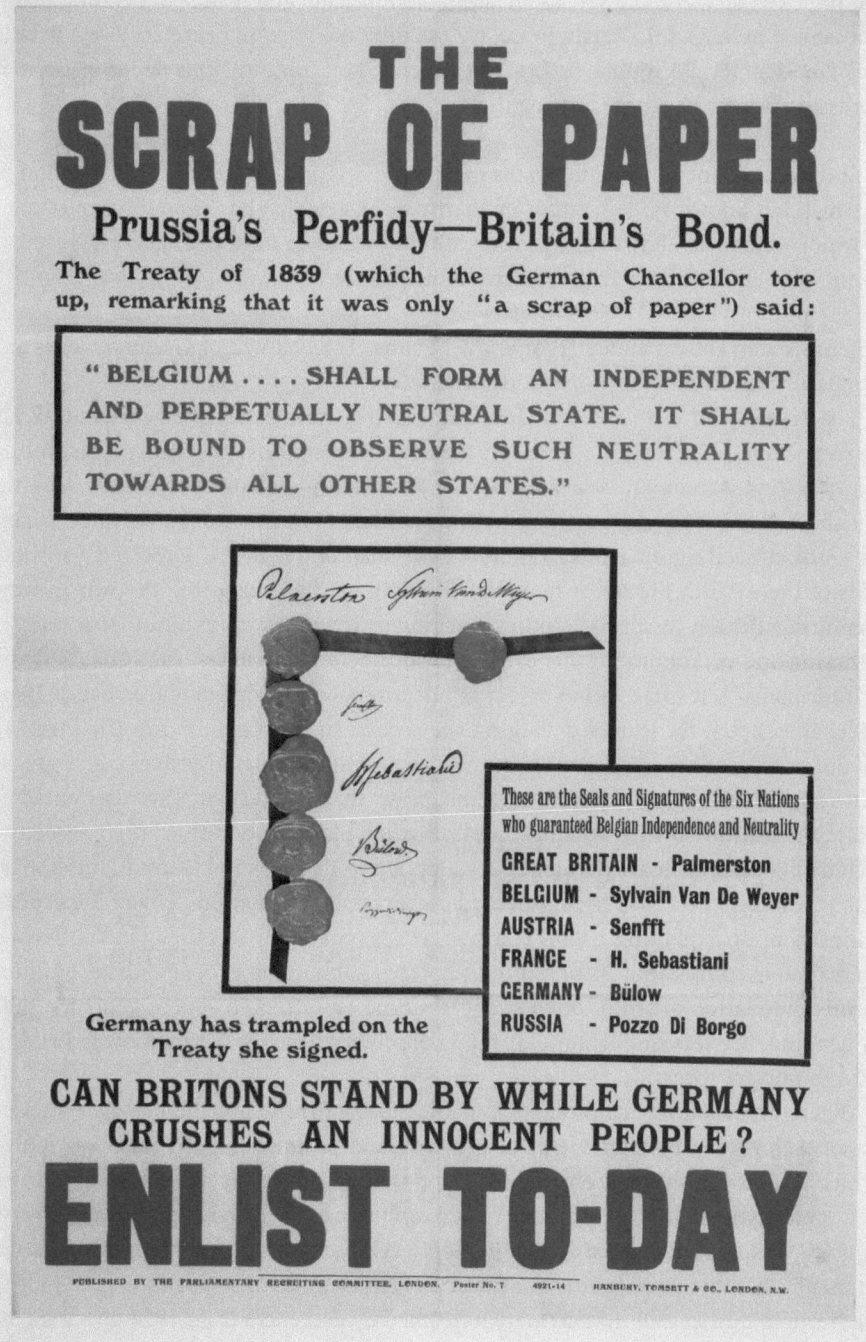

Figure 18 Parliamentary Recruiting Committee poster no. 7, *The Scrap of Paper*, 1914.
Source: Public Domain (Wikimedia Commons).

that the *New York Tribune* saw as an 'admission of fault' and 'ruthlessness' well before it became a propagandist catchphrase. By the time the Foreign Secretary Lord Balfour spoke in Richmond, Virginia, in 1917, he depended on common knowledge of German words and behaviour when insisting that

> Success does not lie along the paths of frightfulness and ruthlessness. That nation which has known no law, either of charity or love, which has cast all scruples to wind, which has allowed no consideration to stand in its way … has raised up outraged civilisation to make certain its own defeat.[8]

Balfour's statement expanded from known truths. The bedrock of German words and actions allowed license for propagandist rhetoric.

The truth of the Armenian Genocide is, likewise, established beyond doubt in respectable scholarship. One of the core collections of witness testimony, incorporating Armenian voices as well as neutral and German observers, was the British parliamentary report compiled throughout 1916 by Arnold Toynbee during his work at Wellington House (as noted in Chapter 1). It was expected (on both sides of the Atlantic) to affect neutral US public opinion regarding the war in ways benefitting Britain. Multiple studies document Toynbee's scrupulous processes in gathering and corroborating his evidence, with help from an international network of informants, but often either reject connections with propaganda or brush them aside, apparently, for fear of devaluing the report. In fact (as noted in Chapter 14), Toynbee, his collaborator Bryce and his propaganda chief, Masterman, were so satisfied with the work's quality and reliability that Masterman first consented to delay publication so that Toynbee could finalize his corroboration, then agreed to exclude material from a separate report supplied to Bryce by the German missionary Johannes Lepsius because Lepsius feared embarrassing his nation.[9] Given the general enthusiasm for exploiting useful German words and deeds in propaganda, this was a remarkable concession. As noted in Chapter 7, subsequent propagandists, building on this foundation of truth, often spent less time on Ottoman acts of genocide than on genuine, but less important, German complicity because Germany was Britain's most important threat.

Where propaganda's truthfulness is harder to confirm is not the heavily criticized atrocities, however, but statements of principle and promises for the post-war future. Armenia, notoriously, was abandoned by post-war diplomats unwilling to burden their country with its protection. Wider ambitions for international harmony or domestic social improvements often did not develop as promised, though this does not automatically show propagandists' insincerity. Pennell notes that appeals to grand ideals like freedom, justice and honour were welcomed by audiences from 1914 onwards, but these concepts' application remained vague for much of the war, until Lloyd George firmly stated Britain's war aims in January 1918. A month earlier, Victor Fisher, leader of the pro-war, 'patriotic labour', British Workers National League (BWNL), took a populist swipe at both wartime critics and the government over this issue:

> The mudlarks of our political life are perpetually indulging in all sorts of innuendos and suggestions as to the baseness, the viciousness, and the essential criminality of their country's War Aims. It would be simple to answer them without ambiguity or equivocation – once and for all. Do we answer them? Not a bit of it. Our All-Wise Statesmen still indulge in anything but lucidity. They are artists in rodomontade, experts in elocutionary clap-trap, exponents of the noble art of rhetorical gymnastics – and the British public loves the show.
>
> The British public, bless it! … would be quite miserable if they had been reminded of the truth in words undiluted by cant.
>
> The truth is that the British public does not want to be reminded of the truth, and the converse of that statement is that it knows the truth without the help of the politicians.

Fisher, though with different sympathies, was as mocking as Hobson of wartime truth's merits. He suggested the public already knew what it thought of the war and its expected outcomes and (echoing Masterman regarding distrust of government) certainly did not need to be officially told what to think. This last point was a common propagandist claim: Britons were so patriotic, they did not need to be reminded to conserve food, but, since they were here … While not directly discussing propaganda, Fisher's argument works for it. Much wartime propaganda retained public performance – on speaking platforms, or film screens. Other parts were created by literary and artistic talent. Presenting war's severe discomforts within an idealistic framework offered more comforting explanations than simply telling people to get on with it because they must. Comparing propagandists with anti-war poets, one modern analyst suggests both were 'asserting a vision of the war, its meaning and its consequences … doing so seriously, and with great emphasis on what they believe[d] to be at stake'.[10] In this interpretation, propagandists believed what they said about the war and the future – these were truthful appeals. When the post-war period brought international strife and domestic upheaval, instead of harmony and upward mobility, however (as Chapter 26 discusses further), cynical interpretations of previous 'truth' offered an explanation for what went wrong. Perhaps everyone was lied to.

Notes

1. George Cockerill, *What Fools We Were* (London: Hutchinson, 1944), 76; Monger, 'A "Not Uncongenial Task"', 12–13; Peterson, *Propaganda for War*, 37.
2. Besides the works cited in Chapter 1, notes 5–9, see Nick Milne, 'Persuasion vs. Deception: The Connotative Shifts of "Propaganda" and Their Critical Implications', in Julian Walker and Christophe Declercq (eds), *Languages and the First World War: Communicating in a Transnational War* (London: Palgrave Macmillan, 2016); Fiona Houston,' "Seducers of the People": Mapping the Linguistic Shift', *Alicante Journal of English Studies*, 31 (2018), quotation at 50.
3. For parliamentary opposition, see Monger, *Patriotism and Propaganda*, 218–31; Lucian [Hobson], 'The Laboratory of War Truth: 1920', *The Nation*, 27 October 1917, 118–19;

Hobson, 'Foreword', in Irene Cooper Willis, *England's Holy War: A Study of English Liberal Idealism during the Great War* (New York: Alfred A. Knopf, 1928), ix.

4 'Local Recruiting', *St Austell Star*, 19 November 1914, 2; 'Recruiting Campaign', *Surrey Advertiser*, 2 December 1914, 2.

5 'For National Service. Lincoln's Propaganda Campaign', *Lincoln Leader and County Advertiser*, 24 March 1917, 3; 'War Loan Campaign. Stirring Speeches at London's Guildhall', *Scotsman*, 30 June 1915, 7; 'War Aims Meeting at Wigan', *Wigan Examiner*, 17 November 1917, 2, cited in Monger, 'Familiarity Breeds Consent?', 510.

6 On the importance of such interactions, see esp. Lawrence, *Speaking for the People*, 164, 178–88.

7 On the NWAC's status, see Monger, *Patriotism and Propaganda*, 37–40; John Horne, 'Remobilizing for "Total War": France and Britain, 1917–1918', in Horne (ed.), *State, Society and Mobilization in Europe during the First World War* (Cambridge: Cambridge University Press, 1997), 200–1. Wellington House briefing notes attributed to Masterman, cited in Badsey, *German Corpse Factory*, 122 and see 125–7 for Parker's activities; TNA INF4/5, Masterman, 'Report', 7 June 1915, 2; Parker, 'United States', 527.

8 Peterson, *Propaganda for War*, 39; Horne and Kramer, *German Atrocities*; Milne, 'Persuasion vs Deception', 219; 'Chancellor Admits Fault by Germany', *New York Tribune*, 12 August 1914, 3. On active restriction of comments on the blockade, see Gullace, 'Sexual Violence', 735–7; Balfour's speech at Richmond, 19 May 1917, in Charles Hanson Towne (ed.), *The Balfour Visit: How America Received Her Distinguished Guest; and the Significance of the Conferences in the United States in 1917* (New York: George H. Doran, 1917), 65.

9 For works discussing the report while rejecting or downplaying propaganda, see, for example, Ara Sarafian, 'Introduction', in Ara Sarafian (ed.), *The Treatment of Armenians in the Ottoman Empire, 1915-1916: Documents Presented to Viscount Grey of Fallodon by Viscount Bryce, Uncensored Edition*, 2nd edn (Princeton: Gomidas Institute, 2005); David Miller, 'The Treatment of Armenians in the Ottoman Empire: A History of the Blue Book', *RUSI Journal*, 150, no. 4 (2005); Michelle Tusan, 'James Bryce's Blue Book as Evidence', *Journal of Levantine Studies*, 5, no. 2 (2015). For an account seeking to discredit the report's evidence because of propaganda connections, via crude treatment of British propaganda, see Justin McCarthy, *The Turk in America: The Creation of an Enduring Prejudice* (Salt Lake City: University of Utah Press, 2010), ch. 10. For fuller discussion of the report's validity and effects within in its propaganda context, see Monger, 'Networking against Genocide'. Lepsius' report appeared in 1919 as *Deutschland und Armenien* (Potsdam: Der Tempelverlag, 1919).

10 Pennell, *Kingdom United*, 57–67; Victor Fisher, 'For What We Are Fighting', *British Citizen and Empire Worker*, 15 December 1917, 353; Milne, 'Persuasion vs Deception', 215.

CHAPTER 21
UNOFFICIAL PROPAGANDA

A good reason for the truthful approach undertaken by official propaganda, outlined in Chapter 20, was the wide range of unofficial propagandists and organizations also promoting their causes. Critics like the UDC and ILP challenged official arguments as well as making their own, while pro-war voices (sometimes less scrupulous in their approach) and charities also joined the clamour. Competing with these voices, official propaganda's fact-based approach kept it within bounds for the most part, though organizers noted their limited control over public speakers – MPs, and ministers in particular, did not take kindly to being confined to preferred topics.[1] Official propaganda sometimes clashed, sometimes cooperated with and sometimes co-opted or adopted unofficial propaganda's personnel or arguments. All this, alongside the further competing and independent voice of the press, made propaganda a heavy presence in wartime society.

Critical propaganda was produced by multiple groups. The UDC, formed after the war's outbreak, demanded greater parliamentary and public oversight over diplomacy and foreign policy to prevent 'secret diplomacy' from creating future wars. ILP members largely rejected the parliamentary Labour party's wider support for the war, led by the pre-war Labour chairman and UDC co-founder (and future prime minister) Ramsay MacDonald, who became a figurehead of wartime opposition. Anti-conscription groups like the No-Conscription Fellowship and groups concerned with state intrusion into everyday life, such as the National Council for Civil Liberties, also challenged official actions while, in Ireland, despite mainstream Irish nationalists' endorsement of the war, advanced nationalists like Sinn Féin increasingly gained sympathy after the poisonously brutal suppression of 1916's Easter Rising. As the war progressed, officials havered between suppressing and indulging critical voices, often judging that publicity attached to censorship or prosecution would amplify them. *The Nation* continued publishing critical commentary like Hobson's satires, discussed previously. Its criticism saw it prohibited from overseas circulation, but domestic sales increased. The Press Bureau's head Edward Cook asserted that censorship was for news, not opinion, while Lloyd George suggested 'nobody cared' what the *Nation* wrote because it was notoriously critical. Brock Millman, assessing leniency towards some published material, suggests examples of restraint were a cynical way to suggest free speech continued in Britain. Meanwhile, harassment of critical propagandists by aggressive counter-propaganda as well as legal means continued, as noted by Millman and others.[2]

Probably the most influential critics were the UDC, founded by the politicians MacDonald, Ponsonby and the pre-war Liberal junior minister Charles Trevelyan; Norman Angell, whose economic writing proposed the impracticality of European war;

and the humanitarian activist E. D. Morel. Early in the war they formed four 'Cardinal Points': populations should be consulted before any international boundaries were redrawn; secret diplomacy should end and parliament should authorize all international arrangements; foreign policy should seek international consensus through an 'International Council', rather than restoring the European balance of power; and peace terms should include substantial disarmament for all nations and oversight of munitions production.[3] The third point became calls for a league of nations, a term coined by the UDC member Goldsworthy Lowes Dickinson. He and others, including Ponsonby, developed the ideas further in the 'Bryce Group', centred on Lord Bryce, who devoted significant time to the topic alongside investigating German and Ottoman atrocities and other tasks. Over time – as discussed further in Chapter 25 – this idea was adopted by the US President, Wilson. War aims propaganda then strongly endorsed the league, attaching itself to Wilson's idealism and popularity while undercutting a key element of wartime dissent by adopting the UDC's idea. Nonetheless, the league's growing prominence as a key war aim demonstrated the impact possible for unofficial, critical propagandists. The UDC, aware of its capacity to affect wider views, earlier printed a leaflet quoting press criticism, matching its own, of Foreign Office secrecy, arguing that its basic principles were accepted even by 'those who are unfriendly to the Union'.[4]

Over time, its focus shifted to public meetings, demands for clear war aims and calls for peace by negotiation on the assumption (based on 'little factual ground', according to a historian of the group) of German desire for negotiated peace. Like the potentially unrealistic ideals discussed in Chapter 20, UDC propagandists pursued this aim with honest conviction. With growing harassment, including Morel's imprisonment for six months in 1917 for evading censorship by sending pamphlets to Switzerland by hand, some UDC members also became more forthrightly critical. In Halifax, in April 1918, Trevelyan described Lloyd George as 'a braggart and a gambler who has failed' and thus had panicked and authorized ill-judged conscription in Ireland. Millman notes that, while the speech was brought to the Home Office's attention and considered 'deplorable', no prosecution followed. Similarly, a digest of reports of 'disloyalty' made by the Chief Constable of Glamorgan Lionel Lindsay included the Home Office note that a speech by UDC-member Helena Swanwick in January 1917 was 'mischievous ... but prosecution not considered desirable', while an earlier file note described Lindsay as a 'very bellicose Chief Constable ... sending case after case' for attention. Lindsay himself felt it obvious that prosecutions should have followed because punishing 'a conceited upstart [here, a Welsh agitator, A. J. Cook] always give[s] universal satisfaction'. Of eighty reports sent by Lindsay up to late 1917 reporting disloyalty (including one against the decidedly pro-war *Daily Mail*!), twenty-nine were prosecuted, suggesting national officials did not entirely share his view.[5]

Such restraint should not suggest endless leniency towards critics, however. André Keil has recently suggested that official propaganda's contrast between British liberal ideals and the tyranny of 'Prussian militarism' (discussed in Chapter 11), combined with limited manpower, made officials reluctant to use DORA powers to prosecute critics. Instead 'pragmatic authoritarianism became a hallmark of [a] very British dictatorship', he suggests. Rather than prosecuting critics, the authorities allowed pro-war groups like Fisher's BWNL to disrupt meetings. The NWAC was also encouraged to organize its own meetings as 'counterblasts' (though largely keeping themselves separate from the unofficial groups). Due to growing attacks on critical meetings, Keil notes the UDC decided by 1917 only to organize meetings in areas where 'sympathetic labour' audiences may offer protection.[6] Even this was not always sufficient, however, as events in 1918 in Leicester showed. Here, a traditional ILP May Day event, addressed by Leicester's MP, MacDonald, was broken up by discharged servicemen who were attending a rival meeting across the market square, organized by the NWAC. A colleague of MacDonald accused Leicester's mayor and a BWNL organizer, Albert Howarth, who spoke at the NWAC's meeting, of stirring up hostility before and on the day. Howarth was arrested but had his case dismissed for inciting violence against the ILP meeting despite admitting doing so on the grounds that the ILP preached sedition. The ILP's *Leicester Pioneer* questioned why neither Howarth was convicted nor the ILP speakers prosecuted under DORA for 'sedition' as a result. One or the other, surely, was necessary if law and order prevailed. Soon after, MacDonald dismissed the NWAC as 'a fraud because it professed to explain what it did not explain' and spent public money excessively on 'paid touts and cheap-jack orators who would espouse any cause for a fee'. Public letter-writers to other Leicester papers divided, meanwhile, some arguing it was right to attack the meeting because MacDonald no longer represented his constituents' views, while others defended the ILP's right to present its arguments.[7] Longer term, local hostility to MacDonald was confirmed by his defeat in the 1918 election. Foreseeing this, MacDonald noted in another column:

> What so many of our war cranks have never seen with their inflaming of hate and riotous immoral passion was that they were destroying the finer strands of the web of civilisation. When they joined the curs of the gutter in yelping at some of us ... they were not attacking us but their own decency ...
>
> Some of us have been fighting for decency as well as for liberty, and we have come within an ace of being beaten. Let them clear us out and put rottenness in our place.[8]

While MacDonald and most British wartime critics were, indeed, temporarily 'cleared out' of politics at war's end, Ireland saw a different outcome. Loyal support for the war by John Redmond's Irish Nationalists, in acknowledgement of the imminent introduction of Home Rule, resulted in their near-total defeat in 1918. Sinn Féin benefitted from its consistent anti-war stance and the poisoning of Irish opinion by repressive military control after the Easter Rising. Early on, Sinn Féin mocked Irish volunteers for the army but shifted to sympathizing with 'misguided' soldiers as the costs of the war became clear. Meanwhile, 'Recruiting Sergeant John Redmond' was condemned in a cartoon in the socialist James Connolly's *Irish Worker* for leading young Irishmen to their deaths. After the Rising, Sinn Féin increasingly tied public anger at growing losses to calls to vote for it as an anti-war party that would prevent similar future deaths. Attacking atrocity propaganda and censorship enabled advanced nationalists to depict Britain's wartime messages as 'built on a framework of lies and immorality'. Despite targeted and increasing censorship, such claims continued throughout the war.[9]

Unofficial propaganda was also conducted by those supporting the war. As noted in Chapter 10, individuals like Harry Lauder took it upon themselves to recruit troops or promote Britain's cause. Existing organizations like the Pilgrims Society also worked to retain US sympathy (Chapter 14), while others like the pro-empire Victoria League and League of Empire, and the National Service League, advocating conscription in Britain, continued their activities in wartime contexts with varying success.[10] Meanwhile, new organizations emerged, responding to the limited initial development of official domestic propaganda besides recruitment. Both the FRM and CCNPO, featured in earlier chapters, took it upon themselves to inform the public of its patriotic obligations. Historian and CCNPO co-founder G. W. Prothero's *Our Duty and Our Interest in the War* provided what rapidly became commonplace explanations for Britain's involvement in the war. Britain fought for national honour and the rights of small states. It was duty-bound to aid neutral Belgium. It fought for liberty and democracy. Prothero brushed aside Britain's alliance with even more despotic Russia, which he claimed was making 'great advances towards a free and constitutional government', as demonstrated by the emancipation of Russia's serfs and the creation of its (admittedly powerless) parliament, the Duma. By contrast, Germany had made 'no constitutional progress for forty years', operating a corrupt franchise. Britain also fought against Prussian militarism. Not fighting would only strengthen militarism's appeal through its success; the war was thus 'our only chance' to destroy it and protect civilization. Finally, this was about national and imperial survival. Britain had to fight because Germany intended to replace it as the world's dominant power and dissolve Britain's empire: 'Either Germany falls, or we fall.'[11] Prothero's emphasis on honour, justice, liberty and democracy and the confrontation with Prussian militarism became familiar propaganda arguments, regularly echoed in NWAC propaganda that asserted Britain's defence of civilizational ideals. The NWAC, likewise, followed the CCNPO in choosing an image of St George slaying a dragon as its logo (see Figure 19), although the CCNPO's poster was more elaborate, with the dragon of Prussian militarism resting on a bed of human bones, while the background depicted a castle ('the Englishman's home') and wooden ships, evoking the historic protection of Britain's shores. It was little surprise that the CCNPO was absorbed, meeting resolution and all, into NWAC operations from 1917.

While Prothero addressed Britons, Christabel Pankhurst visited New York to put Britain's case to the United States, as the WSPU pivoted to supporting the war effort to demonstrate its active citizenship. Pankhurst justified her support by highlighting Germany's even greater hostility to women's suffrage than Britain: 'So long as you have one country which, like Germany, boasts that it is a male nation, a country in which the counsels of women emphatically do not prevail, then you will have the peace-loving nations always on the defensive.' Like Prothero, Pankhurst asserted the war was a fight for British 'national existence'. She argued suffragists supported Britain's cause because they desired British citizenship, which needed protection from German destruction. Wartime

Unofficial propaganda

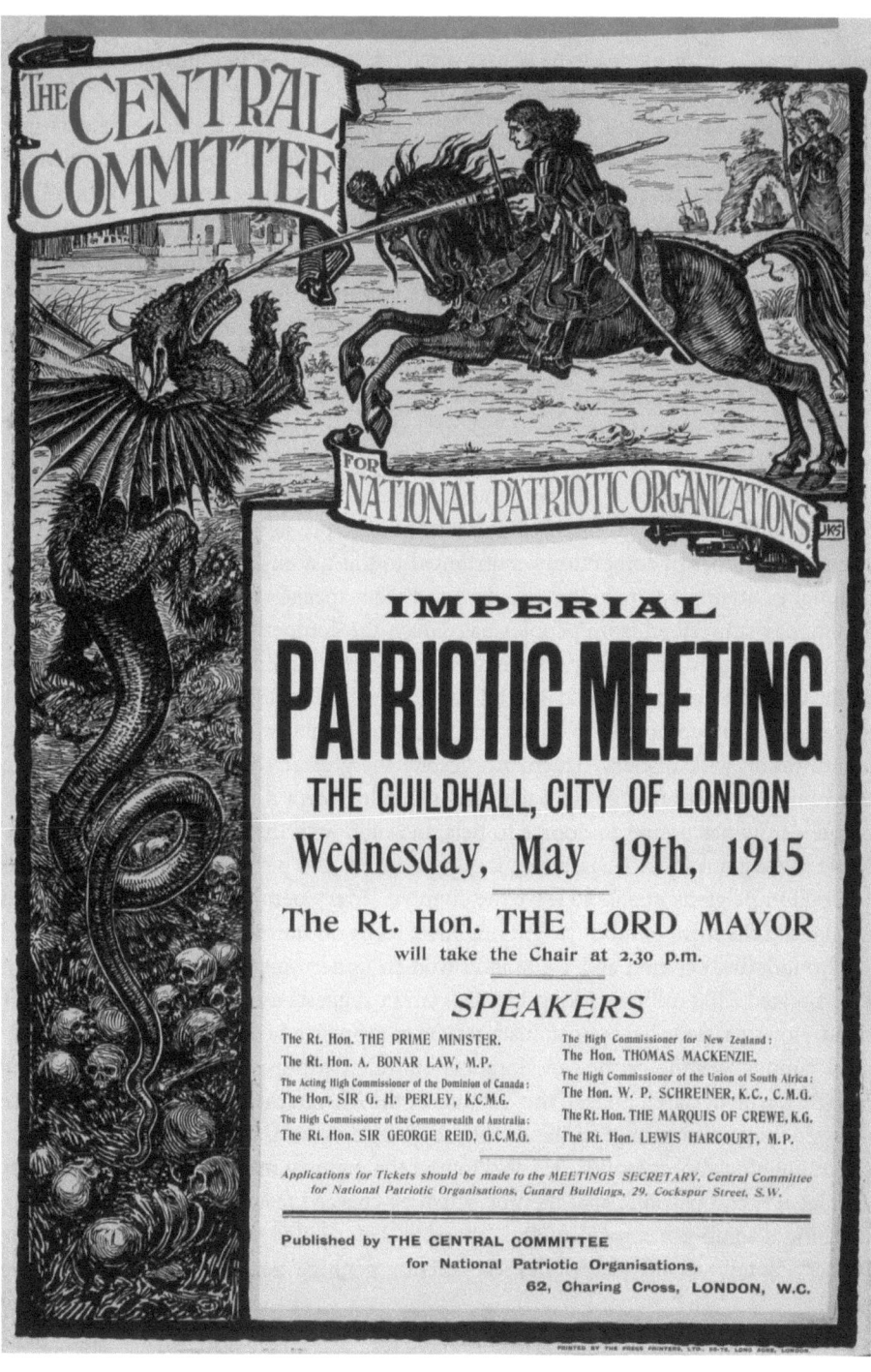

Figure 19 Poster advertising a CCNPO meeting, 1915.
Source: Library of Congress Prints and Photographs Division POS – Gt Brit .S05, no. 1.

service would compel the government to finally acknowledge women's citizenship: 'Do you supposed that it is going to be so easy when this war is over to refuse to acknowledge the rights and duties of women where the work of fulfilling national and Empire responsibility is concerned?' The WSPU's decision to throw itself wholeheartedly into recruitment and pro-war activities was calculated to undercut objections that women did not qualify as citizens through wartime service.[12] Like official propaganda, unofficial propagandists attempted to persuade audiences of the justice of their particular causes.

A final area of wartime propaganda involved charities. Trevor Wilson notes 'constant calls on ... benevolence' from those who could afford it. Besides war savings appeals, covered elsewhere in this book, civilians received 'intolerable' and interminable appeals for charity. Wilson notes at least sixty-nine different charities dedicated to Belgian refugees' relief alone, though Peter Grant suggests Belgian and other refugees' relief made up only 8 per cent of the 17,899 new war charities established between 1916 and 1920. The largest proportions supported comforts for British imperial forces (28 per cent), medical support (25 per cent) and charities for disabled servicemen (13 per cent), reinforcing previous discussion of servicemen's pre-eminence in wartime minds. The sheer number of competitors contributed to the 'astonishing range of fundraising techniques' attempted, including flag days and other special 'days', direct mail to donors and money subscribed from people's pay. Given the competition, some causes missed out. Wilson suggests sympathy for enemy aliens' distress did not extend far past Quakers, while Daniel Steel argues that the relatively small charitable contributions towards Armenian relief, compared to larger donations for Belgians, reflected a lesser sense of identification with distant Armenians, despite the greater scale of harm.[13] Regarding Belgium, Galsworthy suggested each earner should accept a 'self-imposed income tax' of one penny per pound to donate to Belgian relief, with the National Committee for Relief in Belgium (NCRB) asserting it required £500,000 per month to supply food to 1.5 million Belgians unable to leave the country: 'Every penny contributed goes to the Belgians in the form of food ... Pity, ungilded, feeds no starving bodies.'[14]

Around 400,000 men and 1.2 million women undertook war charity work, raising an estimated £400 million. Alongside that, Grant suggests a relatively small amount of fraud. However, financial opportunism related to propaganda certainly existed. Probably most famous was the grifting of Horatio Bottomley, editor of the popular newspaper *John Bull*, who declared himself the 'Tribune of the Man in the Street', whether or not he received the government propaganda role he felt he deserved, and spent much of the war ridiculing official propaganda. He also toured the country making recruiting speeches and, later, broad patriotic speeches for which he charged fees, retaining the bulk while donating a small portion to soldiers' charities. Later jailed for a fraudulent post-war 'Victory Bond' scheme, Bottomley's apparently genuine patriotism was matched by greed.[15]

The wide variety of unofficial propagandists discussing Britain's war at home and abroad added to increasing official material as the war continued. Critical commentary was tolerated to some degree but harassed by both surveillance and physical disruption of public events. Unsurprisingly, a wide variety of both critics and supporters of the war pressed their causes in print and speech, sometimes adapting existing campaigns to wartime, sometimes commencing new ones. Whether promoting public oversight of diplomacy, pressing for Irish nationalism, demonstrating women's citizenship or, like Bottomley, lining pockets, the war offered fruitful opportunities for talented propagandists to advance their cause.

Notes

1. Monger, *Patriotism and Propaganda*, 53.
2. On the *Nation* and censorship, see Monger, 'Press Bureau', 449–50, 457; Alfred E. Havighurst, *Radical Journalist: H.W. Massingham (1860-1924)* (Cambridge: Cambridge University, 1974), 250–6. On free speech cynicism, see Millman, *Managing Domestic Dissent*, 78; on disruption of critical voices, as well as Millman, esp. ch. 6 see Lawrence, 'Public Space, Political Space' and André Keil, 'The National Council for Civil Liberties and the British State during the First World War, 1916-1919', *English Historical Review*, 134, no. 568 (2019).
3. *The Union of Democratic Control: Its Motives, Object, and Policy* (UDC pamphlet B23, 1916), 5–6.
4. Monger, *Patriotism and Propaganda*, 200–2; *What the Press Now Says: More Support for the U.D.C.* (UDC leaflet 17B, 1915).
5. Marvin Swartz, *The Union of Democratic Control in British Politics during the First World War* (Oxford: Clarendon Press, 1971), 64, 74; speech by Trevelyan cited in Millman, *Managing Domestic Dissent*, 255; on Swanwick and Lindsay see TNA HO45/10743/263275, f. 284, 'Glamorgan Chief Constable', 30 November 1917 and f. 274, 'Glamorganshire Chief Constable', 24 November 1917.
6. André Keil, 'A Very British Dictatorship: The Defence of the Realm Act in Britain, 1914-1920', *First World War Studies*, 14, no. 1 (2023), 53, 60; on government and NWAC caution regarding groups like the BWNL, see Lawrence, 'Public Space, Political Space', 296–9; Monger, *Patriotism and Propaganda*, 244–5.
7. For more extensive discussion of the Leicester incident, see Monger, 'Transcending the Nation', 28–32; for MacDonald's comments, see Ramsay MacDonald, 'From Green Benches', *Leicester Pioneer*, 24 May 1918, 4.
8. Ramsay MacDonald, 'From Green Benches', *Leicester Pioneer*, 7 June 1918, 4.
9. Ben Novick, *Conceiving Revolution: Irish Nationalist Propaganda during the First World War* (Dublin: Four Courts Press, 2001), 56–67, 246; Donal Ó Drisceoil, 'Keeping Disloyalty within Bounds? British Media Control in Ireland, 1914-1919', *Irish Historical Studies*, 38 (2012); Monger, 'Press Bureau', 452–5.
10. Hendley, *Organized Patriotism*.
11. G. W. Prothero, *Our Duty and Our Interest in the War* (London: John Murray for CCNPO, 1914), *passim*, quotations at 5, 8, 16.
12. Gullace, *Blood of Our Sons*, 119–26; Christabel Pankhurst, *America and the War* (London: WSPU, 1914), 5–7.
13. Trevor Wilson, *The Myriad Faces of War: Britain and the Great War, 1914-1918* (Cambridge: Polity Press, 1986), 774–5; Peter Grant, 'Charitable Work' in Strachan, *British Home Front*, 300–3; Steel, 'Genocide', 429–30.
14. *'Please Have Pity With Them'* (NCRB pamphlet, n.p.d. [1915]); *'Britain Will not Let Belgium Starve'* (NCRB pamphlet, London, 1915), 4.
15. Grant, 'Charity Work', 300, 305–7; 'My Visit to the Premier', *John Bull*, 19 January 1918, 1; Messinger, *British Propaganda*, 200–12.

CHAPTER 22
VOLUNTARISM

Throughout the war, as many of the unofficial, critical propagandists discussed in Chapter 21 keenly reported, British life became more restricted and controlled. Workplace rights and freedoms were restricted by legislation such as 1915's Treasury Agreement and Munitions of War Act, which, among other things, imposed compulsory arbitration to settle strikes and prohibited workers from switching jobs in war industries without their existing employer's permission, thus hindering them in seeking better pay and conditions elsewhere. DORA not only increased official powers of censorship and surveillance but also interfered with leisure. Early closing hours were introduced in pubs and people were prevented from treating in efforts to increase productivity and reduce grain for brewing. Military conscription was enacted in 1916 when army volunteers dwindled. As Chapter 13 noted, servicemen's wives' separation allowances were removable following accusations of misconduct, while women's intimate lives were regulated by another section of DORA that threatened prison for transmitting venereal disease to soldiers. Finally, in 1918, after years of attempting to sustain a free market in food without, according to Trevor Wilson, 'accepting that the day of voluntary appeals had passed', compulsory rationing was introduced.[1]

Wilson is certainly right that the departure of voluntarism was not accepted. It remained a constant of propaganda throughout the war despite increasing compulsion. Voluntarism, propagandists asserted, set Britain apart. Britain's supposed unpreparedness for war, as Chapter 8 noted, proved its blamelessness. Voluntary participation (by state, empire and the millions who volunteered to serve) then proved British honour, fair play and willing support of the weak. While voluntary efforts clearly were insufficient, propagandists continued to claim that Britons, when an issue's seriousness was properly explained, would respond appropriately. Even after regulation, further voluntary effort was sought. The NWSC's forerunner issued a poster in 1916 requesting alcohol-free Mondays: 'In view of the great sacrifices freely made by our sailors and soldiers, the National Organizing Committee feels sure that all who remain at home will willingly help the Country in this way.' Such attempted persuasion also carried an implied negative motivation, however. If the public had the case clearly put to them and declined to voluntarily change, un-British compulsion might follow.[2]

Obviously, without access to conscripted servicemen, voluntarism was the centrepiece of recruitment propaganda. From the start voluntarism was represented as both virtuous in itself and a way to avoid the evil of compulsion. The PRC's third leaflet reproduced a September 1914 statement by the Parliamentary Committee of the Trades Union

Congress (TUC). Its members welcomed the PRC's creation, and the involvement of Labour figures in it, and asserted that

> in the event of the voluntary system of military service failing … the demand for a national system of compulsory military service will not only be made with redoubled vigour, but may … become irresistible. The prospect of having to face conscription, with its permanent and heavy burden upon the financial resources of the country and … upon nearly the whole of its industries, should in itself stimulate the manhood of the nation to come forward in its defence, and thereby demonstrate to the world that a free people can rise to the supreme heights of a great sacrifice without the whip of conscription.

Voluntarism, for these union advocates, not only demonstrated the special character of Britain's free people but also was essential to longer-term well-being. The alternative, should conscription emerge, was a transition to the 'overbearing and brutal' conditions of militarized Germany. Nonetheless, voluntary enlistment must be matched, they argued, by government support for volunteers' dependents. Thus, workers' voluntarism was presented as part of collective bargaining with the state. Voluntarism was no abstract virtue but a practical defence of workers' rights. 'It is not want of courage that keeps men from enlisting', an appeal from the Joint Labour Recruiting Committee added, 'but a failure to realise the seriousness of the situation'. Workers were 'defending their own interests' by enlisting, protecting 'those personal liberties and privileges which have taken centuries of effort to win'.[3]

Voluntary enlistment from Britain and the empire was heralded abroad as well as at home. In a *New York Times* article in August 1915, converted into a pamphlet, the Wellington House propaganda organizer, Parker, rejected US suggestions Britain had not done enough. He reminded readers that Britain's army in 1914 was less than 500,000 strong:

> There are now in training or in the field 350,000 troops of the overseas dominions alone, while this country … has at least 3,000,000 men in the field or in training …
>
> Is this a discreditable effort for a country which relied on sea-power … and yet has added … land forces outnumbering the regular forces of the United States – also a democratic country with a voluntary system – at least thirty times? …
>
> Great Britain asleep! … No democracy ever produced a voluntary Army approximating three millions in the world's history, not even your United States. You resorted to compulsory service for your civil war. It may be that we shall not get through this war without compulsory service, but the response … has vastly exceeded what was thought possible.

Parker connected the nations by stressing their shared commitment to democracy and voluntarism but elevated Britain's status by noting the United States' earlier resort to conscription. Far from the humblebragging described in Chapter 8, this propaganda openly demanded admiration. Despite Parker's admission that conscription might be needed, voluntarism was identified as the core of British national character: 'inherent goodness has become magnificent merit'.[4]

Parker's reference to the Dominions added to evidence of British virtue. Another PRC pamphlet stressed the willingness of the Dominions, India and Crown Colonies to provide men or supplies, while the NWAC's handbook, published two years after conscription's introduction, nonetheless emphasized voluntary imperial support and the number of voluntary recruits obtained. 'Great Britain has neither the right nor the power to demand military service from her Dominions; it is only of their own free will that these take part in any way in which she may become engaged.' Nonetheless, over a million Dominion soldiers volunteered, proving 'that freedom is a more potent bond than force, that liberty is the surest guarantee of loyalty'. The empire was

> a league of self-governing nations, blended with Dependencies that are in training for self-rule – a colossal experiment in international government with a minimum of compulsion and a maximum of freedom. Thus the silk strands do not snap. They are stronger than the iron bands of Germany.

Britain's voluntary traditions meant its imperial subjects knew the value of their citizenship. Because they were provided free choices, they made them.[5]

Voluntarism was not solely a military virtue, of course. Propagandists sought voluntary effort everywhere. Even as the PRC continued recruiting efforts in 1915, volunteers for other war services were sought. In Grantham, Lincolnshire, Arthur Priestley, the local MP and mayor, addressed workers on behalf of the newly formed Ministry of Munitions:

> We had in conflict to-day, as a piece of national machinery, what was called voluntarism, and what was called compulsion. In other words ... of all the great issues this world conflict was demonstrating, the greatest was whether a self-governing community, based upon the liberty of the individual and the freedom of the nation, could survive in conflict with a military autocracy. The voluntary system was the label of the high civilisation – (hear, hear) – the other was the label of barbarism. The one was based on the higher conception of the destiny of man; the other was based on the power of brute force ... The British people in the British Empire represented to-day the highest form of the true ideal of the emancipation of the human being. It was prepared to sacrifice everything to maintain that attitude ... If the civil power, through the voluntary effort of the individual, the effort of the community, would render that just and right assistance to those who were carrying our flag in the face of the enemy, we had no doubt as to the result.

Priestley told the audience that the meeting thus sought skilled volunteers for Ministry of Munitions work. He was followed by the union official Forsgate Weekley (later mayor of Grantham himself), who warned listeners that 'unless they adopted this voluntary system, severe measures would have to be taken'. He urged all 'skilled mechanics' in private business to volunteer for national munitions service: 'As a nation we were going to see this thing through – (hear, hear) – and to see it through they as civil volunteers must put their backs into it.' Weekley reassured listeners that they would be no worse off financially, though the unions had agreed to 'sacrifice' hard-won workplace privileges. Another speaker urged the audience to 'satisfy Mr. Lloyd George that he need not use compulsion', and a resolution supporting the Ministry's work was carried unanimously. According to the local paper, 100 volunteers were found.[6] Once again, appeals to patriotism and observations on the special nature of British voluntarism accompanied warnings of more forceful measures, should it fail.

Over time, both militarily and industrially, greater levels of compulsion were introduced, yet appeals to voluntarism became no less prominent. As late as mid-1918, following the disastrous introduction and withdrawal of conscription in Ireland, the Irish nationalist Arthur Lynch unsuccessfully attempted to recruit volunteers for a new Irish battalion for the British army, hoping to convert even Sinn Féin supporters to the cause. Instead, Sinn Féin exploited his public meetings to air criticisms of Britain's war, but Lynch's conviction that voluntarism remained plausible is telling. Imposing conscription on a hostile population largely aimed to show British civilians that all parts of the UK bore an equal share of the burden. This having failed, however, Lynch still believed there was an appetite to volunteer.[7]

Elsewhere, calls for voluntary service continued regarding war work, while also affecting people's home lives and leisure time. By 1917, Violet Markham suggested, 'the shams and injustices of the so-called voluntary system were daily more manifest'. Nonetheless the new National Service Department (of which she was deputy-director of the women's section) 'was hailed by all wishful thinkers who hoped … it might still produce the rabbit out of the voluntary hat'. Markham resigned within six months, as it was clear national service was not working, despite the establishment of 945 local committees in England and Wales by July 1917.[8] Calling for voluntary rationing in 1917, meanwhile, the Food Controller Lord Devonport announced he had decided 'a voluntary system is preferable' for economizing on bread, meat and sugar 'until further experience is gained' of whether civilians would show their 'instinct of self-discipline'. This was partly because compulsory rationing required 'very elaborate machinery', which would be wasteful. Britain was 'placed upon its honour' to self-regulate and Devonport was supposedly 'confident that every individual will co-operate loyally', but the complex machinery was being created as a backup. 'Every act of self-denial here', he concluded, aided 'those fighting for us on sea and land'. Here, Devonport leaned on the common example of servicemen's greater sacrifices to encourage voluntary action but also made plain Britons were not entirely trusted. Devonport's scolding tone was echoed by the First Sea Lord, Sir John Jellicoe, who previously commanded Britain's Grand Fleet at the Battle of Jutland. Speaking in Sheffield, he 'bluntly told his audience that if he had his way he would put us all on three-quarter rations' to reduce pressure on the navy. The Conservative *Sheffield Daily Telegraph* suggested this should drive home the importance of voluntary rationing to all. Like the soldier propagandists discussed in Chapter 18, Jellicoe's naval service permitted bluntness, although this was balanced by more generous comments about Sheffield by the South African War Cabinet member, Smuts. A later food control leaflet, telling people to 'think before you eat', took military comparisons a step further, meanwhile, declaring that the 'Cupboard is the Housewife's Trench, and she must defend it. She can pit her knowledge against the Germans quite as effectively as the soldier can point his gun'.[9] Even more than the food economy poster described in Chapter 17, where a woman imagined the risk to sailors while reducing bread consumption, domestic management was here directly compared to military service.

Given the eventual introduction of compulsory rationing, public investment in voluntarism was no more sufficient to address food shortages than to fill the armed forces, yet it continued to be stressed as a particularly British habit. A public message from Lord Rhondda (a successor of Devonport's as food controller) to the US food controller Herbert Hoover stressed Britain's dependence on US food exports. Again, he warned that 'if there is not a marked reduction as the result of our voluntary food economy campaign, the nation must be put on compulsory rations'. This would stain Britain's national character since 'what we ask of them in food economy is scarcely worthy of the name of sacrifice'. Britons, implicitly, should show the United States – the war's emerging superpower – that Britain still led the world in voluntary acceptance of dutiful discomfort. A later pamphlet, circulated by the NWAC, featured a speech by Hoover on US voluntary restrictions, which had 'a moral side ... I do not believe that there is another nation in the world in which the proportion of individuals with a willing sense of self-sacrifice is so high as in this people of ours, and in which a sufficient voluntary reduction could be obtained'.[10] Ostensibly reassuring British readers of their ally's support, such comments also implied a rebuke to British character. The United States, rather than Britain, now seemed to lead the way in voluntary self-sacrifice.

Nonetheless, propagandists never lost faith in the persuasive merits of voluntarism. Despite increasingly tightly regulated work, calls continued for war workers, already accepting extended hours and tougher conditions, to voluntarily do more. The Miners' Federation executive member Vernon Hartshorn wrote in the NWAC's newspaper for industrial workers, *Reality*, in September 1918 that the 'industrial system has necessarily become part of the war machine':

> Though the worker outside the military forces is not working under military regulations his responsibility is not less than that of his soldier or sailor comrade.
> The moral responsibility is, indeed, all the greater, for the carrying out of his duty ... depends on his voluntary recognition of the responsibility which destiny has placed upon him. This responsibility now rests upon every individual.

Workers, despite their increasing regimentation, still exercised free choice. They were, Hartshorn suggested, freer than soldiers yet more burdened. Military discipline left soldiers no choice but to serve, but workers must motivate themselves. Previously, the NWAC reproduced a *Bystander* cartoon by Wilmot Lunt depicting a British worker showing the kaiser his trump card, the ace of spades. A caption beneath noted increased production and workers' enlistments since the start of Germany's 1918 spring offensive, as well as munition workers' voluntary decision to continue work through the Easter holiday. Winston Churchill (then Minister of Munitions), in a speech reproduced as a pamphlet, declared he was 'sure ... that the extra time put in in the Easter holidays – when men and women, wherever needed for 1500 or 1600 firms, wherever asked, worked continuously on at the highest pressure – more than compensated' for any productivity lost to strikes in recent months. Such service should see 'an end of the carping and croaking' about workers' attitudes. Given that a Ministry of Munition's poster had called for 'No Holidays' in 1916, suggesting that this sacrifice would directly demoralize Germany,[11] such actions were hardly spontaneous. Nonetheless, the example suggested that, when things became serious, Britons could still be trusted to volunteer.

Besides attempting to place articles in overseas papers directly, MI7b produced extended analyses of topics that could be adapted by the press. The 1918 Minister of Information, Lord Beaverbrook, retained some samples. One covered military recruitment. Regular comparisons with US actions during its Civil War, and with Abraham Lincoln's ideas, suggest it was meant to influence US opinion. Reflecting on the 'revolutionary nature of this passage to compulsory service', the text congratulated the 1914 War Secretary, Lord Kitchener, for refusing to introduce compulsion immediately:

> The nation did not at first realize, as he did, the magnitude of the task ... and would not have understood the necessity of at once abandoning cherished habits and prejudices. He preferred to educate them by gradually increasing demands for volunteers, according to the system they knew, until the very numbers who had volunteered made it seem unreasonable that all should not be called upon.[12]

The unnamed author summarized the value of voluntarism as a propaganda theme, here. Rather than confront Britons with sudden and shocking change, appeals to voluntarism retained familiar traditions and put the need for compulsion and intrusion in public hands. All Britons could voluntarily serve. Compulsion was only necessary if they rejected this free choice or if the virtuous majority were let down by a minority of 'shirkers'. Such arguments continued throughout the war, even as the state transparently regulated more and more of people's lives. By 1918 it was supposedly clear (as previous chapters have discussed and the next argues further) that everything related to the war and that everyone had critical parts to play. Stressing voluntarism shifted responsibility for compulsion from officials to the public.

Notes

1. For brief discussion of these interventions see Wilson, *Myriad Faces*, 152–3, 169, 226–7, 396–400, 512–14, 538–40 (quotation at 538–9), 648–9 and for those aimed at women, see Chapter 13.

Voluntarism

2   'Don't Take Alcoholic Drinks on Mondays' (National Organizing Committee for War Savings poster, 1916). For fuller discussion of voluntarism and propaganda, see Monger, 'Press and Propaganda'.
3   *Manifesto to the Trade Unionists of the Country* (PRC leaflet no. 3, 1914); 'The Crisis: An Appeal to Free Men' (Joint Labour Recruiting Committee poster, n.d.). On tensions between recruitment and conscription in labour thinking, see John N. Horne, *Labour at War: France and Britain, 1914–1918* (Oxford: Clarendon Press, 1991), 50–2.
4   Gilbert Parker, *Is England Apathetic? A Reply* (London: Darling, 1915), 2, 4, 8.
5   *The Rally of Our United Empire; Aims and Effort*, 54, 7.
6   'The Munitions of War. Public Meeting at Grantham', *Grantham Journal*, 3 July 1915, 8.
7   Monger, 'Press and Propaganda', 503–5.
8   Violet Markham, *Return Passage* (London: Oxford University Press, 1953), 151; TNA NATS1/70, list of National Service committees, 18 July 1917.
9   *Voluntary Rationing: The Food Controller's Appeal to the Nation* (Food Control leaflet no. 1, 1917); 'Prussianism Must Go', *Sheffield Daily Telegraph*, 25 October 1917, 5–6; *How to Get the Most Out of Food* (Food Control leaflet no. 8, 1917).
10 'Lord Rhondda and Sacrifice. Our Reliance on America', *Edinburgh Evening News*, 27 November 1917, 3; Herbert Hoover, *Food in War* (London: W.H. Smith, 1918), 10.
11 Vernon Hartshorn, 'The Civilian Army's Part', *Reality*, 138, 5 September 1918, 4; 'Spades Are Trumps, and – British Labour Plays the Winning Card', *Welcome*, 2, 8 April 1918, 20; Winston S. Churchill, *The Munitions Miracle* (London: NWAC, British Effort Series, 1918), 9; Will Dyson, 'No Holidays' (Ministry of Munitions poster, 1916). On Easter holiday work, see also Gregory, *Last Great War*, 205.
12 PA, Beaverbrook Papers, BBK E/3/5, 'How Great Britain Has Raised Her Armies', 15–16.

CHAPTER 23
WAR WORK

How You Can Serve Your Country, a war savings pamphlet evidently aimed at wealthier British readers, emphasized that every household had a role to play in assisting the economy:

> Every household ... should hold a council of War, and ascertain how much of its total consumption can be temporarily sacrificed. Services should be valued even more highly than goods, as each person doing unnecessary and unproductive work is not only consuming without producing, but is depriving the country of her potential productive power. For instance, in a house of several servants, if, by co-operation in the work of the maids, and simplification of living by the family ... the younger maids were set free to take the place of the men called to the colours or to factory, transport and munition work, the household by co-operative effort would add two units to the army of supply or export production and reduce the consumption of the household. Savings would thus be available for the War Loan, and more goods made for export.

The NWSC's primary goal was investments in war savings, loans and bonds, but here it offered a perspective on valuable 'war work'. Middling and wealthy families need not do without servants altogether but should scale back their domestic staff and send their youngest employees to industrial jobs. The journalist and NWAC propagandist E. M. Goodman likewise, noted that 'we all have, or should have, fewer servants' in 1918 and recommended packing things away to reduce cleaning. Meanwhile, a 'War Work, 1914–1918' collection of lithographs by Archibald Hartrick stressed London Underground staff's war work, with twelve transport roles framed by supposed army equivalents. 'Women Painters', for instance, paired carriage painting with a soldier painting camouflage on a tank, while a lift operator, more tenuously, was tied to soldiers descending into a dugout.[1] Transport work was essential to convey people to workplaces, but Hartrick's lithographs, commissioned by the Underground Electric Railways Co. of London, asserted the equal necessity of all its wartime roles.

'War work' was an elastic concept. For many, like the producers of quotidian propaganda described in Chapter 17 or the advocates of voluntarism described in Chapter 22, since everything related to the war, all work was war work. It all played a part in eventual success. Ethel Tweedie, a pre-war writer and sometime war propagandist and fundraiser, complained in 1916 that servants 'don't yet seem to know there is a war at all' and thus refused to accept either increased work or reduced pay. Nonetheless, she condescendingly reported, domestic servants still contributed:

> Women with brains and education cannot organise and run charities, canteens, or hospitals if the cook neglects to give them their dinner. A nice little dainty-looking dinner served up to her hard-working, brain-fagged mistress is the cook's bit of war work, and is a real help to the country.

Meanwhile, at least some admirable servants 'gratuitously offered to take half wages or none, [or] do double work ... those domestics are truly doing their bit, just as much or more as the woman at the factory'. Despite her patronizing dismissal of servants' need to earn an income, she suggested domestic service added to the war effort, if only by sustaining 'women with brains' like her. Tweedie herself fundraised to erect YMCA Huts, including one in London that catered to Australian and New Zealand troops, staffed by volunteers. 'Those ladies did it all as their bit of war work', and she was miffed when she thought her efforts might go unrecognized by the collection of evidence of women's wartime work undertaken for what became the Imperial War Museum.[2] For Tweedie (who criticized officials' slow embrace of women's war work), all women's work tied to the war in some form.

Tweedie was not the only female propagandist to question servants' patriotism or stress that paid domestic labour was war work. Grace Curnock, press representative for the Women's Section of National Service, likewise called for domestic workers to volunteer for the Women's Army Auxiliary Corps suggesting that '500 girl clerks are to-day unable to leave England' to replace men in the army because of a lack of domestic staff:

> Unless women will volunteer to cook and do the ordinary household work of the hostels where the clerical workers live, the soldiers up the line may ask in vain for the help that has been promised by the women from home.

Curnock sought '200 cooks, 100 housemaids, 100 scrubbers, 50 laundresses and 500 general domestic workers' to come forward for service in France and disprove her assertions of 'lack of patriotism' and 'apathy'.[3] Like Tweedie, Curnock took an uncompromising (if not insulting) view of servants' responsibilities, but her appeal reinforced the idea of a direct connection between the fighting front and domestic labour. Soldiers were wielding pens as clerks rather than rifles. Female clerks could replace them, but these replacements did not have time for their own domestic tasks while doing this important work. Cooks, maids and others could thus take pressure off 'girl clerks' by their own national service. Soldiering remained the ultimate war work, but WAAC volunteers, even for unglamorous domestic work, made it possible.

While many propagandists endorsed the wide applicability of war work, such calls, nonetheless, indicated a hierarchy. A poster designed by Robert Baden-Powell in 1915 clearly indicated the most valued war work. As always, servicemen took pride of place. At the top of a hill stand an infantryman and naval gunner, with Baden-Powell boosting his own organization by having a Boy Scout hand up ammunition. Next are two women – a nurse and a munition worker – with a male industrial worker in the foreground. To the side a well-dressed civilian looks on.[4] These were the obvious exemplars of important war work, which the young man (and, implicitly, young women, too) should seek out, though they omitted other essential workers such as merchant sailors, farm workers, police officers and others. However, wider forms of work were increasingly acknowledged. While (as noted in Chapter 13) munitions work remained the most celebrated element of women's wartime paid work (alongside unpaid mothering), other forms of work were also celebrated, albeit often with an eye to the supposedly novel. *"Carry On"*, a collection of photographs of women's war work, noted that 'two-thirds of the 500 processes in the making of munitions on which they are now engaged had never been performed by a woman':

> But it is not in munition work alone that the face of British industry has been transformed by the extension of women labour. As post-women and police, as bakers and farm-workers, as motor drivers and 'bus conductors – in almost every occupation of which the mind can think – British women are now cheerfully 'carrying on' while their men-folk are away.

Besides munitions and the occupations mentioned in the foreword, the photographs showed women in shipyards, aircraft factories, electrical plants and hospitals, on railways and roads, as dentists, painters and window cleaners. While one selection stressed the 'heavy work' done by women, against supposed norms, more acute propagandists like Goodman scoffed that 'a woman who can do a hard day's washing does not think too much about a hard day at the factory'.[5]

Despite celebrating civilian war work, propaganda later in the war was conducted with considerable suspicion of many war workers. Industrial workers, particularly, were believed (with limited evidence, Adrian Gregory points out) to be losing faith in and commitment to the war. Such anxieties only became stronger after the Russian Revolutions. Goodman's employer, the NWAC, was established in mid-1917 to cover domestic propaganda and particularly targeted industrial audiences, although it operated in all areas of England and Wales including, as Chapter 12 noted, sparsely populated rural areas. Distribution of its weekly newspaper, *Reality*, focused on industrial areas and it published several articles and pamphlets by prominent labour figures. Similar to the bluntness with which servicemen were presumed able to speak as propagandists, fellow workers and union officials sometimes also used uncompromising terms. In *A Call to War Workers of the Engineering and Shipbuilding Industries*, the Amalgamated Society of Engineers member F. H. Rose issued 'a call from the work bench' as someone not employed by either government or the union. Rose noted engineering's particular importance in this industrial war, before condemning

> the decadence of the skilled worker … There has been an absence of motive and a lack of enthusiasm; a disposition to get time in rather than to get work out … If

trade privileges and union regulations are more to us than the blood of our own begotten, a miracle only can bring a victory.

In such circumstances, it would not be deserved. 'The road to victory can only be made by our unremitting labour, and solidified by our skill and devotion', he concluded. While Rose's final point encouraged engineers' pride in their valuable skills, most of his pamphlet condemned thoughts of anything but victory. Even valid complaints were not unique to engineers, and they had special skills and responsibilities in wartime.[6]

Such browbeating was intended as a necessary hard word in war workers' ears but was unlikely to endear its author to many engineers in 1918, though Rose was elected a Labour MP in 1918. Another pamphlet, by the former TUC president Harry Gosling, suggested members of his rivermen's union sorted out disagreements with an immediate, honest fight in their barge so that 'the thing is ended'. This was, he felt, 'the British way', and Rose's uncompromising critique may have been taken in similar spirit. Nonetheless, Gosling took a different tone, stressing how much the war demonstrated labour's importance and assuring readers that there would be pressure for much better conditions after the war. Further, he argued that union officials like himself, by contributing to wartime committees, improved connections across classes:

> The Trades Unions of England have given every worker possible to help in the war. Trades Union officials, great and small, are all of them largely involved in voluntary war work. They are members of different committees. On these committees they meet … people drawn from quite other classes of society. The lighterman finds himself sitting next to, and working in co-operation with, the titled lady and the high military official. He discovers that they are people very like himself … They in turn realise that the mysterious 'labour agitator' is not so terrible an individual as they imagined. It is not necessary to put away their best silver or fine china when he comes to their houses … They reach a common understanding over common work for the welfare of their country.

By engaging in such war work, Gosling argued, union officials were building lasting connections that would assist workers after the war in rebuilding a better and fairer Britain. Such a mixture of arguments was typical of the NWAC's wider propaganda narrative – workers were praised, difficulties were sympathized with and promises were made for the future, but they were also reminded that there was hard work to be done now.[7]

Gosling's emphasis on voluntary committee roles as war work, like Tweedie's on 'women with brains', pointed to an element of 'war work' beyond regular employment. Wartime propagandists suggested it was not sufficient merely to accept longer and more demanding work. Civilians should also find ways to do war work domestically or in place of their leisure time. A 1918 War Office Topical Budget newsreel, for example, depicted 'British Schoolboys at War Work. Gathering in Flax crop during holidays', while a National Service press notice encouraged women and girls to spend summer evenings collecting stray wool from country hedgerows. Propagandists like Goodman stressed that, as important as women's work in various new occupations was, housewifery remained essential and part of war work. Women at home assisted the war effort by making the most of food scraps, preserving fruit, repairing or repurposing their family's clothes, recycling materials and other things. Another NWAC propagandist imagined a scene with a VC-winning soldier visiting his home town. Rather than celebrate his own valour, he suggests heroism is 'doing the job which happens to lie alongside' and asks his neighbours what they are doing. While one young woman works at a munitions factory, Mrs Tibble says all her time is spent raising six children, while an older man laughingly describes his work on an allotment, sometimes with help, but 'I done enough myself to make these old bones of mine ache something awful at times. My 'taters were as good as anyone's, and my beans was the best on our 'lotments.' The soldier then provides the moral of the story, praising them all as heroes doing their part in the 'home offensive'.[8] Percy Brebner's homespun tale asserting the equal merit of all wartime efforts featured (like Goodman's columns for women) in war supplements provided to provincial newspapers throughout the UK (Table 1), thus obtaining wide circulation.

Anticipating Gregory's rejection of workers' supposed unreliability by more than seventy years, Caroline Playne noted that the 'British working classes as a whole upheld the war from its outbreak to the end, exceptions were but a small minority'. Nonetheless, she asserted, the burden became increasingly heavy:

> War work almost always made excessive demands on the capabilities and powers of endurance of those engaged in it. Urgent appeals continued to be issued throughout the war to men and women to do their utmost, and events added to the urgency of the appeals.[9]

Propagandists attempted to offset the obvious negative consequences of excessive war work by assuring people that the burdens were temporary and would lead to a brighter future. As noted above, labour voices like Gosling stressed workers would gain from the increased connections of union officials with elite society through wartime committee work, while others like the South African War Cabinet member, Smuts, toured industrial areas calling for better futures for all parts of society as the natural reward for wartime service, provided the hard work continued till victory. Increasingly, during 1918, promises were accompanied by genuine workplace concessions.[10] Nonetheless (as Chapter 26 discusses further), promises of a better future created expectations that, when later disappointed, encouraged views of deceitful propaganda.

Reassurance of only temporary changes to Britain and the workplace offered a less promising future for many women. While some undertook war work 'for the duration', fully expecting to withdraw after the war, others eagerly sought 'new work opportunities at higher wages than those available in traditional venues like domestic service', first in munitions work, then elsewhere. What Curnock presented as women's lack of patriotism in declining to join the WAAC, Janet Watson interprets as working women's pragmatic pursuit of better pay in war industries.[11] Such women were less likely to relish a return

Table 1. Appearances of Percy James Brebner, 'The Home Offensive', in provincial newspaper *War Supplements* on 1–2 November 1918 identified in *British Newspaper Archive*, 4 May 2024.

	County	Area of UK	No of examples in BNA
	Berkshire	England	3
	Brecknockshire	Wales	1
	Buckinghamshire	England	1
	Cumberland	England	1
	Derbyshire	England	1
	Durham	England	1
	Gloucestershire	England	2
	Kent	England	3
	Lancashire	England	1
	Leicestershire	England	1
	Lincolnshire	England	2
	Nottinghamshire	England	1
	Oxfordshire	England	1
	Roxburghshire	Scotland	1
	Somerset	England	4
	Staffordshire	England	1
	Stirlingshire	Scotland	1
	Sussex	England	5
	Tyrone	Ireland	2
	West Lothian	Scotland	1
	Worcestershire	England	1
	Yorkshire	England	1
TOTALS	22	17 x England; 1 x Ireland; 3 x Scotland; 1 x Wales	36

to the pre-war status quo. Recognizing this, propagandists like Goodman emphasized that, even if women did not keep their new roles, they would benefit from good wartime wages, as well as learning useful skills that could serve other purposes while dwelling on their duties as (finally recognized) citizens. As women's post-war ejection from many industrial roles showed, urgent appeals for patriotic war work were, like so many other elements of wartime propaganda, geared to immediate needs. Once victory was attained, both the propaganda and the war work stopped.

Notes

1. *How You Can Help Your Country* (NWSC pamphlet no. 82, n.d.), 12; Margaret Osborne [E. M. Goodman], 'The Woman's Part. How to Tackle Spring Cleaning Difficulties in War Time', *Nuneaton Observer War Supplement*, week ending 11 May 1918, 2; [Archibald Hartrick] *War Work, 1914-1918: Playing the Game* (n.p.d.).
2. Mrs Alec-Tweedie, 'Women and War Economy', *English Review*, 89 (April 1916), 353, 357; Mrs Alec-Tweedie, *Women and Soldiers* (London: John Lane, 1918), 55; IWM, MS Women, War and Society, 1914-18: The Women at Work Collection, B.O.3 13/2, Tweedie to Lady Norman, 13 October 1917.
3. TNA NATS1/1286, 'The Servant's Chance', draft notice sent to '6 Evening Papers' on 12 July 1917.
4. Robert Baden-Powell, 'Are You In This?' (PRC poster no. 112, 1915).
5. 'Foreword', *"Carry On": British Women's Work in War Time* (London: Harrison, Jehring, n.d. [1917]); [Goodman], 'The Woman's Part. Not Too Old at Forty – or Even Sixty', *Nuneaton Observer War Supplement*, week ending 4 May 1918, 2; On Goodman's propaganda, see Monger, 'Nothing Special?'.
6. F. H. Rose, *A Call to War Workers in the Engineering and Shipbuilding Industries* (London: Hayman, Christy & Lilly, 1918), 8, 20; on workers' attitudes to the war, see Gregory, *Last Great War*, esp. ch. 6; on the NWAC's foundation and organization, see Monger, *Patriotism and Propaganda*, chs. 1-2.
7. Harry Gosling, *Peace: How to Get and Keep It* (London: Cassell, n.d. [1917]), 14; for the NWAC's narrative, see Monger, *Patriotism and Propaganda*, esp. chs. 4, 7.
8. IWM, *War Office Topical Budget*, 369-1, September 1918; TNA NATS1/1286, press notice, 'War Work for Children', sent to newspapers 11 May 1917; Monger, 'Nothing Special?'; Percy James Brebner, 'The Home Offensive', in, for example, *Westerham Herald War Supplement*, week ending 2 November 1918, 2.
9. Playne, *Society at War*, 113.
10. For some discussion of propaganda promises for the future, see Monger, *Patriotism and Propaganda*, ch. 8; for concessions, see Gregory, *Last Great War*, ch. 6, esp. 204-5.
11. Watson, *Fighting Different Wars*, 33-4.

CHAPTER 24
X – CENSORSHIP

First, a disclaimer. X did not indicate censorship in the First World War. Other letters did, particularly the 'D' of the Press Bureau's D notices, prohibiting publication of sensitive information. X did already have symbolic status as the unknown – in mathematical equations, for instance – and was sometimes over-typed to obscure deleted words in typewritten correspondence, but its associations with censorship relate to mid-twentieth-century film classification. A previous, general, First World War-related A to Z selected x-rays, while commercial propaganda in support of Belgian relief aimed at children (discussed in Chapter 3), opted for 'Xmas' and a picture of a soldier buying the *Strand* magazine's Christmas edition.[1] Nonetheless, with xenophobic propaganda already covered in earlier chapters, purists must forgive the anachronistic use of X for this chapter on wartime censorship!

Peterson suggests Britain's first act of propaganda was actually one of censorship, namely, cutting the undersea cables connecting Germany and the United States. From then, he suggests, British censorship and propaganda were 'Siamese twins of public opinion [which] were from that time to dictate what the American people were to think'. Peterson saw censorship as 'negative propaganda' in the sense of obstructing enemy communication, alongside Britain's institution of 'positive propaganda' – the communication of its own perspective on the war. British mail censorship also allowed insights into enemy communication to the United States, while he suggested censorship of Britain's press, via the Press Bureau, also helped control US opinion, which drew its European news from censored British sources.[2]

Certainly, the PB's rapid establishment indicated official intentions to control what was said about the war. British officials learned from press coverage of the South African war at the turn of the century that some management was necessary. Lord Kitchener, appointed secretary for war in August 1914, particularly resented press intrusion into military affairs after criticism of his conduct in South Africa (which, given the substantial deaths in concentration camps instituted at his orders, was merited) with the result, noted in Chapter 6, that he obstructed press access to the fighting fronts for some time. More broadly, however, Britain's armed forces Ministries had already established the Admiralty, War Office and Press Committee in 1912 to reduce friction with newspapers through clearer communication. While this continued into the war, Churchill, then First Lord of the Admiralty, announced the PB's formation on 7 August 1914. Its leadership changed twice before the colonial administrator Sir Frank Swettenham and the journalist Sir Edward Cook took charge of what became a team of 300 censors in May 1915. Cook took pains to distinguish the PB's work from wider censorship. It had no hand in cable or postal censorship, he noted, which were the War Office's concern, as was censorship of soldiers' letters. Likewise, despite issuing B and C notices, providing information newspapers *could* publish, Cook added that the PB had no power to issue its own information – it simply distributed notices on behalf of government departments. Meanwhile, the PB's D notices spelled out things that newspapers must not discuss.[3]

Demm suggests one focus of British press censorship was on industrial disputes, connected to the issues surrounding war work discussed in Chapter 23, which he claims were 'regulated by numerous D-notes'. However, this is not borne out by comprehensive analysis of the PB's D notices. Only 14 of 747 wartime notices addressed industrial disputes, and one of these, in August 1917, cancelled all previous restrictions, following editors' protests that obscuring such information was counter-productive. Editors were reminded that DORA prohibited the encouragement of strikes and warned to use careful judgement in any coverage, but no restrictions on reporting were issued during the most acute period of industrial dissent in the winter of 1917–18. As discussed in much fuller detail elsewhere, wider references to industrial venues usually restricted commentary for fear of making factories targets for air raids.[4] This fitted the wider security focus governing most notices. The most common subjects for censorship were military and naval topics (where the restriction generally prohibited newspapers from publishing information about the location of units or ships, which might increase enemy knowledge of British forces' movements) and the movements of notable people. While the latter category of prohibition was occasionally used for personal convenience – as when Lloyd George asked for a weekend visit to his country home not to be mentioned so that he would not be disturbed – most, again, wished to avoid creating targets, whether of the people themselves or the places they visited. Even things that seemed absurd, such as prohibiting weather forecasts, were justified by Cook as precautions against providing militarily useful information to the enemy.

As previously noted, some notices went beyond straightforward security concerns. The notice, described in Chapter 5, prohibiting images of white nurses tending to non-white troops, for instance, reflected racial prejudice more than any serious question of discipline, while D611 (Figure 20), issued 12 December 1917, instructed newspapers not to report damage done to paintings in the National Gallery, supposedly to avoid copycat incidents. The soldier in question, Private Robin Pearce, apparently damaged nine works – including paintings by Claude, Hogarth, Rembrandt, Turner and Van Dyck– with a trenching tool. The National Gallery Board, including the War Cabinet member Lord Curzon considered it 'obviously undesirable in the public interest, both as regards the repute of the army and the safety of public collections, that this action by an isolated soldier should be given publicity' and thus asked the PB to issue a notice prohibiting discussion of the event or subsequent court proceedings while taking steps to patrol the gallery more carefully.[5] The incident was duly excluded from press coverage.

As an aside to this incident, the Gallery Board's minutes were signed off by Lord Lansdowne, a former Conservative Foreign Secretary then, supposedly, in public disgrace following a letter to the *Daily Telegraph* in November calling for negotiated peace. Despite the damage to his political reputation, he continued to sit on the Board

X – Censorship

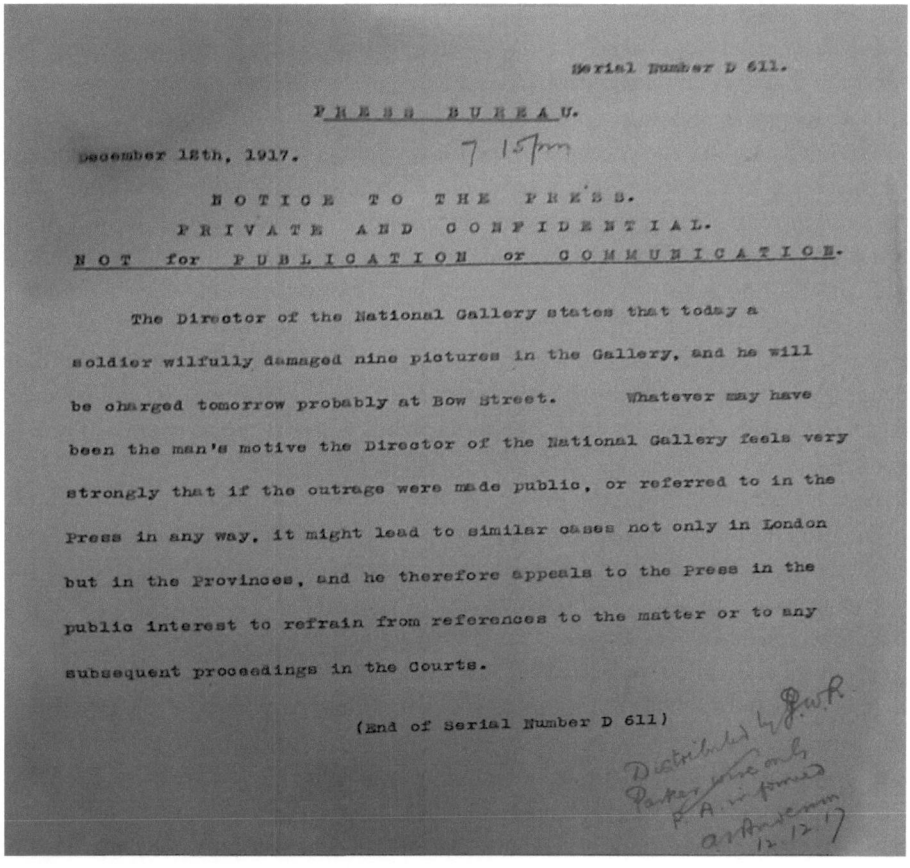

Figure 20 Press Bureau D notice D611, 12 December 1917.
Source: TNA HO139/45.

with Curzon, a key government figure. This reflected the web of social connections within the British Establishment. Such connections also existed between press proprietors and politicians, assisting censorship. One reason it could remain relatively light and largely focus on protecting information with security implications was the reliance on editors undertaking voluntary self-censorship in the 'national interest'. While regulations existed (and were occasionally used) to punish transgressions, many did not transgress in the first place because of a sense of social and wartime duty, not only to withhold sensitive material but also to support the war effort.[6] Newspapers of the day already maintained discreet silence over certain things, such as the extramarital affairs of prominent politicians like Asquith and Lloyd George. Wartime restrictions, justified by security or appeals to the 'national interest', were thus not often challenged.

This network of informal and social, as well as professional, contact between editors, politicians and officials meant the PB acted as an additional channel of communication. Cook and Swettenham maintained regular contact with editors via groups like the

Newspaper Proprietors' Association, headed by Sir George Riddell, editor of the *News of the World* and a close friend of Lloyd George. This allowed regular opportunities for editors to challenge unwelcome intrusions. Mostly, these related to attempted censorship of tone or opinion rather than sensitive information. When a 1915 notice asserted that 'exaggerated accounts of successes' in the press might encourage public complacency, for instance, Riddell retorted that 'if the public are being unduly soothed and elated, this responsibility lies with the Government', which supplied the insufficient information on which press reports were based.[7] Over time, the PB established a functional relationship with, at least, the metropolitan press, declining to censor statements of opinion, both when unwisely requested by government departments and when editors themselves criticized rival papers' commentary. Even strong wartime critics like the leading ILP figure Philip Snowden acknowledged that the PB's policy involved 'no unnecessary interference with the expression of opinions', while a report on an organization less particular about civil liberties (MI7) claimed 'political censorship did not exist … the Bureau, though nominally under the Home Office, carried out in reality the instructions of the Admiralty, War Office and Ministry of Munitions'. Riddell concluded there was 'no doubt the war killed Cook', who suffered from constant criticism from both government Departments and the press. Although he noted that tensions continued throughout the war, he accepted that 'it is surprising the system worked as well as it did'.[8]

Meanwhile, despite their censorship of sensitive military information, restrictions were applied rather more tightly to major dailies than to provincial papers, which published soldiers' letters reporting on their conditions. Describing the experience of local troops at the 1915 Battle of Loos, the *Northampton Daily Chronicle*'s headline, '7th Northamptons Cut Up', hardly obscured the situation. Thus, John Bourne suggests, censorship was, in some respects, 'astonishingly lax'.[9] As has been previously argued, this was less true in Ireland, both before and after the 1916 Easter Rising, where censorship was generally stricter. Arthur Griffith, founder of Sinn Féin, had his newspaper, *Scissors and Paste*, which rearranged British press material to negative effect, suppressed in 1915. After the Rising, a special Irish Press Censorship Office was established to monitor Irish commentary. Despite this, Donal Ó Drisceoil suggests, critical commentary remained. While the PB issued special 'Ireland' D notices in 1917–18, often restricting reports of Sinn Féin's activities, Irish dissent could not be wholly censored.[10] As Chapter 22 noted, some government propaganda actions, such as Arthur Lynch's attempt to recruit Irish volunteer soldiers, actually provided platforms for Sinn Féin dissent.

In largely avoiding censoring opinion, the PB struck a tolerable balance between government and editors. This corresponded with the view of the leading Liberal and 1916 home secretary, Herbert Samuel, who indicated that press commentary 'which could be regarded as unpatriotic' was acceptable, provided it did not incite things such as strikes. This does not mean, however, that wartime censorship – nor even Samuel's direction – was universally benign. While press commentary remained relatively vibrant and, as seen in previous chapters, critical voices could mock officialdom, censorship of other media could be stricter. Millman notes that, while Samuel led the Home Office, direct censorship of ideas remained too much, but interference with their distribution was another matter. People distributing anti-conscription material began to be arrested and imprisoned, meaning that 'to hold an opinion was not illegal, but to express it in such a manner as to make an anti-war critique effective might be'. Millman charts the harassment of the No-Conscription Fellowship's leaders, suggesting that spells in prison broke the resolve of intellectuals like Fenner Brockway and Clifford Allen, with the Fellowship's activities only continuing because of the activism of its volunteer women. In choosing whether to suppress publications, he suggests, the author's fame was a key consideration. 'While, for example, George Bernard Shaw was certainly annoying, he was also famous' and likely to publicize widely any censorship he might experience.[11] A further squeeze was placed on critical commentary by new DORA regulations that required publishers of all publications to be identified and made them potentially liable for prosecution, thus reducing publication venues by intimidating publishers.

When a member of the public complained to the PB about the monthly paper, *Satire*, published by a deaf anarchist, Leonard Motler, Cook had it inspected by the Department of Public Prosecutions. Its front-page cartoon (Figure 21) depicted John Bull as a profiteer (denoted by his top hat and cigar) lounging on top of the world with a priest and soldier, while the octopus of capitalism strangles workers. Nonetheless, the only element identified as breaching DORA was a brief passage, 'Fables for Fools', which attacked war loans as a valueless sham. Since prosecution would only likely result in a small fine, no action was initially planned. The PB's original complainant, the artist Frank L. Emanuel, having heard nothing, wrote again, observing that

> although 'Satire' was quite unknown in your office – though openly sold in London – the number I left you with is the tenth. The paper is one of many of the same type which may be equally unknown to you. They may be bought at a socialist bookshop in Charing X [sic] road + in Red Lion Street + probably at hundreds of other places.

Emanuel threatened to send his letter to the press or his MP. Cook replied that submission of material for advance censorship was voluntary – authors and publishers published at their own risk and members of the public could report things they considered seditious. Despite initially tolerating the paper, however, closer inspection by the Director of Public Prosecution suggested Motler's paper was running an 'illegal lottery', which resulted in prosecution.[12]

Despite such interference, critical voices continued to appear throughout the war, sometimes finding ways to embarrass official censorship. Imprisonment of critics was not unchallenged. When the philosopher Bertrand Russell was imprisoned for six months after disparaging comments about US troops, the *Manchester Guardian*'s editor C. P. Scott protested that

> Mr. Russell's jest about American troops was tactless and misplaced ... How many tactless and stupid things are said daily by people of all parties and every shade of opinion about the war! If every such expression laid a man open for prosecution

Figure 21 Cover of *Satire*, vol. 1, no. 10 (October 1917) in Press Bureau correspondence re. seditious propaganda.
Source: TNA HO139/23.

the gaols would be too few. The petition [by 'representative Labour men' against the sentence] rightly lays stress on the immense importance of liberty of expression in war as in peace. Controversial questions are not suspended in war-time; on the contrary, some of them become more than ordinarily acute. We need a full measure of freedom to discuss them ... The real function of press censorship in war is to prevent news reaching the enemy, but for articles accused of giving information writers have been let off with a fine, while any indiscretion in a peace advocate is visited with long terms of imprisonment. There is neither equality nor freedom in this. The moral effect is bad, and the curtailment of reasonable discussion is dangerous.

Scott's protest acknowledged a genuine role for censorship but condemned unequal persecution. Excessively punitive censorship thus risked backfiring on officials. Not only, as Millman suggests, did holding back from censorship help authorities assert that free speech still operated in Britain, but censors also knew that respected voices like Scott's could challenge perceived persecution, potentially giving the critical cause more attention than it would otherwise have received. Elsewhere, despite the UDC's Secretary Morel being imprisoned for technical infringement of censorship rules regarding overseas distribution, Marvin Swartz notes that it continued publishing. Having submitted all its existing pamphlets for PB review in November 1917, it republished them with 'passed by censor' on the front cover, embarrassing the Home Secretary (by then Sir George Cave) by giving the implication of official endorsement. A further change to the relevant DORA regulation followed swiftly.[13]

Christopher Nevinson spent the war as an official war artist hired by Wellington House. Though producing propaganda material such as his depictions of war work for the *Britain's Effort and Ideals* series, he was also irked by censorship. However, a War Office official's attempt to prohibit his display of the painting *Paths of Glory*, depicting the bodies of British soldiers, provoked a confrontation in early 1918. The official's intervention was the equivalent of the kind of censorship of 'opinion' that the PB carefully avoided. The reality that British soldiers died was hardly news to the public in 1918 and the bodies were not depicted disrespectfully. Nevinson displayed the picture anyway, with a strip of paper labelled 'Censored' across the centre of the painting, while complaining to Masterman that war artists required independence since 'my work would be valueless as an artist and propagandist otherwise.' Masterman agreed that only something giving away militarily sensitive information should be censored. Nevinson's disobedience ultimately drew more attention than the painting would likely have received if displayed in its original form. Despite a War Office scolding, moreover, Sue Malvern suggests Nevinson ultimately 'enhanced his standing as an avant-garde artist by appearing to be persecuted and misunderstood'.[14] As the retorts of Scott, the UDC and Nevinson differently show, a key reason for censorship to take as light a touch as possible was the capacity for embarrassment it could cause. If censorship increased attention to the object to be censored, it was self-defeating.

Notes

1. The National World War I Museum and Memorial, online exhibition, *WWI A-Z: An A-Z Guide to the War that Shaped the 20th Century* (https://www.theworldwar.org/learn/educator-resource/wwi-z-z-guide-war-shaped-20th-century, n.d. – accessed 6 May 2024); *Belgian Relief Fund*, 'X'.
2. Peterson, *Propaganda for War*, 12–16.
3. For press criticism of Kitchener and the army in the South African War, see Paula M. Krebs, *Gender, Race and the Writing of Empire: Public Discourse and the Boer War* (Cambridge: Cambridge University Press, 1999). For fuller details of the AWOPC and the PB's establishment, see Wilkinson, *Secrecy and the Media*, 3–62. Sir Edward Cook, *The Press in War-Time: With Some Account of the Official Press Bureau* (London: Macmillan, 1920), 33–5.
4. Demm, *Censorship and Propaganda*, 17. The outline of PB D notices that follows summarizes the far more detailed account in Monger, 'Press Bureau', which is available online, with open access.
5. TNA HO139/45, D611, 12 December 1917; National Gallery, London, NG1/8, Board Minutes (25 January 1910–8 January 1918), 13 December 1917, 384–5.
6. Sanders and Taylor, *British Propaganda*, 18–31.
7. See Monger, 'Press Bureau', 455–60, for fuller discussion of these points.
8. Philip Snowden's autobiography, quoted in Monger, 'Press Bureau', 452; TNA INF4/1B, 'Military Press Control: A History of the Work of M.I.7, 1914–1919' (1920), 13; Lord Riddell, *Lord Riddell's War Diary, 1914–1918* (London: Ivor Nicholson & Watson, 1933), 24–5.
9. David Stevenson, *1914–1918: The History of the First World War* (London: Allen Lane, 2004), 273; John Bourne, *Britain and the Great War, 1914–1918* (London: Edward Arnold, 1989), 206–7. On local papers, soldiers' letters and civilians' wider knowledge of conditions, see also McCartney, *Citizen Soldiers*, 104–10.
10. Virginia E. Glandon, *Arthur Griffith and the Advanced Nationalist Press: Ireland, 1900–1922* (New York: Peter Lang, 1985), 147–53; Ó Drisceoil, 'Keeping Disloyalty within Bounds?'; Monger, 'Press Bureau', 452–5.
11. Millman, *Managing Domestic Dissent*, 77–83.
12. TNA HO139/23, Press Bureau Correspondence – Seditious propaganda: HO139/23/96/32, correspondence regarding *Satire*, 15 October 1917–1 January 1918.
13. 'The Sentence on Mr. Bertrand Russell', *Manchester Guardian*, 17 May 1918, 4; Swartz, *Union of Democratic Control*, 191–2.
14. Sue Malvern, *Modern Art, Britain and the Great War* (New Haven: Yale University Press, 2004), 49–55; C. R. W. Nevinson, *Paint and Prejudice* (New York: Harcourt & Brace, 1938), 142–8.

CHAPTER 25
YANKS

One critical voice which felt the intrusion of British censorship discussed in Chapter 24 was H. W. Massingham, editor of the *Nation*, whose newspaper was prohibited from overseas circulation in 1917, prompting substantial protests. Massingham's attitude to the war was complex. He distressed his more radical friends by strongly supporting British intervention in 1914, although the *Nation* continued publishing liberal opinion across the spectrum. He later returned to a radical critique of government after the introduction of conscription in 1916, becoming a prominent critic of Lloyd George.[1] Before this, however, he wrote an 'open letter' to US readers, stating that

> while British feeling about America's relation to the war has varied from time to time; it has had one characteristic element: the desire to secure and retain your sympathy ...
>
> Your diplomatic service is in one way modeled on our own; but within the last few months we have had good cause to admire its unequalled efficiency and public spirit ...
>
> No country but yours could have conceived and executed such a work of disinterested humanity [as the provision of food to Belgium] ...
>
> So far, therefore, as the exercise of moral force is concerned, Britain's attitude can only be one of gratitude to the American government and nation, and of relief that so powerful a neutral force is available to save the older world ... This is a conflict, not between armies but between nations, or rather between two governing systems and their dependencies in five continents ...
>
> America, therefore, was 'in the war' from the moment the first gun was fired. Her commerce, her credit, her international obligations, were all caught up in its fatal whirl.[2]

While not produced for a propaganda organization, his observations chime with arguments commonly made by propagandists seeking US favour. Britons desired sympathetic US attitudes and admired its humanitarian instincts, greatness and efficiency, illustrated by its relief of Belgium. Britons thus owed the US gratitude and valued its intervention, although, like the Archbishop of York's observations to US audiences (see Chapter 2), Massingham partly linked US achievement to British examples. Finally, he insisted the United States was already, in 1915, part of the war. Variations on such arguments were made by propagandists of multiple stripes. Propaganda regarding the United States havered between admitting British vulnerability and need of transatlantic help (deepened by increasing US financing of the war) and residual assumptions that the United States was a culturally junior partner. Nonetheless, regular appeals to US audiences, as well as later celebrations of US intervention, indicated growing acceptance that Britain could no longer oversee world affairs independently. Effectively, wartime propagandists signalled the passage of self-appointed world leadership from London to Washington, sometimes consoled by assumptions that the latter's outlook derived from British sources.

As discussed previously, official propagandists targeted the United States early and often, with the MP and novelist Gilbert Parker leading Wellington House's efforts and contacting thousands of influential Americans. However, not only official propagandists sought US favour. Swartz notes that the UDC eagerly associated itself with the United States and President Wilson. As noted in Chapter 21, the UDC was an early advocate of a league of nations. It rejoiced when Wilson's December 1916 peace note urged belligerents to consider the idea. After US entry into the war, UDC member Norman Angell wrote a leaflet citing similarities between Wilson's speeches and UDC policies. His 'Fourteen Points' speech of January 1918 was also considered 'a vindication of its own position' and, despite concerns about Wilson's anti-German views once the United States was in the war, the UDC considered him 'an invaluable ally in the campaign for a liberal peace'. However, there was an interesting circularity in evolving attitudes to the league. The concept owed most to the work of the academic Goldsworthy Lowes Dickinson. Dickinson convened the 'Bryce Group', including UDC executive members Ponsonby, Angell and Hobson, which met at Lord Bryce's house to develop the scheme. Swartz notes that it was really Bryce's presence, with his intellectual credentials and popularity as a recent ambassador, that brought the league to US prominence and influenced Wilson. Former president Theodore Roosevelt dismissed Dickinson's earlier suggestion of international resolution without force: 'As for Lowes Dickinson and his kind ... Some of the things for which they strive are right and proper. The same things are striven for with infinitely more efficiency and sanity by serious men such as James Bryce.' Thus, a cornerstone of critical UDC propaganda owed influence substantially to a figure frequently criticized for his association with atrocity propaganda. Dickinson was further encouraged by the Foreign Secretary Sir Edward Grey to look to the United States, 'telling him that such a League would be welcomed by England, but that it should be initiated in the United States'.[3] The circle was completed in 1917–18 when official propagandists latched onto Wilson and the league to vindicate Britain's wider war effort. Depending on perspective, this either undercut or bolstered the UDC by officially co-opting its most prominent idea.

NWAC propaganda stressed US examples and the league from the start of its campaigns. At the first War Aims meeting in Bristol, in September 1917, the Lord Mayor reminded his audience of German atrocities, before dwelling on US participation. He quoted the American Federation of Labour's statement supporting the war effort: 'Either democracy will endure and men be free, or autocracy will triumph and men be enslaved. We declare in this crisis that the one fundamental need is unity of action.' The Federation thus denounced labour opposition or any resort to strikes. Later, Alderman F. Sheppard argued,

Men like himself who always advocated peace, felt that they must support the cause of the Allies against German brutality. He hoped that when it ended there would be set up something like a League of Nations that would prevent any mad monarch from embroiling the world in war again ... He referred to the war aims of the Allies, and expressed agreement with the Lord Mayor that if we had not gone to the help of France and Belgium we might have got rich as the result of their troubles, but it would have been a mean and unmanly thing to do.[4]

The Bristol speakers, in a rhetorical combination typical of NWAC arguments, linked German crimes and US entry. Citing US labour's endorsement of the war and disavowal of industrial action reminded British workers of their obligation to knuckle under, while Sheppard's reference to the league promised a more stable future for the world, which he linked back to Britain's original, honourable decision to support France and Belgium. Later, Grey produced a widely circulated pamphlet arguing that the league's success depended on governments and leaders embracing it wholeheartedly. Further, however,

Germany had to be convinced that force does not pay ... and that when the world is free from the menace of these literary rulers, with their sharp swords, shining armour, and mailed fists, Germany will find peaceful development assured ... Till Germany feels this to be true, there can be no League of Nations in the sense intended by President Wilson.[5]

Grey, here, followed his own advice to Dickinson to present the league as a US, and especially Wilsonian, initiative. This flattered US opinion by implicitly accepting Wilson's depiction of US entry as a disinterested, humanitarian act and harnessed US priorities to Britain's wider goal of eradicating 'Prussian militarism'.

More than this, propagandists insisted that Americans generally, and Wilson specifically, were essentially British. The NWAC republished an interview by Sir Mark Sykes, an influential intelligence officer and member of the War Cabinet secretariat. 'If one thing can give courage' to war-weary Britons, he suggested, it was that 'one calm man has been watching our travail; that man has blood in his veins of English stock; he is not passionate nor easily moved, he has been calculating and slow in his deliberation', much like the humblebragging Britons described in Chapter 8. 'His name is President Wilson.' Wilson himself, meanwhile (who actually had Scottish and Scots-Irish lineage), happily tied US and British heritage closely, comparing George Washington, in a multiply reproduced speech, to 'the Barons of Runnymede' who compelled King John to accept Magna Carta in the thirteenth century. Similarly, a pamphlet by the League of Nations Society, which emerged from the Bryce group, labelled the league 'An International Magna Charta'. While Wilson represented US 'wisdom and culture', the organization followed a *British* precedent. US entry, Wilson and the league all validated Britain's war effort in official interpretations, while even Wilson himself and independent, dissenting opinion, stressed close British–US ties. Wilson's ambassador to the UK, in a speech reprinted as a propaganda pamphlet, claimed, dubiously, that 'no American can feel otherwise but at home anywhere in England'. As Peterson notes, in emphasizing connections 'the British captured the American flag and waved it in front of themselves',[6] but they were sometimes encouraged by prominent Americans.

Trying to tie the United States to Britain commenced before US entry. From the start, efforts were made to appeal to US fellow-feeling, humanitarian instincts or self-interest. As noted previously, *King Albert's Book*, ostensibly a multinational tribute to Belgium, doubled as an appeal to world – and particularly (as its editor, Hall Caine, asserted later) US – opinion. While British commentators emphasized the special nobility of Britain's support for neutral Belgium, they also made clear that Britain and its allies could not resolve the war alone. World opinion should be stimulated, and other nations should recognize the war's importance, Britain's virtue and the need to intervene. Only the former prime minister Earl Rosebery appealed outright to US interests, arguing that Germany aimed to destroy Britain's empire, after which 'the liberties and prosperity of America would alarm the jealousy of the tyrant', but wider calls for both admiration and help aimed squarely at US attitudes.[7] Similarly, Bryce and Toynbee's parliamentary report on the Armenian Genocide was supported by Masterman at Wellington House because of its potential US impact. Bryce's popularity, together with the network of US collaborators he and Toynbee called upon, provided what Masterman called an 'unrivalled opportunity' for US attention. Their key contact, the missionary organizer James Barton, was keen to publicize the genocide due to previous missionary service in the region and sympathy with Armenian Christians, as well as the threat to his organization's schools and missions. He thus eagerly drove publicity in the United States, rather than Parker or others. Barton's contacts, including leading US businessmen and Wilson himself, ensured the report was trailed in the *New York Times' Current History* before publication, while Wilson approved two days' official fundraising for Armenia. As discussed elsewhere in greater detail, Bryce and Toynbee's main aim was to highlight Armenians' plight and encourage efforts to help. Barton's endeavours heightened what could be accomplished by British publicity alone. British efforts to document the crimes tied Britain and the United States in common humanitarian concern, with hopes that the neutral United States, unburdened by war costs, could act. Sure enough, US fundraising dwarfed that in Britain. Once again, this effectively acknowledged that US intervention was needed in international affairs.[8] Propagandists during the United States' neutral period thus indicated, at best, desire for US partnership or, perhaps, to defer some international matters to US leadership.

Alongside these substantial projects, and the many other publications Wellington House distributed in the United States,[9] individuals besides Parker provided British perspectives to the United States, sometimes at US request. Roosevelt – who felt the United States must join the war – eagerly corresponded with British connections. He warned Bryce in 1915 against excessively promoting the league or accepting official justifications of neutrality, which he felt comforted Britain's enemies. This was particularly serious from Bryce who had an influence in America that no other Englishman has … [especially] among well-meaning people who, unless guided aright, go into any kind of foolish nominal peace movement and who are eager to find some excuse for saying that the United States has no duty to perform that will entail risk or hardship …

I have earnestly advised the British Government … to yield as far as possible to America's demands – and this for England's sake. But in a public argument from you what is needed is an emphatic appeal to the American people not to be neutral between right and wrong.

Later, Roosevelt contacted the novelist and activist Mary Humphry Ward, asking that 'some writer like yourself … put vividly before our people what the English people are doing … the effort, the resolution and the self-sacrifice'. Ward obliged with *England's Effort*, published the following year and praised by the former US ambassador to Britain, Joseph Choate, partly because Ward was 'a staunch believer in the greatness of America's future'. Influential pro-war Americans like Roosevelt and Choate thus encouraged British propagandists to flatter US egos while firmly promoting Britain's war effort.[10] Propagandists like Ward, meanwhile, knew how to attract US favour.

Meanwhile, notable Britons toured the United States, independently or at official request, to put Britain's case directly. Besides entertainer-propagandists like Lauder and Bairnsfather, activists like Christabel Pankhurst and clerics like the Archbishop of York (all discussed previously), leading intellectual and literary figures like the classicist Gilbert Murray and the poet John Masefield toured. Murray, another enthusiastic league advocate, paired academic lecturing in 1916 with discussion of the war but was wary of touring the United States again alongside Lord Northcliffe's 'mission' in 1917, which might allow the press baron to claim credit for his work. Northcliffe's instability was commented on by close colleagues too, with the editor of his paper, the *Times*, telling a friend he thought Northcliffe would do a good job in the United States 'if he doesn't chuck it in a huff'.[11] Masefield, meanwhile, toured in 1918, confiding to an American friend, that he felt he was 'wasted' speaking to general audiences and 'I don't feel I've done any good here'. He feared military recruits would 'wish me the devil, me & my England' if he promoted British efforts too fervently. Nonetheless, he toured for ten weeks, publishing his speeches.[12]

Such ongoing efforts as Northcliffe and Masefield's, after US entry into the war, showed continuing British concern about US attitudes. Wilson's designation of the United States as an 'associated power', rather than an ally, deliberately kept it aloof from its 'old world' partners. Given Britain's dependence on US financial as well as military support, communication remained surprisingly deferential. Lord Balfour, undertaking an early mission in 1917, showed himself 'deeply conscious of America's susceptibilities and sensitivenesses [*sic*]' and eager to maintain 'the constant statement that the British had come to serve, not to interfere'. Readers in Logan, Utah, were assured that there was 'a certain modesty about the expressions of the wishes of the visitors. They wish to act on suggestions which come from the United States and only to make suggestions of their own if they find that such are welcome.'[13] Such caution, perhaps expected of minor functionaries, is more surprising from

Figure 22 Roland Hill, 'Some Pitcher', *Welcome*, 3 July 1918, 163.
Source: Bodleian Library, University of Oxford (author's photograph).

a former prime minister and current foreign secretary of an imperial nation accustomed to global authority. Within Britain, meanwhile, propagandists celebrated US culture. A demonstration of baseball between US army and navy teams was reportedly watched by over 10,000 spectators, while a cartoon in *Welcome* (Figure 22) showed Uncle Sam heaving a pitch towards a sweating Hindenburg, with Britain's John Bull as catcher, ready to receive the ball, again suggesting a necessary, if complex, partnership. Pitchers had the glamorous role, with a regular propaganda column in *Welcome* noting, in explaining baseball, that 'if a baseball pitcher has a lapse the fat is in the fire'. Nonetheless, a pre-war guide noted, the 'best work of a pitcher can be rendered ineffective if he does not receive the support of the catcher', who was 'the man who is practically in control of the field'. Roland Hill's cartoon, then, perhaps subtly suggested US greatness still needed British guidance. Meanwhile, another column noted George V's planned attendance at a 4 July baseball demonstration, adding that it was 'a jolly good job [George III's] German mercenaries got it in the neck' on the 'first Fourth of July'.[14]

British propagandists of all stripes – official and unofficial, supportive and critical of their nation's war efforts – urgently and regularly put their case to US audiences. A recent study notes the persistence of interwar views that British propaganda somehow tricked the United States into the war. Rather than investigating Britain's propaganda towards the United States, however, Stephen Badsey suggests it remains common to assume 'baseless and deceitful lying' was its contribution to US intervention.[15] However, closer investigation of British propaganda towards US audiences (in Chapters 2 and 8, as well as here) shows persistent anxiety to win US sympathy by emphasizing US and British cultural closeness and suggesting – increasingly strongly – that it was time for the United States to accompany, if not take over, British world leadership.

For US Independence Day, 1918, the Ministry of Information advertised an event celebrating 'Anglo-Saxon Fellowship' in Westminster, inevitably addressed by Bryce, as well as Churchill. Bryce, in what the *Daily News* called a 'quiet, thoughtful speech', noted that Britain entered the war to defend neutral Belgium:

> When Germany followed up her first crime by perpetrating upon non-combatants and neutrals a succession of outrages unheard of before, it had been America's turn. Seeing every principle of right overridden, every sentiment of humanity cast to the winds, America had come forth in her strength. A new star had blazed forth in the sky ... a star whose light would know no fading. The common sense of duty and the common spirit which had arisen ... would bring America and Britain still closer together.[16]

Bryce's celebration of US intervention noted that Britain led the way, invoked atrocities and predicted greater future partnership. Nonetheless, this 'new star ... whose light would know no fading' suggested his acceptance that the United States was now the brightest force in the world. British propaganda appeals to the neutral United States, followed by missions and celebrations of its wartime partnership suggested at least partial, and perhaps willing, recognition of a passed torch.

Notes

1. Havighurst, *Radical Journalist*, 226–68.
2. H. W. Massingham, 'An Open Letter to the American People', *Atlantic Monthly*, 115, no. 5 (May 1915), 701–2.
3. Swartz, *Union of Democratic Control*, 97–8, 131–40; Theodore Roosevelt to Susan Dexter Dalton Cooley, 2 December 1914, in Elting T. Morison (ed.), *The Letters of Theodore Roosevelt*, vol. 8 (Cambridge, MA: Harvard University Press, 1954), 855; George Macaulay Trevelyan, *Grey of Fallodon: Being the Life of Sir Edward Grey Afterwards Viscount Grey of Fallodon* (London: Longmans, Green, 1937), 312–13.
4. 'War Aims Campaign. First Meeting in Bristol', *Western Daily Press*, 18 September 1917, 5.
5. Viscount Grey of Fallodon, *The League of Nations* (2nd million, London: W.H. Smith, n.d. [1918]), 8.
6. Mark Sykes, 'What Britain Has Done', *Reality*, 18 December 1917, 4; Monger, *Patriotism and Propaganda*, 145; *An International Magna Charta* (n.p.d. [1917]), 10; Walter Hines Page, *The Union of Two Great Peoples* (London: Hodder & Stoughton, 1917), 2; Peterson, *Propaganda for War*, 35.
7. Monger, 'Speaking to or for the People?', quotation at 101.
8. Monger, 'Networking against Genocide', esp. 308–9.
9. The Hoover Institution Library attributes over 400 items in its collection to Wellington House: Trevor Wood, *Inventory of the Great Britain, Foreign Office, Wellington House publications*, Hoover Institution Archive finding aid XX230, Online Archives of California (2008–14).

10 Roosevelt to Bryce, 31 March 1915; Roosevelt to Ward, 27 December 1915, both in Morison, *Letters of Theodore Roosevelt*, 915–17, 998; Joseph H. Choate, 'Preface', in Mrs. Humphry Ward, *England's Effort: Letters to an American Friend* (New York: Charles Scribner's, 1916), vi.
11 BLO, Gilbert Murray Papers, MS Gilbert Murray 486/1-3, notes of 1916 tour of US; MS Gilbert Murray 125, Bryce to Murray, 12 September 1917; Geoffrey Dawson Papers, MS Dawson 66, Dawson to Mike Furse, 20 June 1916.
12 Masefield to Florence Lamont, 27 March 1918, in Corliss Lamont and Lansing Lamont (eds), *Letters of John Masefield to Florence Lamont* (New York: Columbia University Press, 1979), 63; John Masefield, *The War and the Future* (New York: Macmillan, 1918).
13 Charles Hanson Towne, *The Balfour Visit: How America Received Her Distinguished Guest; and the Significance of the Conferences in the United States in 1917* (New York: G.H. Doran, 1917), 12; 'Are Glad to Talk', *Logan Republican*, 15 May 1917, 5. On British financial dependence on the United States, see Burk, *Britain, America and the Sinews of War*.
14 Monger, 'Sporting Journalism', 392; J. E. McManus, 'Sport and Play', *Welcome*, 5 June 1918, 117; John J. McGraw, *Science of Baseball* (New York: Richard K. Fox, 1904), 17; J. E. McManus, 'Sport and Play', *Welcome*, 12 June 1918, 129. Both Hill and McManus were paid contributors to the NWAC's Publications Department.
15 Stephen Badsey, 'American Neutrality and Belligerent Propaganda: Contested Histories', in Edward Corse and Marta García Cabrera (eds), *Propaganda and Neutrality: Global Case Studies in the Twentieth Century* (London: Bloomsbury Academic, 2023), 29.
16 'Independence Day. Memorable Celebrations in all Parts of the Country', *Daily News*, 5 July 1918, 5; for the Ministry of Information's announcement, see the advertisement 'Independence Day', *Daily News*, 4 July 1918, 4.

CHAPTER 26
ZERO-SUM BIAS

By January 1918, the labour movement had wearied of uncertainty regarding Britain's wartime goals. Since the war's outbreak, successive governments had declined to state complete war aims, instead insisting – as in Grey's genuinely held conviction that a league of nations was necessary, discussed in Chapter 25– that Germany must be fully beaten before satisfactory peace was possible. In December 1917, partly inspired by US President Wilson's views, heavily promoted by both official and critical propagandists (as discussed in the previous chapter), the Labour Party and TUC issued its own joint statement of war aims. It proclaimed that British labour was involved in the war to 'make the world safe for democracy', echoing Wilson's famous justification for US intervention. Further, 'there should be henceforth on earth no more war', and the statement demanded a league of nations. It also made limited commitments to territorial changes, though disavowing imperial gains for Britain or its allies. Likewise, it stated carefully that 'inhuman and ruthless conduct' by 'particular governments' should be fully investigated. The labour statement was rapidly and positively adopted by official propaganda. A pamphlet by the Liberal MP C. A. McCurdy – a regular NWAC propagandist – added a preface that stressed the terms were 'very different from the "Peace without annexations or indemnities" which Germany so insincerely offered'. A few days later, Lloyd George made his own war aims speech (shortly before Wilson's famous Fourteen Points speech), which closely resembled the labour statement. Millman sees Lloyd George's speech as 'much more a palliation of dissent than a statement of British policy', while a recent analysis suggests the speech, 'suffused with moralism', actually 'provided a flexible basis for concluding a range of deals with other Allied leaders', which was then pinned down by Wilson's statement.[1]

Within a couple of weeks, Lloyd George addressed another labour audience, explaining the government's manpower plans to trade unionists. He noted the labour statement and claimed he and Wilson had 'laid down what was substantially the same programme of demands' (leaning, typically, on Wilson's popularity to enhance his own status). This programme was met with 'acclaim' among Britain's allies but had, he said, been treated in Germany as a sign of weakening British resolve:

> Is there a single condition laid down by you in your Trade Union aims to which you have had any response from anybody in Germany, who has got any authority to speak? Not one ...
> There has been no civilian answer at all.

Figure 23 Cover of the *Globe*, 18 January 1918.
Source: British Library.

I spoke here a fortnight ago. President Wilson's speech was delivered a few days after that. Both speeches have been thoroughly discussed in the German papers. But no civilian Minster has said a word …

If it means anything it means this: that the Prussian military power is dominant. The answer which is to be given to civilisation is an answer which will be given from the cannon's mouth.

In such circumstances, unions must accept the manpower demands: 'the people must either go on or go under'. In the Conservative *Globe* (Figure 23), Lloyd George's conclusion was a banner headline. Above left, a war savings advert encouraged readers to 'hasten victory' by investing in war bonds. Below that, a speech by the Food Controller Lord Rhondda suggested food economy was the alternative to 'famine' – there was no risk of this provided people stopped unnecessary consumption.[2] All these arguments reflected a common element of propaganda commentary – all-or-nothing, zero-sum assumptions. As previous chapters noted, propagandists assured audiences that everything, no matter how large or small, was related to the war. War bonds, in this logic, remained a choice, but each individual chose whether or not to 'hasten victory'; food consumers chose whether or not to hasten famine; workers chose to win or lose the war by their actions. Rational audiences, the messages implied, would recognize the zero-sum alternative and act accordingly.

A core aim of this book has been to demonstrate that British First World War propaganda was much more varied than casual assumptions and stereotypes suggest. Propagandists used different media and arguments to appeal to their audiences. They did this because they were trying to persuade individuals and groups to accept varying actions or ideas over time; because it made communication more dynamic than endless repetition of the same claim or image; and because propaganda used the skills of many contributors, granted varying levels of creative freedom. Propagandists increasingly met critical audiences on their own terms. Disgruntled workers were sympathized with more than scolded; US audiences were humbly, not haughtily, addressed by official British representatives. Persuasion, however, rested on a fundamental bedrock of certainty and conviction. Britain's war was just. It was fought against a determined enemy, which had overridden normal conventions of warfare and politics and must be defeated and removed for the world to return to peace. Everyone's duty was to the war effort, whether protecting national character, cosmopolitan civilization or material self-interest. We can disagree on specific conditions, propagandists argued, but we all want a better world after the war. Ending the war early, with Germany still under military domination, would simply mean returning to the battlefield in the near future. Better to fight what H. G. Wells earlier described as 'the war that will end war' than do it all over again. Audiences were increasingly promised that wartime discomforts were necessary, but temporary, and would be rewarded later.

Needless to say, such convictions were not borne out by subsequent history. Despite the kaiser's abdication, establishment of a German republic, initially led by a socialist government, and the construction of the much-heralded League of Nations, Britain did indeed fight another devastating war with Germany within a generation. Wider promises of social improvements were not fulfilled at home, either, as economic downturn encouraged austerity, debt reduction and demands for 'anti-waste' at the expense of reform. Lloyd George himself went from a charismatic war leader to an unusually brazen seller of honours, willing to contemplate involving Britain in a new conflict with Turkey, and resigned in 1922. Wells subsequently regretted that the 'broken promise' of his phrase became a 'taunt of the out-and-out pacifist' for those willing to consider that war might ever be worthwhile or necessary, though he still believed this himself.[3]

Later disproof of many wartime claims and promises does not automatically mean they were insincere, however. Unless it is assumed that not only the relatively small number of central propagandists who wrote and spoke such ideas but also the far wider number of local contributors to recruiting, war savings, national service, food economy, war aims and other events conspired to lie to their audiences, such claims should be assumed, usually, to represent genuine wartime conviction.[4] Propagandists' regular habit of presenting all-or-nothing, zero-sum choices to audiences provided clear, readily understood messages during wartime, often serving useful, short-term persuasive purposes, prompting the interwar analyst Lasswell's previously discussed cynical observation on avoiding ambiguity. Public meetings and pamphlets generally aimed to convey clarity, certainty and reassurance, not to debate all possible competing views. Domestic material, particularly, sought immediate consent and postponed disputes till later. However, propaganda's zero-sum biases had serious consequences, explored in the rest of this chapter. Not only did they help poison the reputation of Britain's wartime propaganda, but they may also have influenced (or, at least, not challenged) wartime determination to continue the war effort at the expense of other alternatives.

As discussed at various points in previous chapters, despite approaching topics from multiple angles, propagandists often used binary comparisons: civilization vs barbarism; right or might; liberty or tyranny; victory or defeat; patriotism or pacifism. Such labels were transparent simplifications. The British Empire, containing over 400 million subjects of varying enthusiasm, really had little to learn from Germany about imposing 'might', for instance, but the binary suggested Britain was restrained by international law while German conduct was restrained only by force. As Gullace pointed out regarding the use of atrocities to enliven drier accounts of international law, propagandists like Masterman were eager to prevent approving comments on Britain's blockade of Germany because they undercut the wider contrast drawn between the nations' conduct.[5]

Over time, such polarizing rhetoric may have closed off possible alternatives in the minds (or at least expressed thoughts) of propagandists. Throughout the war, some commentators, including Bryce, continued to distinguish 'two Germanies', as John Ramsden notes. Germany itself, with its artistic and scientific heritage, might be recoverable if the poison of Prussian militarism could be drawn from its body. Bryce, Chapter 11 noted, advised against condemning Germany in reporting the Armenian Genocide because he hoped it might intervene. Wells, as late as 1918, resigned from his enemy propaganda role because he wanted to appeal to 'good Germans' while his department head Northcliffe condemned all Germans equally.[6] While particular emphasis continued to be laid on Prussian militarism throughout the war, the common claim that wider Germany was in thrall to it, and could only be released by destroying the regime that supported it, closed down any serious engagement with negotiated or compromise peace. Peter Chalmers Mitchell, the London Zoo scientist put to work by MI7b, wrote his report analysing German propaganda content to help British propagandists develop effective, informed arguments. His analysis of German socialists, however, offered little hope of an alternative political regime. German majority socialists, he argued, had since mid-1916 become 'more and more imperialistic, becoming, in fact, only the left wing of the Government block' – there was little to hope for from them. The critical minority, meanwhile, included

> Honest ... men of high personal character, passionate conviction and wide knowledge. They have cast off painfully and slowly, not only the wave of German patriotism, but the long associations with their comrades of the majority, and the high hopes that German Socialism would open up a new heaven and a new earth for the peoples of all countries. They are now absorbed by pure idealism. For the moment they are a factor on the side of the Allies.

Nonetheless, Chalmers Mitchell, reporting in mid-1917 in the context of growing suspicion of socialism as the Russian revolutions proceeded, wrote German minority socialists off because their ideas attacked 'the fabric of modern society'. Meanwhile, he claimed 'very few English or Neutral writers, and no German writers, advocate pacifism without betraying a preference for the German side'. Thus, all suggestions for negotiation leaned towards German gains. Small wonder, then, that propagandists like McCurdy dismissed calls such as the Reichstag's for a peace with no annexations or indemnities as 'insincere' or that a former Conservative Foreign Secretary, Lansdowne, who suggested a negotiated peace in late 1917, was largely lumped in as one more (at best, misguided) 'pacifist' in public discussion. Official propagandists adopted one of the UDC's leading goals, strongly promoting a league of nations in 1918 but rarely acknowledged these critics' hand in the scheme – why bother if they were all 'pro-German'? As noted elsewhere, Chalmers Mitchell's complacent convictions and zero-sum biases did little to suggest propagandists might persuade, rather than dismiss, groups like German socialists, British pacifists or Irish nationalists.[7]

Having embraced the league, most propagandists showed little doubt it would achieve Wells's end to war, provided the German regime was fully defeated. Zero-sum arguments thus mutually reinforced each other. Britain could not make any compromise peace with Germany because Germany was fundamentally rotten. Having seen the war through to an end, however, the new league, if it could not 'abolish the possibility of war', could at least treat war like 'slavery and the duel – make it discreditable, disreputable, criminal' to the world's 'common conscience'.[8] In turn, with the league monitoring world affairs, Britain could invest less in defence and more in social reform. Not only did government increasingly turn to 'domestic appeasement' from 1917, conceding to public complaints, as Gregory notes, but it also encouraged civilians to expect more in future. Leading figures like Lloyd George and Smuts, as well as lower-ranking politicians and other propagandists, assured the public there would be a 'new world', free of 'class war, industrial injustice'. Instead, a 'cleaner, healthier Britain' would emerge. British propaganda in the final year or more of war actively encouraged an aspirational patriotism in its civilians. While, as seen previously, civilians were regularly told that their burdens were trivial compared to servicemen's, in other ways late-war propaganda stopped telling workers to know their place and be grateful. They *should* expect better, they deserved it because of their wartime service and they would get it.[9]

John Galsworthy, drawing up 'The Balance Sheet of the Soldier-Workman' in 1917, predicted that opportunities would be plentiful for a time as various parts of the economy, like house-building, suspended during wartime, were revived. 'In a word, the demand for labor, at the moment, will be overwhelming.' However, he suspected that the 'vast reconstructive process' would slow down:

> The soldier-workman will go back, I believe, to two or three years at least of good wages, and plentiful work. But when, after that, the pinch begins to come, it will encounter the quicker, more resentful blood of men who in the constant facing of danger have left behind them all fear of consequences ... Can the workmen of the future possibly be as patient and law-abiding as they were before the war, in the face of what seems to them injustice? I don't think so.

This was a real risk, because

> somewhere back of the mind of every workman there is, even during his country's danger, a certain doubt whether all war is not somehow hatched by the aristocrats

and plutocrats of one side, or both. Other feelings obscure this instinct during the struggle, but it is never quite lost.[10]

British propagandists promised civilians better conditions as the reward for wartime sacrifice. Servicemen deserved happier lives even more, given their elevated status. Yet Galsworthy doubted the promises could be kept.

As is well known, his analysis was correct. New wars rapidly raged: Greece fought Turkey; there were civil wars in Russia and Ireland and paramilitaries enacted brutal violence across Europe in the five years after the Armistice. An economic downturn saw Britain's government halt ambitious social housing schemes and other reforms. Neither international nor domestic promises were fulfilled, and workers briefly declared a general strike in 1926. Already, by 1919, during the brief post-war boom, industrial relations were weakening. In September, the National Union of Railwaymen launched a national strike after the President of the Board of Trade (a former wartime Director of National Service), Sir Auckland Geddes, attempted to impose wage cuts. At a railwaymen's meeting in Glasgow before the strike, Frank Hodges of the Miners' Federation complained that 'during the last three months there had been a propaganda which had for its purpose the antagonising of the rest of the working class to the miners, a subtle, clever, carefully-planned propaganda', which claimed that 'the mining industry were engaged in a perfectly selfish task, having for their object an entirely selfish end, regardless of the rest of the community'. Such arguments echoed wartime calls for equal sacrifice. Accepted during the wartime emergency, workers were now less willing to be scolded about community obligations. A few weeks later, the Union's head J. H. Thomas, MP (who had accompanied Balfour on his 1917 US Mission as a labour representative and addressed US meetings), protested that the *Times* suggested the government's dispute with the railwaymen:

> 'must be a fight to a finish'. Is it realised what that sort of utterance means? It can mean nothing else than that the Government should treat those 500,000 railwaymen, many of whom fought for the liberties and lives of the citizens of this country in our common struggle against Prussian militarism, as if they were foreign enemies … they are using against their own countrymen the methods of propaganda which they used in wartime against the foreign enemy.[11]

Railwaymen, Thomas argued, fought for the ideals propounded in wartime propaganda, only to find themselves its targets after the war. Emerging cynicism towards propaganda is unsurprising in these circumstances. Most Britons accepted wartime justifications for the conflict and its impacts on their lives and maintained their efforts throughout. They were promised their sacrifices would be worthwhile. However, wars continued and working lives became harder. The Union's newspaper (Figure 24) explicitly contrasted wartime promises with its perception of 1919's realities, with Lloyd George depicted as 'the bubble merchant' conjuring 'promises of a new world', 'work for all' and a 'housing scheme' from 'soft soap' before a 'houseless, workless, foodless' worker.[12] Predictably,

THE "BUBBLE" MERCHANT: "Don't worry—gaze upon the beauty of these!"
SICK-AND-TIRED WORKER: "All wind—give me the real thing, or clear out!"

Figure 24 Cartoon in the *Railway Review* (National Union of Railwaymen), 3 October 1919, 9.
Source: Modern Records Centre, University of Warwick, National Union of Railwaymen archive, MSS.127/NU/4/1/7.

appeals to further selflessness fell flat when people felt demonized and let down or believed propaganda arguments were recycled in their direction. They tolerated wartime deprivations out of faith in the cause and duty, but the war was over.

Disappointing raised expectations was arguably more important, particularly for working people, to propaganda's declining post-war reputation than Ponsonby's denunciation of 'lies' about atrocities or US criticism of efforts to involve it in the war. Nonetheless, its reputation was not yet terminal. If young people, facing the war's longer political and economic consequences, increasingly saw 'propaganda as a trap to catch them', as the former propagandist Violet Markham suggested, and some propaganda veterans regretted their past work, others remembered their (and, more tellingly, their colleagues') work proudly – even enthusiastically, in the case of authors Keble Howard and G. K. Chesterton. It was, I have argued elsewhere, 'no guilty secret' to have been a propagandist.[13] Nonetheless, as domestic, European and world affairs darkened through the 1920s and 1930s, the certain convictions expressed in zero-sum wartime arguments made it easy to see propaganda as deceptive, manipulative and ill-intentioned. Thus, British propaganda was largely successful during the war – it helped attract neutral sympathy and intervention, recruit people to fight and work, promote investments and maintain public consent to the war's end. Longer term, failure to deliver the genuinely stated ideals and goals encouraged cynicism, which only deepened with the advent of a second, even more destructive and vicious global war.

Notes

1. *The War Aims of the British People: An Historic Manifesto* (London: Hodder & Stoughton, n.d. [1918]), quotations from statement at 11, 17; McCurdy at 9; Millman, *Managing Domestic Dissent*, 172; B. J. C. McKercher, 'The Quest for Stability: British War Aims and Germany, 1914–1918', *Diplomacy and Statecraft*, 30, no. 2 (2019), 214–15.
2. 'Go On or Go Under' and 'We Shall Not Starve', *The Globe*, 18 January 1918, 1, continued 8.
3. Kenneth O. Morgan, 'Lloyd George's Government: A Study in "Prime Ministerial Government"', *Historical Journal*, 13, no. 1 (1970), 153–6; H. G. Wells, *Experiment in Autobiography: Discoveries and Conclusions of a Very Ordinary Brain (since 1866)*, vol. 2 (London: Faber and Faber, [1934] 1984), 667.
4. As in Chapter 20, Nick Milne's reflections in 'Persuasion vs. Deception' are useful here.
5. Gullace, 'Sexual Violence', 735–8.
6. Ramsden, *Don't Mention the War*, 122–8; for Wells, see the discussion and references in Chapter 6.
7. Chalmers Mitchell, 'Report', 29–31, 12; Monger, 'Know Your Enemy'.
8. C. A. McCurdy, *Freedom's Call and Duty: Addresses Given at Central Hall, Westminster, May and June, 1918* (London: W.H. Smith, 1918), 26–7, 30.
9. Gregory, *Last Great War*, 204–5; W. H. Somervell, MP, speaking at Keighley, 10 August 1918, cited in Monger, *Patriotism and Propaganda*, 204, and see the wider discussion of these issues from 200–12.
10. John Galsworthy, 'The Balance Sheet of the Soldier-Workman', *North American Review*, 206, no. 745 (December 1917), 851, 855, 856.
11. Henry Pelling, *A History of British Trade Unionism* (Harmondsworth: Penguin, 1963), 159–63; 'Nationalisation Movement. Miners and the Trade Union Congress', *The Scotsman*, 8 September 1919, 7; Lyddon, *British War Missions*, 163–5; 'Driven to Strike. Mr Thomas on the Men's Case', *Scotsman*, 30 September 1919, 5.
12. 'Batt', untitled cartoon, *Railway Review*, 3 October 1919, 9.
13. Monger, 'A "Not Uncongenial Task"', quotations at 3, 4.

BIBLIOGRAPHY

Note: specific unpublished files from different archives are detailed in chapters' notes. Newspapers and articles about propaganda events are not individually recorded but are fully detailed in the notes.

Published Primary materials

A. G. G. (of the Daily News), *The Blast of Truth*, NWAC Searchlight series, no. 13, 1918.
A Kalendar of Kultur, London: NWAC leaflet no. 15, [1917].
Angell, Norman, *The Prussian in Our Midst*, London, UDC pamphlet no. 15, n.d.
Anonymous, *'Carry On': British Women's Work in War Time*, London: Harrison, Jehring, n.d. [1917].
Anonymous [J. E. Hodder-Williams], *Jack Cornwell: The Story of John Travers Cornwell, V.C., 'Boy – 1st Class'*, Toronto: Hodder and Stoughton, 1918.
Anonymous [A. R. Orage], *Shall WE GO ON? A Socialist's Answer*, London: W.H. Smith, 1918.
Anonymous [A. R. Orage], *A Socialist Talks It Over*, NWAC *Searchlight* pamphlet no. 5, 1918.
Baden-Powell, Robert, 'Are You In This?', PRC poster no. 112, 1915.
Bairnsfather, Bruce, *Fragments from France*, New York: G. P. Putnam's, 1917.
Basu, Bhupendranath, *Why India Is Heart and Soul with Great Britain*, London: Macmillan, 1914.
'Britain Will Not Let Belgium Starve', NCRB pamphlet, London, 1915.
'But Why Did You Kill Us?', Parliamentary Recruiting Committee leaflet no. 44, n.d. [1915].
Caine, Hall (ed.), *King Albert's Book: A Tribute to the Belgian King and People from Representative Men and Women Throughout the World*, London: Hodder and Stoughton, 1914.
Caine, Hall, *Our Girls: Their Work for the War*, London: Hutchinson, 1916.
Chesterton, G. K., *Autobiography*, London: Hutchinson, 1936.
Churchill, Winston S., *The Munitions Miracle*, London: NWAC, 1918.
Cockerill, Sir George, *What Fools We Were*, London: Hutchinson, 1943.
Colville, K. Newton, 'The Farrier. A Character Sketch', *Taranaki Herald*, 4 April 1918, 7.
Cook, Sir Edward, *The Press in War-Time: With Some Account of the Official Press Bureau*, London: Macmillan, 1920.
'Don't Take Alcoholic Drinks on Mondays', National Organizing Committee for War Savings poster, 1916.
'Don't Waste Bread', Ministry of Food poster F.C. 18, n.d. [1917].
Dyson, Will, 'No Holidays', Ministry of Munitions poster, 1916.
Fight for Right Movement, *For the Right: Essays and Addresses*, New York: G. P. Putnam's, 1918.
Galsworthy, John, 'American and Briton', *Yale Review*, 8, no. 1, 18–32.
Galsworthy, John, *A Sheaf*, New York: C. Scribner's, 1916, 250–62.
Galsworthy, John, 'A "Credo" for Keeping Faith', *Current History*, 1, no. 1, New York: New York Times, 1914, 102–3.
Galsworthy, John, 'Diagnosis of the Englishman' [originally published in the *Amsterdamer Revue*, 1915], in Galsworthy, *A Sheaf*, New York: C. Scribner's, 1916, 250–62.
Galsworthy, John, 'The Balance Sheet of the Soldier-Workman', *North American Review*, 206, no. 745 (1917), 841–57.

Bibliography

Galsworthy, John, *Another Sheaf*, London: Heinemann, 1919.
Galsworthy, John, 'The Sacred Work', in Galsworthy, *Another Sheaf*, 3–10.
Garrett Fawcett, Millicent, *The Women's Victory – and After: Personal Reminiscences, 1911–1918*, London: Sidgwick & Jackson, 1920.
Germany Condemned by Her Own Ambassador, NWAC Searchlight series, no. 18, 1918.
'Go! It's Your Duty, Lad', Parliamentary Recruiting Committee poster no. 109, n.d. [1914].
Grey of Fallodon, Viscount, *The League of Nations*, London: W.H. Smith, n.d. [1918]
Hanson Towne, Charles, *The Balfour Visit: How America Received Her Distinguished Guest; and the Significance of the Conferences in the United States in 1917*, New York: George H. Doran, 1917.
Hartshorn, Vernon, 'The Civilian Army's Part', *Reality*, 138, 5 September 1918, 4.
Hines Page, Walter, *The Union of Two Great Peoples*, London: Hodder & Stoughton, 1917.
Hitler, Adolf, *Mein Kampf*, trans. Ralph Mannheim [1925–6], Boston: Houghton Mifflin, 1972.
Holmes, Sergeant H. V., *An Infantryman on Strikes*, n.p.d. [NWAC, 1918].
How to Get the Most Out of Food, Food Control leaflet no. 8, 1917.
How You Can Help Your Country, NWSC pamphlet no. 82, n.d.
Howard, Keble, *The Quality of Mercy*, n.p.d. [Ministry of Information, 1918].
Howard, Keble, *The Zeebrugge Affair*, New York: George H. Doran, 1918.
Howard, Keble, *An Author in Wonderland*, London: Chatto & Windus, 1919.
Humphry Ward, Mrs. [Mary], *England's Effort: Letters to an American Friend*, New York: Charles Scribner's, 1916.
Independent Labour Party, *The Perils of Conscription: An Appeal to the Organised Workers of Great Britain*, 5 June 1915, n.p.d.
Independent Labour Party, *British Prussianism: The Scandal of the Tribunals*, London: National Labour Press, 1916.
Jebb, Richard, *The Imperial Conference: A History and Study*, vol. 2, London: Longmans, Green, 1911.
The "Land & Water" Edition of Raemakers' Cartoons, 2 vols, London: Land & Water, 1916.
Lamont, Corliss, and Lansing Lamont (eds), *Letters of John Masefield to Florence Lamont*, New York: Columbia University Press, 1979.
Lauder, Harry, *Roamin' in the Gloamin*, Philadelphia: J.B. Lippincott, 1928.
Lucian [J. A. Hobson], 'The Laboratory of War Truth: 1920', *Nation*, 27 October 1917, 8–9.
Lucian [J. A. Hobson], 'D.O.R.A. in 1920', *Nation*, 3 November 1917, 155–7.
Ludendorff, Erich, *My War Memories, 1914–1918*, London: Hutchinson & Row, 1919.
MacGill, Patrick, 'The Samaritan in Khaki', *The Queenslander* (Brisbane), 2 March 1918, 43.
MacGill, Patrick, 'Mud', *Mercury* (Hobart), 3 April 1918, 6.
MacGill, Patrick, 'The Give and Take of War', *The Telegraph* (Brisbane), 30 May 1918, 5.
Manifesto to the Trade Unionists of the Country, PRC leaflet no. 3, 1914.
Markham, Violet, *Return Passage*, London: Oxford University Press, 1953.
Masefield, John, *The War and the Future*, New York: Macmillan, 1918.
Mathews, Basil, *The Vista of Victory*, London: Hodder & Stoughton, 1917.
McCurdy, Charles A., *Freedom's Call and Duty: Addresses Given at Central Hall, Westminster, May and June 1918*, London: W.H. Smith, 1918.
McCurdy, Charles A., *Guilty! Prince Lichnowsky's Disclosures*, NWAC, German Aims Series, 1918.
McCurdy, Charles A., *To Restore the Ten Commandments*, London: Hodder & Stoughton, 1918.
McManus, J. E., 'Sport and Play', *Welcome*, weekly article series, 1918.
Milne A. A. [as A. A. M.], 'The Infantryman's Friend', *Otago Witness*, 13 February 1918, 55.
Milne, A. A., 'A Specialist. The Battalion Signalling Officer', *Newcastle Morning Herald and Miners' Advocate*, 1 April 1918, 6.
Milne, A. A., 'One of the Boys', *Mercury* (Hobart), 1 May 1918, 8.

Bibliography

Milne, A. A., 'Blighty', *Wanganui Chronicle*, 18 October 1918, 7.
Milne, A. A., 'A Day at Lords', *The Mercury* (Hobart), 19 October 1918, 8.
Montague, C. E., *Disenchantment*, London: Chatto & Windus, 1922.
'More Aeroplanes are Needed', Ministry of Munitions poster, 1918.
Morison, Elting T., *The Letters of Theodore Roosevelt*, vol. 8, Cambridge: Harvard University Press, 1954.
National War Aims Committee, *Aims and Effort of the War*, London: NWAC, 1918.
National War Savings Committee, *Second Annual Report* (1 June 1918) in TNA, NSC1/3.
National War Savings Committee, *Sound Advice: A Two-Minute Talk on the Wisdom of Investing in National War Bonds*, NWSC, 1918.
National War Savings Committee, *Keep it Up!*, leaflet no. 302, 1918.
Nervo, Amado, 'Algo sobre la Kultur y la Cultura', *América-Latina*, 10, 15 December 1915, 29–30.
Nevinson, C. R. W., *Paint and Prejudice*, New York: Brace Harcourt, 1938.
'On Her Their Lives Depend', Ministry of Munitions poster, 1916.
Pankhurst, Christabel, *America and the War*, London: WSPU, 1914.
Pankhurst, E. Sylvia, *The Home Front*, London: Cresset Library, [1932] 1987.
Parker, Gilbert, *Is England Apathetic? A Reply*, London: Darling, 1915.
Parker, Gilbert, 'The United States and the War', *Harper's Monthly Magazine*, 136, no. 814 (1918), 521–31.
Paxson, Frederick L., Edward S. Cordin and Samuel B. Harding (eds), *War Cyclopedia: A Handbook for Ready Reference on the Great War*, Committee on Public Information, Red White and Blue series, no. 7, Washington: Government Printing Office, 1918.
Pincombe, W. J., *Britain and Gallant Belgium: A Talk to the School Children of Britain*, Victoria League leaflet no. 6, London: J. Wyman, n.d.
Playne, Caroline E., *Society at War, 1914–1916*, Boston: Houghton Mifflin, 1931.
'Please Have Pity with Them', NCRB pamphlet, n.p.d. [1915].
Prothero, G. W. *Our Duty and Our Interest in the War*, London: John Murray for CCNPO, 1914.
Reality (NWAC newspaper for civilians, 1917–18).
Redmond, William, 'From the Trenches: A Plea and a Claim', in *Major William Redmond*, London: Burns & Oates, 1918.
Riddell, Lord, *Lord Riddell's War Diary, 1914-1918*, London: Ivor Nicholson & Watson, 1933.
Roberts, Field-Marshal Earl, *The Supreme Duty of the Citizen at the Present Crisis: The Last Message to His Fellow-Countrymen*, London: Williams & Norgate, n.d. [1915].
Samuel, Herbert, speech to National Liberal Federation, in *National Liberal Federation. Proceedings in Connection with the Meeting of the General Committee of the National Liberal Federation, Held at Manchester, September 26th and 27th, 1918, with The Resolutions and the Speeches Including That Delivered by the Right Hon. H.H. Asquith, K.C., M.P., in the Free Trade Hall*, London: Liberal Publication Department, 1918.
Sanders, William Stephen, *Those German Peace Offers*, NWAC, German Aims series, no. 3, 1918.
Sarafian, Ara (ed.), *The Treatment of Armenians in the Ottoman Empire, 1915–1916: Documents Presented to Viscount Grey of Fallodon by Viscount Bryce, Uncensored Edition*, 2nd edn, Princeton, NJ: Gomidas Institute, 2005.
Scraps of Paper: German Proclamations in Belgium and France, London: Hodder & Stoughton, 1916.
Sleath, F. J., 'The Challenge from the Sky', *Dominion*, 26 November 1917, 7.
Sleath, F. J., 'Fogged. An Airman's Adventure', *Lyttelton Times*, 9 January 1918, 9.
Sleath, F. J., '"That a Man Should Lay Down His Life". A Sacrifice in the Desert', *Dominion*, 9 January 1918, 4.

Bibliography

Smuts, General, *The British Commonwealth of Nations: A Speech Made by General Smuts on May 15th, 1917*, London: Hodder & Stoughton, 1917.
Smuts, General, *Smuts' Message: The World Awakened*, London: NWAC, 1918.
Speed, Lancelot, *Britain's Effort*, Ministry of Information (film), 1918.
'Step Into Your Place', PRC poster no. 104, 1915.
Stuart, Campbell, *Secrets of Crewe House*, London: Hodder & Stoughton, 1920.
'The Crisis: An Appeal to Free Men', Joint Labour Recruiting Committee poster, n.d.
The Empire and the War: The Voice of the Dominions, Empire Parliamentary Association, 1917.
The Rally of Our United Empire, PRC leaflet no. 14, 1914.
The Union of Democratic Control: Its Motives, Object, and Policy, UDC pamphlet B23, 1916.
The Voice of Ireland: Being an Interview with John Redmond, M.P., and Some Message from Representative Irishmen Regarding the Sinn Fein Rebellion, London: Thomas Nelson, 1916.
The Weekly Bulletin of the Ministry of National Service, 1917–18.
"To a Victorious Conclusion." The Prime Minister's Appeal to the Nation. London: PRC pamphlet no. 5, 1914.
Towne, Charles Hanson (ed.), *The Balfour Visit: How America Received Her Distinguished Guest; and the Significance of the Conferences in the United States in 1917*, New York: George H. Doran, 1917.
Tweedie, Ethel [Mrs Alec-Tweedie], 'Women and War Economy', *English Review*, 22, April 1916, 353–9.
Tweedie, Ethel [Mrs Alec-Tweedie], *Women and Soldiers*, London: John Lane, 1918.
Twelve Good Reasons Why Every Able-Bodied Man Should Enrol for National Service, Department of National Service, n.d.
Voluntary Rationing: The Food Controller's Appeal to the Nation, Food Control leaflet no. 1, 1917.
Welcome (NWAC newspaper for soldiers, 1918).
Wells, H. G., *Experiment in Autobiography: Discoveries and Conclusions of a Very Ordinary Brain (since 1866)*, vol. 2, London: Faber and Faber, [1934] 1984.
What the Press Now Says: More Support for the U.D.C., UDC leaflet 17B, 1915.

Secondary materials

Abbenhuis, Maartje, Neil Atkinson, Kingsley Baird and Gail Romano (eds), *The Myriad Legacies of 1917: A Year of War and Revolution*, Cham: Palgrave Macmillan, 2018.
Anderson, Stuart, *Race and Rapprochement: Anglo-Saxonism and Anglo-American Relations, 189--1904*, London: Associated University Presses, 1981.
Archibald, David, and Maria Velez-Serna, 'Kilts, Tanks, and Aeroplanes: Scotland, Cinema, and The First World War', *NECSUS: European Journal of Media Studies*, 3, no. 2 (2014), 155–75.
Audoin-Rouzeau, Stéphane, and Annette Becker, *1914–1918: Understanding the Great War*, trans. Catherine Temerson. London: Profile Books, 2002.
Aulich, Jim, and John Hewitt, *Seduction or Instruction? First World War Posters in Britain and Europe*, Manchester: Manchester University Press, 2007.
Badsey, Stephen, 'Battle of the Somme: British War-Propaganda' *Historical Journal of Film, Radio and Television*, 3, no. 2 (1983), 99–115.
Badsey, Stephen, 'Propaganda and the Defence of Empire, 1856–1956' in Greg Kennedy (ed.), *Imperial Defence: The Old World Order 1856–1956*, London: Routledge, 2008, 218–33.
Badsey, Stephen, *The British Army in Battle and Its Image*, London: Continuum, 2009.
Badsey, Stephen, *The German Corpse Factory: A Study in First World War Propaganda*, Warwick: Helion, 2019.

Bibliography

Badsey, Stephen, 'American Neutrality and Belligerent Propaganda: Contested Histories' in Edward Corse and Marta García Cabrera (eds), *Propaganda and Neutrality*, London: Bloomsbury Academic, 2023, 23–34.

Bar-Yosef, Eitan, 'The Last Crusade? British Propaganda and the Palestine Campaign, 1917–18', *Journal of Contemporary History*, 36, no. 1 (2001), 87–109.

Barnes, Felicity, *New Zealand's London: A Colony and Its Metropolis*, Auckland: Auckland University Press, 2013.

Bennett, Jessica, and Mark Hampton, 'World War I and the Anglo-American Imagined Community: Civilization vs. Barbarism in British Propaganda and American Newspapers', in Joel H. Wiener and Mark Hampton (eds), *Anglo-American Media Interactions, 1850–2000*, Basingstoke: Palgrave MacMillan, 2007, 155–75.

Beaven, Brad, *Visions of Empire: Patriotism, Popular Culture and the City, 1870–1939*, Manchester: Manchester University Press, 2012.

Blades, Barry, *Roll of Honour: Schooling and the Great War, 1914–1919*, Barnsley: Pen & Sword, 2015.

Bowman, Stephen, *The Pilgrims Society and Public Diplomacy, 1895–1945*, Edinburgh: Edinburgh University Press, 2018.

Buitenhuis, Peter, *The Great War of Words: Literature as Propaganda, 1914–18 and After*, London: B.T. Batsford, 1989.

Burk, Kathleen, *Britain, America and the Sinews of War, 1914–1918*, London: George Allen & Unwin, 1985.

Burns, Arthur, 'The Authority of the Church' in Peter Mandler (ed.), *Liberty and Authority in Victorian Britain*, Oxford: Oxford University Press, 2006, 179–200.

Cabanes, Bruno, *The Great War and the Origins of Humanitarianism, 1918–1924*, Cambridge: Cambridge University Press, 2014.

Colclough, Stephen, '"No Such Bookselling Has Ever Before Taken Place in This Country": Propaganda and the Wartime Distribution Practices of W.H. Smith & Son', in Mary Hammond and Shafquat Towheed (eds), *Publishing in the First World War: Essays in Book History*, Basingstoke: Palgrave Macmillan, 2007, 27–45.

Cook, Tim, 'Documenting War and Forging Reputations: Sir Max Aitken and the Canadian War Records Office in the First World War', *War in History*, 10, no. 3 (2003), 265–95.

Cooper Willis, Irene, *England's Holy War: A Study of English Liberal Idealism during the Great War*, New York: Alfred A. Knopf, 1928.

Corse, Edward, and Marta García Cabrera (eds), *Propaganda and Neutrality: Global Case Studies in the Twentieth Century*, London: Bloomsbury Academic, 2023.

Cox, Mary Elisabeth, *Hunger in War and Peace: Women and Children in Germany, 1914–1924*, Oxford: Oxford University Press, 2019.

Das, Santanu, *India, Empire, and First World War Culture: Writings, Images, and Songs*, Cambridge: Cambridge University Press, 2018.

Dehne, Phillip, 'How Important Was Latin America to the First World War', *Iberoamericana*, 14, no. 53 (2014), 151–64.

Demm, Eberhard, *Censorship and Propaganda in World War I: A Comprehensive History*, London: Bloomsbury Academic, 2019.

Donson, Andrew, 'Children and Youth', in Ute Daniel, Peter Gatrell, Oliver Janz, Heather Jones, Jennifer Keene, Alan Kramer and Bill Nasson (eds), *1914-1918 Online: International Encyclopedia of the First World War*, Berlin: Freie Universität Berlin, 2014.

Epsler, Richard, 'Caroline Playne: The Activities and Absences of a Campaigning Author in First World War London', *London Journal*, 41, no. 3 (2016), 249–65.

Fuller, J. G., *Troop Morale and Popular Culture in the British and Dominion Armies, 1914–1918*, Oxford: Clarendon Press, 1991.

Bibliography

Fyfe, Hamilton, *Northcliffe: An Intimate Biography*, London: George Allen & Unwin, 1930.
García Cabrera, Marta, 'International Propaganda in Spain during the First World War: State of the Art and New Contributions', in John Griffiths (ed.), *Communication and the First World War*, Abingdon: Routledge, 2020, 188-218.
García Cabrera, Marta, 'The British Film Campaign in Spain during the First World War (1914-1918)', *War & Society*, 41, no. 4 (2022), 308-22.
Glandon, Virginia E., *Arthur Griffith and the Advanced-Nationalist Press, Ireland, 1900-1922*, New York: Peter Lang, 1985.
Goldfarb Marquis, Alice, 'Words as Weapons: Propaganda in Britain and Germany during the First World War', *Journal of Contemporary History*, 13, no. 3 (1978), 467-98.
Gosling, Luci, 'Saving Face – Beauty for Women Workers during the First World War', *Picturing the Great War: The First World War Blog from Mary Evans Picture Library*, 16 December 2013: https://blog.maryevans.com/2013/12/saving-face-beauty-for-women-workers-during-the-first-world-war.html.
Grant, Peter, 'Charitable Work', in Hew Strachan (ed.), *British Home Front and the First World War*, Cambridge, Cambridge University Press, 2023, 296-313.
Grayzel, Susan R, *Women's Identities at War: Gender, Motherhood, and Politics in Britain and France during the First World War*, Chapel Hill: University of North Carolina Press, 1999.
Griffiths, John (ed.), *Communication and the First World War*, Abingdon: Routledge, 2020.
Griffiths, John, 'Fake News or an Education in War? Communicating War Aims to the British Public in its Early Phases: The Oxford Pamphlets, 1914-1915', in Griffiths, *Communication and the First World War*, 87-118.
Grimshaw, Sabine, 'The Responsibility of Women: Women's Anti-War Writing in the Press, 1914-1916', *Women's Writing*, 24, no. 1 (2017), 80-93.
Gullace, Nicoletta, 'Sexual Violence and Family Honor: British Propaganda and International Law during the First World War', *American Historical Review*, 102, no.3 (1997), 714-47.
Gullace, Nicoletta, *'The Blood of Our Sons': Men, Women and the Renegotiation of British Citizenship during World War One*, New York: Palgrave, 2002.
Gullace, Nicoletta, 'Allied Propaganda and World War I: Interwar Legacies, Media Studies, and the Politics of War Guilt', *History Compass*, 9, no. 9 (2011), 686-700.
Gregory, Adrian, *The Last Great War: British Society and the First World War*, Cambridge: Cambridge University Press, 2008.
Grosvenor, Chris, '"He Sees Now What He Looked Like": Soldier Spectators, Topical Films, and the Problem of Onscreen Representation during World War I', *Film History*, 30, no. 4 (2018), 84-106.
Gust, Wolfgang, *The Armenian Genocide: Evidence from the German Foreign Office Archives, 1915-1916*, New York: Berghahn Books, 2014.
Hammond, Michael, '*The Battle of the Somme* (1916): An Industrial Process Film That "Wounds the Heart"', in Michael Hammond and Michael Williams (eds), *British Silent Cinema and the Great War*, Basingstoke: Palgrave Macmillan, 2011, 19-38.
Hancock, Simon, 'Duty and Personal Advantage Combined: The War Savings Movement in Pembrokeshire during the First World War', *Welsh History Review*, 31, no. 3 (2023), 428-47.
Haste, Cate, *Keep the Home Fires Burning: Propaganda in the First World War*, London: Allen Lane, 1977.
Havighurst, Alfred E., *Radical Journalist: H.W. Massingham (1860-1924)*, London: Cambridge University Press, 1974.
Hendley, Matthew, *Organized Patriotism and the Crucible of War: Popular Imperialism in Britain, 1914-1932*, London: McGill-Queen's University Press, 2012.
Hiley, Nicholas, 'Sir Hedley Le Bas and the Origins of Domestic Propaganda in Britain, 1914-17', *European Journal of Marketing*, 21, no. 8 (1987), 30-46.

Bibliography

Hiley, Nicholas, 'The British Cinema Auditorium' in Karel Dibbets and Bert Hogenkamp (eds), *Film and the First World War*, Amsterdam: Amsterdam University Press, 1995, 160-70.

Hiley, Nicholas, '"Kitchener Wants YOU" and "Daddy, What Did YOU Do in the Great War?" The Myth of British Recruiting Posters', *Imperial War Museum Review*, 11 (1999), 40-58.

Hiley, Nicholas P., '"The British Army Film", "You!" and "For the Empire": Reconstructed Propaganda Films, 1914-1916', *Historical Journal of Film, Radio and Television*, 5, no. 2 (1985), 165-82.

Hockenhull, Stella, 'Everybody's Business: Film, Food and Victory in the First World War', *Historical Journal of Film, Radio and Television*, 35, no. 4 (2015), 579-95.

Hoover, A. J., *God, Germany and Great Britain: A Study in Clerical Nationalism*, New York: Praeger, 1989.

Hopkin, Deian, 'Domestic Censorship in the First World War', *Journal of Contemporary History*, 5, no. 4 (1970), 151-69.

Horne, John N., *Labour at War: France and Britain, 1914-1918*, Oxford: Clarendon Press, 1991.

Horne, John (ed.), *State, Society and Mobilization in Europe during the First World War*, Cambridge: Cambridge University Press, 1997.

Horne, John, and Alan Kramer, *German Atrocities, 1914: A History of Denial*, New Haven: Yale University Press, 2001.

Houston, Fiona, '"Seducers of the People": Mapping the Linguistic Shift', *Alicante Journal of English Studies*, 31 (2018), 33-52.

Huxley, Aldous, 'Notes on Propaganda', *Harper's Magazine*, 174 (1936), 32-9.

Hynes, Greg, 'Propaganda, Perspective, and the British World: New Zealand's First World War Propaganda and British Interactions, 1914-1918', University of Canterbury, MA Thesis, 2013.

Hynes, Greg, 'We New Zealanders Pride Ourselves Most of All Upon Our Loyalty to Our Empire, Our Country, Our Flag: Internalised Britishness and National Character in New Zealand's First World War Propaganda', in Michael Walsh and Andrekos Varnava (eds), *Great War and the British Empire: Culture and Society*, London: Ashgate, 2017, 81-102.

Hynes, Samuel, *A War Imagined: The First World War and English Culture*, New York: Colliers, 1992.

Ihrig, Stefan, *Justifying Genocide: Germany and the Armenians from Bismarck to Hitler*, Cambridge, MA: Harvard University Press, 2016.

Irish, Tomás, 'Petitioning the World: Intellectuals and Cultural Mobilization in the Great War', in Catriona Pennell and Filipe Ribeiro de Meneses (eds), *A World at War, 1911-1949: Explorations in the Cultural History of War*, Leiden: Brill, 2019, 42-60.

Jarboe, Andrew, 'Indian and African Soldiers in British, French and German Propaganda during the First World War', in Troy R. E. Paddock (ed.), *World War I and Propaganda*, Leiden: Brill, 2014, 181-96.

Jenkins, Philip, *The Great and Holy War: How World War I Changed Religion For Ever*, Oxford: Lion, 2014.

Jones, Max, *The Last Great Quest: Captain Scott's Antarctic Sacrifice*, Oxford: Oxford University Press, 2003.

Jowett, Garth, and Victoria O'Donnell, *Propaganda and Persuasion*, 4th edn, London: Sage Publications, [1986] 2006.

Keil, André, 'The National Council for Civil Liberties and the British State during the First World War', *English Historical Review*, 134, no. 568 (2019), 620-45.

Keil, André, 'A Very British Dictatorship: The Defence of the Realm Act in Britain, 1914-1920', *First World War Studies*, 14, no. 1 (2023), 51-70.

Kennedy, Rosie, *The Children's War: Britain, 1914-1918*, Basingstoke: Palgrave Macmillan, 2014.

Kennedy, Rosie, 'Children', in Hew Strachan (ed.), *The British Home Front and the First World War*, Cambridge, Cambridge University Press, 2023, 564-82.

Bibliography

Kramer, Alan, *Dynamic of Destruction: Culture and Mass Killing in the First World War*, Oxford: Oxford University Press, 2007.
Krebs, Paula M., *Gender, Race and the Writing of Empire: Public Discourse and the Boer War*, Cambridge: Cambridge University Press, 1999.
Lammasniemi, Laura, 'Regulation 40D: Punishing Promiscuity on the Home Front during the First World War', *Women's History Review*, 26, no. 4 (2017), 584–96.
Lasswell, Harold, *Propaganda Technique in the World War*, London: Kegan Paul, Trench, Trubner, 1927.
Lawrence, Jon, *Speaking for the People: Party, Language and Popular Politics in England, 1867-1914*, Cambridge: Cambridge University Press, 1996.
Lawrence, Jon, 'The Transformation of British Public Politics after the First World War', *Past and Present*, 190, no. 1 (2006), 185–216.
Lawrence, Jon, 'Public Space, Political Space', in Jay Winter and Jean-Louis Robert (eds), *Capital Cities at War: Paris, London, Berlin 1914-1919*, vol. 2, *A Cultural History*, Cambridge: Cambridge University Press, 2007, 280–312.
Lawrence, Jon, *Electing Our Masters: The Hustings from Hogarth to Blair*, Oxford: Oxford University Press, 2009.
Lyddon, W. G., *British War Missions to the United States, 1914-1918*, London: Oxford University Press, 1938.
McCartney, Helen B., *Citizen Soldiers: The Liverpool Territorials in the First World War*, Cambridge: Cambridge University Press, 2005.
McCartney, Helen B., 'The First World War Soldier and His Contemporary Image in Britain', *International Affairs*, 90, no. 2 (2014), 299–315.
McKercher, B. J. C., 'The Quest for Stability: British War Aims and Germany, 1914–1918', *Diplomacy and Statecraft*, 30, no. 2 (2019), 201–27.
McKernan, Luke, *Topical Budget: The Great British News Film*, London: BFI, 1992.
McKernan, Luke, 'Propaganda, Patriotism and Profit: Charles Urban and British Official War Films in America', *Film History*, 14, no. 3–4 (2002), 369–89.
McNeill, William H., *Arnold Toynbee: A Life*, Oxford: Oxford University Press, 1989.
Maartens, Brendan, 'The Great War, Military Recruitment, and the Public Relations Work of the Parliamentary Recruiting Committee', *Public Relations Inquiry*, 5, no. 2 (2016), 169–85.
Maartens, Brendan, 'For "Common Christianity": War, Peace and the Campaign of the Irish Recruiting Council, 1918, *English Historical Review*, 136, no. 579 (2021), 364–94.
Madigan, Edward, '"Sticking to a Hateful Task": Resilience, Humour, and British Understandings of Combatant Courage', *War in History*, 20, no. 1 (2013), 76–98.
Malvern, Sue, *Modern Art, Britain and the Great War*, New Haven: Yale University Press, 2004.
Mandler, Peter, *The English National Character: The History of an Idea from Edmund Burke to Tony Blair*, New Haven: Yale University Press, 2006.
Marcus, Jane (ed.), *The Young Rebecca: Writings of Rebecca West, 1911-17*, London: Virago, 1982.
Marrin, Albert, *The Last Crusade: The Church of England in the First World War*, Durham, NC: Duke University Press, 1974.
Mason, Tony, 'English Rugby Union and the First World War', *Historical Journal*, 45, no. 2 (2002), 797–817.
May, Ernest R., *The World War and American Isolation: 1914–1917*, Cambridge: MA: Harvard University Press, 1959.
Mayhew, Alex, 'English Patriotism and the Implicit Nation: Homelands and Soldiers' National Identity during the Great War', *English Historical Review*, 138, no. 594–5 (2024), 1277–306.
Messinger, Gary S., *British Propaganda and the State in the First World War*, Manchester: Manchester University Press, 1992.

Bibliography

Miller, David, 'The Treatment of Armenians in the Ottoman Empire: A History of the Blue Book', *RUSI Journal*, 150, no. 4 (2005), 36–43.

Millman, Brock, *Managing Domestic Dissent in First World War Britain*, London: Frank Cass, 2000.

Milne, Nick, 'Persuasion vs. Deception: The Connotative Shifts of "Propaganda" and Their Critical Implications', in Julian Walker and Christophe Declercq (eds), *Languages and the First World War: Communicating in a Transnational War*, London: Palgrave Macmillan, 2016, 209–25.

Monger, David, 'Sporting Journalism and the Maintenance of British Servicemen's Ties to Civilian Life in First World War Propaganda', *Sport in History*, 30, no. 3 (2010), 374–401.

Monger, David, 'Soldiers, Propaganda and Ideas of Home and Community in First World War Britain', *Cultural and Social History*, 8, no. 3 (2011), 331–54.

Monger, David, *Patriotism and Propaganda in First World War Britain: The National War Aims Committee and Civilian Morale*, Liverpool: Liverpool University Press, 2012.

Monger, David, 'Nothing Special? Propaganda and Women's Roles in Late First World War Britain', *Women's History Review*, 23, no. 4 (2014), 518–42.

Monger, David, 'Transcending the Nation: Domestic Propaganda and Supranational Patriotism in Britain, 1917–18', in Troy R. E. Paddock (ed.), *World War I and Propaganda*, Leiden: Brill, 2014, 21–42.

Monger, David, 'Familiarity Breeds Consent? Patriotic Rituals in British First World War Propaganda', *Twentieth Century British History*, 26, no. 4 (2015), 501–28.

Monger, David, 'Propaganda at Home (Great Britain and Ireland)', in Ute Daniel, Peter Gatrell, Oliver Janz, Heather Jones, Jennifer Keene, Alan Kramer and Bill Nasson (eds), *1914-1918 Online: International Encyclopedia of the First World War*, Berlin: Freie Universität Berlin, 2016: https://encyclopedia.1914-1918-online.net/article/propaganda_at_home_great_britain_and_ireland.

Monger, David, 'Networking against Genocide during the First World War: The International Network behind the British Parliamentary Report on the Armenian Genocide', *Journal of Transatlantic Studies*, 16, no. 3 (2018), 295–316.

Monger, David, 'Tangible Patriotism during the First World War: Individuals and the Nation in British Propaganda', *War & Society*, 37, no. 4 (2018), 244–61.

Monger, David, 'Know Your Enemy: Peter Chalmers Mitchell, British Military Intelligence and the Understanding of German Propaganda in the First World War', *History*, 103, no. 358 (2018), 777–99.

Monger, David, 'The Press Bureau, "D" Notices, and Official Control of the British Press's Record of the First World War', *The Historical Journal*, 65, no. 2 (2022), 435–61.

Monger, David, 'A "Not Uncongenial Task": British Propaganda Veterans and Propaganda's Post-First World War Reputation', *First World War Studies*, 13, no. 1 (2022), 1–23.

Monger, David, 'Speaking to or for the World? Britain, Presumed Authority and World Opinion at the Start of the First World War', *Historical Research*, 96, no. 1 (2023), 82–102.

Monger, David, 'The Press and Propaganda', in Hew Strachan (ed.), *The British Home Front and the First World War*, Cambridge: Cambridge University Press, 2023.

Moody, Paul, '"Improper Practices" in Great War British Cinemas', in Michael Hammond and Michael Williams (eds), *British Silent Cinema and the Great War*, Basingstoke: Palgrave Macmillan, 2011, 49–63.

Moore, Gregory, 'The Super-Hun and the Super-State: Allied Propaganda and German Philosophy during the First World War', *German Life and Letters*, 54, no. 4 (2001), 310–30.

Morgan, Kenneth O., 'Lloyd George's Premiership: A Study in "Prime Ministerial Government"', *Historical Journal*, 13, no. 1 (1970), 130–57.

Bibliography

Moss, Stella, '"Wartime Hysterics"?: Alcohol, Women and the Politics of Wartime Social Purity', in Jessica Meyer (ed.), *British Popular Culture and the First World War*, Leiden: Brill, 2008, 147-71.
Novick, Ben, *Conceiving Revolution: Irish Nationalist Propaganda during the First World War*, Dublin: Four Courts Press, 2001.
Nuttall, Paul A., 'Sir Archibald Salvidge and the Failed Realignment of British Politics, 1918-1922', *Northern History*, 60, no. 1 (2023), 74-93.
Ó Drisceoil, Donal, 'Keeping Disloyalty Within Bounds? British Media Control in Ireland, 1914-1919', *Irish Historical Studies*, 38, no. 149 (2012), 52-69.
O'Gorman, Aoife, '*Wissenschaft* at War: British and German Academic Propaganda and the Great War', unpublished DPhil thesis, University of Oxford, 2016.
Paddock, Troy R. E. (ed.), *World War I and Propaganda*, Leiden: Brill, 2014.
Paris, Michael, 'Film/Cinema (Great Britain)', in Ute Daniel, Peter Gatrell, Oliver Janz, Heather Jones, Jennifer Keene, Alan Kramer and Bill Nasson (eds), *1914-1918 Online, International Encyclopedia of the First World War*, Berlin, Freie Universität Berlin, 2014.
Pelling, Henry, *A History of British Trade Unionism*, Harmondsworth: Penguin, 1963.
Pennell, Catriona, *A Kingdom United: Popular Responses to the Outbreak of the First World War in Britain and Ireland*, Oxford: Oxford University Press, 2012.
Pennell, Catriona, 'Presenting the War in Ireland', in Troy R. E. Paddock (ed.), *World War I and Propaganda*, Leiden: Brill, 2014, 42-65.
Peterson, H. C., *Propaganda for War: The Campaign Against American Neutrality, 1914-1917*, Norman: University of Oklahoma Press, 1939.
Ponsonby, Arthur, *Falsehood in War-Time: Containing an Assortment of Lies Circulated Throughout the Nations during the Great War*, London: Allen & Unwin, 1928.
Putnis, Peter, and Kerry McCallum, 'Reuters, Propaganda-Inspired News, and the Australian Press during the First World War', *Media History*, 19, no. 3 (2013), 284-304.
Ramsden, John, *Don't Mention the War: The British and the Germans since 1890*, London: Little, Brown, 2006.
Read, J. M., *Atrocity Propaganda, 1914-1919*, New Haven: Yale University Press, 1941.
Reeves, Nicholas, *Official British Film Propaganda during the First World War*, London: Croom Helm, 1986.
Reeves, Nicholas, 'Cinema, Spectatorship and Propaganda: "Battle of the Somme" (1916) and Its Contemporary Audience', *Historical Journal of Film, Radio and Television*, 17, no. 1 (1997), 5-28.
Reeves, Nicholas, *The Power of Film Propaganda: Myth or Reality?*, London: Cassell, 1999.
Reisenauer, Eric, 'A World in Crisis and Transition: The Millennial and the Modern in Britain, 1914-1918', *First World War Studies*, 2, no. 2 (2011), 217-32.
Riedi, Eliza, and Tony Mason, '"Leather" and the Fighting Spirit: Sport in the British Army in World War I', *Canadian Journal of History*, 41, no. 3 (2006), 485-516.
Rinke, Stefan, 'Propaganda War (Latin America)' in Ute Daniel, Peter Gatrell, Oliver Janz, Heather Jones, Jennifer Keene, Alan Kramer and Bill Nasson (eds), *1914-1918 Online, International Encyclopedia of the First World War*, Berlin, Freie Universität Berlin, 2015.
Robertson, Emily, 'Propaganda and "Manufactured Hatred"': A Reappraisal of the Ethics of First World War British and Australian Atrocity Propaganda', *Public Relations Inquiry*, 3, no. 2 (2014), 245-66.
Robertson, Emily, 'Propaganda at Home Australia', in Ute Daniel, Peter Gatrell, Oliver Janz, Heather Jones, Jennifer Keene, Alan Kramer and Bill Nasson (eds), *1914-1918 Online: International Encyclopedia of the First World War*, Berlin: Freie Universität Berlin, 2015.

Bibliography

Rogan, Eugene, 'Rival Jihads: Islam and the Great War in the Middle East, 1914–1918', *Journal of the British Academy*, 4, no. 1 (2016), 1–20.

Roper, Michael, *The Secret Battle: Emotional Survival in the Great War*, Manchester: Manchester University Press, 2009.

Sanders, M. L. and Philip M. Taylor, *British Propaganda during the First World War, 1914–18*, London: Macmillan, 1982.

Schulze, Frederick, 'Brazil', in Ute Daniel, Peter Gatrell, Oliver Janz, Heather Jones, Jennifer Keene, Alan Kramer and Bill Nasson (eds), *1914–1918 Online: International Encylopedia of the First World War*, Berlin: Freie Universität Berlin, 2015.

Scully, Richard, *British Images of Germany: Admiration, Antagonism & Ambivalence*, Basingstoke: Palgrave Macmillan, 2012.

Sharma, Lubina, 'Anti-Imperialist Pamphleteering: Understanding Global Jihad in Wartime India, 1914–1918', *British Journal for Military History*, 8, no. 1 (2022), 152–66.

Singha, Radhika, 'India's Silver Bullets: War Loans and War Propaganda, 1917–18', in Maartje Abbenhuis, Neil Atkinson, Kingsley Baird and Gail Romano (eds), *The Myriad Legacies of 1917: A Year of War and Revolution*, Cham: Palgrave Macmillan, 2018, 77–102.

Slight, John, 'Reactions to the Ottoman Jihad Fatwa in the British Empire, 1914–18', in Robert Johnson and James Kitchen (eds), *The Great War in the Middle East: A Clash of Empires*, London: Routledge, 2019, 256–74.

Smith, Michelle, 'Be(ing) Prepared: Girl Guides, Colonial Life, and National Strength', *Limina*, 12 (2006), 1–12.

Smith, Richard, 'Propaganda, Imperial Subjecthood and National Identity in Jamaica during the First World War' in Troy R. E. Paddock (ed.), *World War I and Propaganda*, Leiden: Brill, 2014, 89–112.

Smither, Roger, 'Anticipating the Blitz Spirit in First World War Propaganda Film: Evidence in the Imperial War Museum Archive', in Michael Hammond and Michael Williams (eds), *British Silent Cinema and the Great War*, Basingstoke: Palgrave Macmillan, 2011, 160–9.

Smither, Roger, 'Film/Cinema', in Ute Daniel, Peter Gatrell, Oliver Janz, Heather Jones, Jennifer Keene, Alan Kramer and Bill Nasson (eds), *1914–1918 Online: International Encyclopedia of the First World War*, Berlin: Freie Universität Berlin, 2015.

Steel, Daniel, 'Genocide and the "Clean Fighting Turk" in First World War Britain and Ireland', *Historical Research*, 94, no. 264 (2021), 419–39.

Stobart, Jon, 'Identity, Competition and Place Promotion in the Five Towns', *Urban History*, 30, no. 2 (2003), 163–82.

Strachan, Hew, 'John Buchan and the First World War: Fact into Fiction', *War in History*, 16, no. 3 (2009), 298–324.

Sutcliffe, Marcella P., 'Reading at the Front: Books and Soldiers in the First World War', *Paedagogica Historica*, 52, nos. 1–2 (2016), 104–20.

Swartz, Marvin, *The Union of Democratic Control in British Politics during the First World War*, Oxford: Clarendon Press, 1971.

Tato, Maria Ines, 'Luring Neutrals. Allied and German Propaganda in Argentina during the First World War', in Troy R. E. Paddock (ed.), *World War I and Propaganda*, Leiden: Brill, 2014, 322–44.

Thom, Deborah, *Nice Girls and Rude Girls: Women Workers in World War I*, London: I.B. Tauris, 1998.

Trevelyan, George Macaulay, *Grey of Fallodon: Being the Life of Sir Edward Grey Afterward Viscount Grey of Fallodon*, London: Longman, Green, 1937.

Tusan, Michelle, 'James Bryce's Blue Book as Evidence', *Journal of Levantine Studies*, 5, no. 2 (2015), 35–50.

Bibliography

Vincent, C. Paul, *The Politics of Hunger: The Allied Blockade of Germany, 1915–1919*, Athens: Ohio University Press, 1985.

Waites, Bernard, *A Class Society at War: England, 1914–1918*, Leamington Spa: Berg, 1987.

Wallace, Stuart, *War and the Image of Germany: British Academics, 1914–1918*, Edinburgh: John Donald, 1988.

Waller, Philip, *Writers, Readers, and Reputations: Literary Life in Britain, 1870–1918*, Oxford: Oxford University Press, 2006.

Walsh, Michael, and Andrekos Varnava (eds), *The Great War and the British Empire: Culture and Society*, London: Ashgate, 2017.

Ward, Paul, *Red Flag and Union Jack: Englishness, Patriotism and the British Left, 1881–1924*, Woodbridge: Boydell Press, 1998.

Ward, Paul, 'Women of Britain Say Go: Women's Patriotism in the First World War', *Twentieth Century British History*, 12, no. 1, 2001, 23–45.

Ward, Paul, 'Empire and the Everyday: Britishers and Imperialism in Women's Lives in the Great War', in Philip Buckner and R. Douglas Francis (eds), *Rediscovering the British World*, Calgary: University of Calgary Press, 2005, 267–84.

Watson, Alexander, and Patrick Porter, 'Bereaved and Aggrieved: Combat Motivation and the Ideology of Sacrifice in the First World War', *Historical Research*, 83, no. 219 (2010), 146–64.

Watson, Janet S. K., *Fighting Different Wars: Experience, Memory, and the First World War in Britain*, Cambridge: Cambridge University Press, 2004.

Wessels, André, 'Afrikaner (Boer) Rebellion (Union of South Africa)', in Ute Daniel, Peter Gatrell, Oliver Janz, Heather Jones, Jennifer Keene, Alan Kramer and Bill Nasson (eds), *1914–1918 Online: International Encyclopedia of the First World War*, Berlin: Freie Universität Berlin, 2015.

Whittaker, Jason, *Jerusalem: Blake, Parry, and the Fight for Englishness*, Oxford: Oxford University Press, 2022.

Wilkinson, Alan, *The Church of England and the First World War*, London: SPCK, 1978.

Wilkinson, Nicholas, *Secrecy and the Media: The Official History of the United Kingdom's D-Notice System*, London: Routledge, 2009.

Wilson, Trevor, 'Lord Bryce's Investigation into Alleged German Atrocities in Belgium, 1914–1915', *Journal of Contemporary History*, 14, no. 3 (1979), 369–83.

Wilson, Trevor, *The Myriad Faces of War: Britain and the Great War, 1914–1918*, Cambridge: Polity Press, 1986.

Winter, Jay, and Antoine Prost (eds), *Capital Cities at War: Paris, London, Berlin, 1914–1919*, vol. 2, *A Cultural History*, Cambridge: Cambridge University Press, 2007.

Wood, Trevor, *Inventory of the Great Britain, Foreign Office, Wellington House Publications*, Hoover Institution Archive finding aid XX230, Online Archives of California, 2008–2014.

Woollacott, Angela, '"Khaki Fever" and Its Control: Gender, Class, Age and Sexual Morality on the British Homefront in the First World War', *Journal of Contemporary History*, 29, no. 2 (1994), 325–47.

INDEX

Angell, Norman 89–90, 167, 200
Anti-Semitism 80–1
Archbishop of York (*see* Lang, Cosmo)
Armenian Genocide 8–9, 53, 88, 113–14, 144
  compared to atrocities in Belgium 88
  humanitarianism and 113–14, 172, 202
  parliamentary report on 8, 86, 113, 164, 202
Asquith, Herbert 33, 38, 106, 153, 161, 193
Atrocities (chapter 1 *passim*)
  definition of 5
  reality of 8, 53, 162, 164
  purposes within propaganda 9–11, 29
Australia 40

Bairnsfather, Bruce 63, 156
Beaverbrook, Lord (Max Aitken) 40, 71
  as Minister of Information 37, 69, 117, 121, 180, 121
  film and 47–8, 119
Belgium 13, 14, 24, 33, 62
  Britain fighting for 30, 54, 142, 170, 201, 202
  German atrocities in 5, 7, 45, 85, 110, 142–3
  humanitarian relief 14, 21–2, 112, 146, 172, 199
Britain (chapters 2 and 8 *passim*)
  and civilizational values 14–17, 141, 170, 208, 210
  rights of 'small nations' 17, 24–5, 29
  landscape of 17–18, 78
  national character 61–3, 64–5
British Workers National League (BWNL) 164–5, 169
Bryce, James 15, 54, 117–18, 142–3
  Armenia and 8, 86, 113, 164, 202
  League of Nations and 168, 200, 201
  United States and 54, 113, 202–3, 205
  views on Germany 86, 210
'Bryce Report' on German atrocities 1, 9, 23, 144
  later reputation of 8, 113, 162
Buchan, John 69, 120, 121

Caine, Hall 15, 48, 106, 109, 202
Cavell, Edith 5–7, 104
Censorship (chapter 24 *passim*) 38, 41, 70–2, 118–19
  Ireland and 194
  of war critics 194–7
  topics censored 144, 192–3
Chalmers Mitchell, Peter 53, 86–7, 127
Chesterton, G. K. 117

Children (chapter 3 *passim*)
  as vehicles for propaganda 21–2
  propaganda about 21–4, 25–6, 136
  propaganda towards 24–5
  expectations of 25
Churchill, Winston 180, 191, 204
Central Committee for National Patriotic Organizations (CCNPO) 62, 119, 120, 147, 170, 171
Conscription 16, 17, 170, 175, 176–7
  anti-conscription 16, 167, 195, 199
  Ireland and 38, 168, 178
  within the empire 38
Cook, Edward 118–19, 167, 191–2, 193–4, 195
  censorship philosophy 71, 167, 192
Critical propagandists 81, 89–90, 119, 141, 153–4
  suppression of 138, 168–9, 194–7
Curnock, Grace 31–2, 103, 127, 184

Daily life (chapter 17 *passim*) 146
  'business as usual' 103, 133, 134
Defence of the Realm Act (DORA) 71, 81, 106, 168, 192
Department of Information (DI) 69, 117, 120
  film and 47
  press and 121–2, 126
Dissent *see* Critical propagandists
Duty (chapter 4 *passim*) 25, 73, 146, 209, 213
  community and 31–2
  'shirkers' 32, 81, 180
  to Belgium 170
  to servicemen 30–1
  women and 105

Empire, British (chapter 5 *passim*)
  Muslims within 38
  German threat to 170
  voluntarism and 177
Empire, Ottoman
  Germany and 89
  jihad proclamation 38, 56, 143–4
  see also Armenian Genocide

Fight for Right Movement (FRM) 15, 87, 119, 153, 170
  and *Jerusalem* 18
Film chapter (6 *passim*) 40–1

Index

Battle of the Somme 45, 47, 50, 72, 111, 138
   overseas distribution 49-50, 111
Food economy 10, 17, 49, 73-4, 77-8, 105, 136
   local propaganda 96, 98
   voluntarism and 178-9

Galsworthy, John 29, 64, 125, 211-12
Garrett Fawcett, Millicent 101, 103
Germany (chapter 7 *passim*)
   British blockade of 7, 54, 112, 162
   Hindenburg, Paul von 79-80
   Hitler, Adolf 7
   Kaiser Wilhelm II 56, 57, 58, 79, 144, 209
   Kultur (chapter 11 *passim*)
   against 'civilization' 86, 87, 88, 90
   atrocities and 85, 86, 88
   comparisons with Britain 89-90
   Bernhardi, Friedrich von and 86, 87
   Nietzsche, Friedrich and 87, 89, 90, 142
   Ludendorff, Erich 7, 79
   positive depictions 53, 86, 144, 146, 210
   Prince Lichnowsky 55-6, 162
   'scrap of paper' 9, 54-5, 87, 88, 162-4
   U-Boat campaign 111, 112-13, 136
Gandhi, Mohandas 38-9
Goodman, E. M. 33, 105, 106, 187, 189
   NWAC and 103, 126, 136, 183
Grey, Edward 54, 200, 201

Henderson, Arthur 16, 81-2
Hobson, J. A. 81, 160, 167, 200
Humour (chapter 10 *passim*)
   Britishness and 62-3
   Germany and 56-8, 79-80
   women and 77-8

Independent Labour Party (ILP) 16, 90, 167, 169, 194
India 48-41, 49-50
Ireland 49, 54, 154, 212
   censorship and 71, 194
   conscription and 38, 168, 178
   Sinn Féin 167, 169-70, 178, 194
   voluntarism and 16-17, 34

Kipling, Rudyard 41, 63, 125
Kitchener, Lord 45, 71, 98, 180
Kultur see Germany

Lang, Cosmo (Archbishop of York) 13-14, 144, 146, 147
Lansdowne, Lord 192-3, 211
Latin America 110-11
League of Nations 39, 63, 88, 200-1, 209, 211
   UDC and 168, 200, 211

Lloyd George, David 126, 192, 193, 211
   as Prime Minister 45, 48
   post-war career 209, 212-13
   and propaganda organization 69, 119, 121
   and war aims 164, 184, 207-8
   as Minister of Munitions 103, 133, 178
   as War Secretary 45
   press and 69, 71, 119, 127, 194
   quoted in propaganda 65, 138, 151, 153
   war critics and 167, 168, 199
Lusitania 7, 23, 113, 144

MacDonald, Ramsay 167, 169
Markham, Violet 73, 103, 178
Masterman, Charles 45, 109-10, 111, 126, 164
McCurdy, Charles 21, 142
MI7b 13, 15-16, 56-7, 62, 137, 152, 154
   Bairnsfather and 63, 71, 78, 155
   Chalmers Mitchell and 86, 87, 210
   independence from DI and MI 117, 121-2
   RCI and 37, 122
   scale of work 37
   topical analyses 71-2, 180
   see also Milne, A. A.
Middle East 38, 80, 126, 143-4
   Jerusalem 144, 145
Milne, A. A. 17, 30-1, 39, 55-6, 78, 137
Ministry of Information (MI) 40, 121, 130, 205
   suspicions of 69-70
   film and 40-1, 49
   relationship with propaganda organizations 55, 69, 117
   views on propaganda 122
Morel, E.D. 153-4, 168, 197
Murray, Gilbert 87-88, 124-5, 153

National War Aims Committee (NWAC) 3
   CCNPO and 119, 120, 147, 170
   film and 47, 48, 49
   government connections 160, 162
   independence from MI 55, 69, 117, 121
   local propaganda 25, 33, 65, 70, 93, 94, 96, 129
   PRC and 118, 120, 127
   propaganda for soldiers 105, 155
   propaganda for industrial workers 138, 143, 185
   propaganda methods 33, 65
   propaganda themes 10, 17, 80, 96, 170, 200, 201
National War Savings Committee (NWSC) 31, 70, 75, 126, 128, 144, 183
   food control and 95-6, 119
   local committees 93-4, 95-6
   overlap with NWAC 33, 120
National Service, Directorate/Department/Ministry of 48, 73, 98
   Women's Section 24, 31-2, 73, 103, 136, 178, 184

Index

national service 133, 137, 146-7, 178
  film propaganda 45, 46, 48
  local propaganda 73, 98-9, 136, 178
  propaganda towards women 31-3, 74, 77, 103-4, 184, 186-7
  propaganda towards workers 33-4, 81-2, 161
New Zealand 40-1, 56, 78
Northcliffe, Lord (Alfred Harmsworth) 117, 121, 129
  anti-Germanism 53, 210
  propaganda 'mission' to the United States 127, 203

Oxford pamphlets 86, 142
Owen, Wilfred 153

'Pals' battalions 99
Parker, Gilbert 109, 112, 161, 176-7, 200
Parliamentary Recruiting Committee (PRC) 38, 73, 105, 110, 153, 177
  cross-party support for 15-16, 118
  Labour involvement 175-6
  localized propaganda 94-5, 161
  open propaganda 161
  posters 17, 23, 40, 62, 105, 161
Peel, Dorothy 77-8, 103, 105, 125
Pember Reeves, Maude 103, 105
Ponsonby, Arthur 9, 81, 167, 168
  influence on propaganda's later reputation 8, 213-4
Press Bureau (PB) 70-1, 118
  criticisms of 69, 70, 195, 197
  censorship by 38, 41, 71, 143, 192-3, 194-5
  limitations on censorship 192-3, 194, 197
  relationship with press 71, 193-4
Press and propaganda 69-70, 70-2, 121, 126-7, 193-4
Propaganda
  advertising and 21-2, 30
  as persuasion 1, 73, 118, 162
  later reputation 1, 7-8, 70, 159-60
  open propaganda 161-2
  'propaganda machine' 2, 117-8
Propaganda and truth (chapter 20 *passim*) 121, 168
  military reality 47, 72, 154, 194, 197
  promises of post-war future 164, 165, 187
  wartime scepticism 160, 164-5, 169
Propagandists (chapter 16 *passim*) 122
  advertisers 126, 127
  and business interests 69-70
  journalists 126-7, 129-30
  local figures 94-5, 98, 99, 127, 129
  motivations 125-6, 130
  religious leaders 141, 144, 146-7
  women 103
Prussian militarism *see* Germany; *Kultur*

Racism 41
Raemaekers, Louis 5, 6
Recruiting 23, 30, 105, 118
  local efforts 94-5, 98, 99
  voluntarism and 175-77
  see also Parliamentary Recruiting Committee
Religion (chapter 18 *passim*)
  clerical propagandists 141, 144, 146-7
  holy war 143-44, 147
  Islam 38, 143
  Kultur and 142-3
Riddell, George 71, 119, 194
Roosevelt, Theodore 200, 202-3
Royal Colonial Institute (RCI) 37, 122
Russia 170

Sacrifice 143, 151, 152-4
Scotland 26, 49, 104, 146
Shakespeare, William 18
Shaw, George Bernard 195
Smuts, Jan Christiaan 37, 39-40, 179
Soldiers and Servicemen (chapter 19 *passim*) 137, 184
  airmen 151-2
  'contemptible little army' 62-3
  propaganda about 30, 40-1, 133, 134, 137, 187
  women and 101, 102, 104, 184
  propaganda towards 17-18, 25-6, 77, 79-80, 155
  women in 80, 104, 105
  sacrifice and 143, 151, 152-4
  sailors 23-24, 151
  soldier-propagandists 56, 72, 154-5
South Africa 38
Spain 49, 111

Toynbee, Arnold 8, 113-4, 125
Trades Union Congress (TUC) 176-7, 186, 207
Turkey *see* Empire, Ottoman

Union of Democratic Control (UDC) 89-90, 119, 141, 167-8
  and League of Nations 168, 200, 211
  'pro-German' charges 211
  tensions with Labour 81-2, 169
United States of America (chapters 14 and 25 *passim*) 146
  and German atrocities 54
  Anglo-American values 13-14, 63-4, 112, 205
  Civil War 180
  film and 50
  global authority 200, 202

Victoria League (VL) 37, 38
Voluntarism (chapter 22 *passim*) 15-17, 33-4, 125-6
  and Britishness 176-7, 178

Index

and Ireland 34, 178
contrast with Germany 98

Wales 147
War aims 164–5, 168, 200–1
   opposition to negotiated peace 86, 88–9, 142, 211–2
   see also National War Aims Committee
War Office Cinematograph Committee (WOCC) 40, 47, 48, 119
War savings 75, 136, 143, 155
   see also National War Savings Committee
Wellington House (War Propaganda Bureau) 1, 17, 29, 37, 49, 118, 126
   concealing official connections 162
   propaganda methods 109–10
Wells, H. G. 53, 86
Wilson, Woodrow 54, 168, 202, 203, 207–8
   League of Nations and 63, 168, 200–1

Women (chapter 13 *passim*) 30, 31–3, 67, 183–5, 187, 189
   as propagandists 31–3, 103
   domestic servants 183–4
   farm work 73, 74, 103–4
   girls 25
   mothers 104–5, 106, 187
   munition workers 102, 103, 105–6, 185
   nurses 104
   soldiers and 101, 104, 179
   suffrage 32–3, 101, 103, 170, 171
Women's Army Auxiliary Corps (WAAC) 31, 32, 184, 187
Women's Social and Political Union (WSPU) 103, 170
Workers 130–1, 153, 211–2
   propaganda towards 33–4, 63, 138, 177–8, 207–8
   propaganda discouraging industrial action 143, 185–6, 200–1
   voluntarism and 175, 179–80